THE AWAKENED LIFE

CHAKRA HEALING

BETSY RIPPENTROP, PhD, AND EVE ADAMSON

ALPHA

Publishing: Mike Sanders
Senior Acquisitions Editor: Janette Lynn
Art Director: William Thomas
Book Producer: Lee Ann Chearneyi/Amaranth@LuminAreStudio.com
Copy Editor: Rick Kughen
Cover Designer: Jessica Lee
Book Designer/Layout: Ayanna Lacey
Indexer: Celia McCoy
Proofreader: Lisa Starnes

Published by Penguin Random House LLC
002-317435-NOV2020
Copyright © 2020 by Amaranth

International Standard Book Number: 978-1-46549-335-4
Library of Congress Catalog Card Number: 2020930830

22 21   5 4 3 2

Interpretation of the printing code: The rightmost number of the first series of numbers is the year of the book's printing; the rightmost number of the second series of numbers is the number of the book's printing. For example, a printing code of 20-1 shows that the first printing occurred in 2020.

Printed in the United States of America

Note: This publication contains the opinions and ideas of its authors. It is intended to provide helpful and informative material on the subject matter covered. It is sold with the understanding that the authors, book producer, and publisher are not engaged in rendering professional services in the book. If the reader requires personal assistance or advice, a competent professional should be consulted.

The authors, book producer, and publisher specifically disclaim any responsibility for any liability, loss, or risk, personal or otherwise, which is incurred as a consequence, directly or indirectly, of the use and application of any of the contents of this book.

All identifying information, names, and details of client cases have been changed to protect the confidentiality of clients with whom Dr. Rippentrop has worked. Client stories provided in the book are often conglomerates of different cases to provide examples of how chakra work can be informative and therapeutic in the counseling setting.

Most Alpha books are available at special quantity discounts for bulk purchases for sales promotions, premiums, fund-raising, or educational use. Special books, or book excerpts, can also be created to fit specific needs.

For details, write: Special Markets, Alpha Books, 1745 Broadway, New York, NY 10019.

Reprinted and updated from *The Complete Idiot's Guide to Chakras*

A WORLD OF IDEAS:
SEE ALL THERE IS TO KNOW

www.dk.com
First American Edition, 2020

Contents

Chapter 8: **Sacral Chakra (*Suadhisthana*): Creating Passion** 95

Chapter 11: **Throat Chakra (*Vishuddha*): Express Yourself**............... **155**

Chapter 12: **Third Eye Chakra (*Ajna*): In Sight** **173**

Foreword

I was on a train going from Grand Central Station in New York City up to New Canaan, Connecticut. I dug into a book I had just bought impulsively—just as you have perhaps bought this one. I found myself immediately fascinated: there were juicy new power words to learn, ways to say things that sounded a little mysterious but, according to the author, were as clear as the Liberty Bell clanging for my personal freedom, my individuality as a birthright gift from the gods! "I'm a Capricorn ♑ because the Sun ☉ was located in that sign when I was born! I mean business. I get things done. (I can be pretty melancholic sometimes, but don't tell anyone.) But I'm in there for the long haul. I age well!"

My brain was racing through the pages to pick up more things about my Capricorn ♑ nature. There was something pointed out about my tremendous attraction to any Pisces ♓ woman who ever lived. I filed that away (and remembered it regularly throughout 27 years with two Pisces ♓ ladies!).

There was a lot about my incompatibility with Aries ♈ people. (And I knew that that explained everything about my relationship with my mother, God take her soul!)

Okay, when I finally settled down, I saw that astrology had *reasons* for these generalities. I saw those reasons were tied to the miracle of creation and to millennia of keen observations by wise people. And I saw that the mysteries of being were easily converted into strategies of becoming—I was hooked!

By the time I had arrived at New Canaan on that hot summer day, I didn't need a cool drink as much as I needed a pencil and paper. I was going to follow the guidelines in the book and start to build my birth chart—the portrait of my birth in space and time and the portrait of who I am (the nice stuff, the tough stuff—all of it!).

Books, lines, and thinkers: how hooked was I? I studied, studied, and studied, and gradually I realized that nothing was more interesting to me in the world than astrology—and it probably was also in a previous life, as I was learning. I saw how I could appreciate myself, my purpose in life, and how I could help others to do the same. Time and space now started to mean something more than three meals a day, a raise now and then, college education for the children, and the IRS.

And that book, with the neat lines and the quotes from all the wise men from Ptolemy to Newton to Einstein to J. P. Morgan, was nowhere near as good as this one you're holding right now.

Watch out! Be warned: Madeline Gerwick has the lines that will hook you, too; she's one of those wise thinkers in astrology who really knows what she's talking about.

And Madeline and her book producer at Amaranth, Lee Ann Chearneyi, have style. This book is a breeze. For example (getting back to the Pisces issue, please), their "Fish Facts" talks about Pisces' (delightful) character trait to live largely in the world of the imagination, the realm of dreams, and where objects and events seem to have no connection to outer reality. (I, the Capricorn ♑ warlord of accomplishment, love it!) But then they tack on the lines that show you the substance within all the fun: "Above all, Fishes [Pisces] are here to give their help, love, and whatever else is needed—not just to those like themselves, but to anyone in need." Isn't that lovely? Isn't that valid? And that's just the beginning. How do all the traits, powers, and interrelationships among the planets within the signs reflect your life, the details of your progress, the outlines of your dreams, and the dynamics of your relationships?

Well, my fateful train ride those many years ago took me to write some 24 technical astrological texts of my own, to lecture throughout the world, and to appreciate this *Astrology: The Awakened Life* guide to the field I love. I can tell you for sure that when I introduce newcomers to this fascinating world of astrology, I will recommend this book. They, and you, will be thrilled with Madeline Gerwick's introduction to seeing stars. It's expert, it's charming, and it's easy.

All aboard!

—Noel Tyl
World-renowned astrologer and cofounder of the Association for Astrological Networking, astrology's global organization

Introduction

You know who you are. You've looked in the mirror thousands of times. You've got a name, physical qualities, things you do. People you know recognize you when they see you. But what's going on *inside*? Is there more to you than you can see in that mirror, more than your friends and family know, more than everyone sees in your pictures and posts on social media, or more than even *you* have dreamed?

Your Life Force Energy

You *are* more than just a body. You are a confluence of energies, like a network of rivers and streams burgeoning with life. You are part of something bigger—the Universe—and yet, you are also ultimately a unique, individual Spirit. Don't worry if you don't see it all just yet. You've got a secret code, a key inside you that can guide you toward greater self-realization. You've got chakras.

In ancient Sanskrit, the word *chakra* means "wheel," and these seven spinning energy vortexes inside your body, located along your spine from the bottom of your pelvis to the crown of your head, reveal more about you than any reflection or description ever could. Your chakras constantly open and close, widen and narrow, and turn and spin, taking in and releasing life force energy according to *your* life, *your* experiences, and who *you* are at any given moment. They are wheels of light, and they are all about you. Get to know them, and you get to know and heal yourself.

About the Authors

We've written this book to help you make the most of the chakras you hold inside you. We are Dr. Betsy Rippentrop and Eve Adamson. What do we know about chakras?

Betsy Rippentrop, Ph.D. is a certified yoga instructor, a licensed psychologist, hypnotherapist, and Reiki practitioner, as well as a trained *Anusara* yoga teacher. Betsy teaches yoga classes as well as specialized trainings on yoga and the mind. She has published academic papers on the relationship between spirituality and health, women's health, and chronic pain management. Dr. Rippentrop describes the treatment she offers as yoga-based psychotherapy; she sees clients in her clinical practice based at Heartland Yoga in Iowa City. Visit her website at www.dryogamomma.com.

Betsy uses the chakras in her psychology practice to help her clients better understand themselves and heal. She measures clients' chakras early in treatment to serve as a baseline, and routinely monitors clients' chakras throughout treatment to help them understand their patterns and progress. In this book, she'll show you how to measure your chakras, too. Betsy also utilizes her chakra knowledge to help her yoga students understand the subtle energies in their bodies and how yoga can help neutralize imbalances they may have.

Co-author Eve Adamson is a writer and devoted yoga practitioner who has written many popular books on health and wellness topics, including co-authoring the bestselling *The Mediterranean Diet* by Marissa Cloutier, MS, RD., and Eve Adamson (Harper, 2004). Eve lives and writes in Iowa City.

Eve checks in almost daily with her own chakras, to get a better sense of what she is feeling—for example, whether she's imbalanced, assertive, moody, or particularly insightful on any particular day.

Together, Betsy and Eve guide you through your own chakras, introducing you to your chakras and helping you get to know and understand these vital energy centers as you heal. We'll show you how to use your chakras, how to decode the messages they write in your physical body, and how to keep in touch with yourself through these spinning centers of your own life force. Hip pain? Neck pain? Fallen arches or sore throat? Sudden sadness or unexplained joy? The answers to healing lie within those spinning wheels.

Healing with Chakras

This is a journey of healing self-knowledge—one that can catapult you to the next level of your personal evolution.

Throughout this book, we also discuss how blocks and overloads in our chakras may lead to certain physical and/or mental health problems. We acknowledge that many factors come into play regarding a person's likelihood of developing illness or disease (such as genetics, lifestyle, diet, and weight). Yet we believe that when chakras are out of balance for extended periods of time, this energy disparity increases the likelihood of developing disease. If you break apart the word disease, it actually becomes dis-ease, or a lack of ease, a lack of balance.

Nobody wants to become ill, but disease and illness are opportunities, even if they don't feel that way. This is your body's way of alerting you, of protecting you, of telling you that something is off-kilter and needs to be addressed. If you have a disease or health condition, there is no blame here. You have been doing the best you can in your life with the information you had. You are now receiving new information from your body in the form of symptoms. Use this new information to improve your life, to seek balance, to take better care of yourself, to acknowledge and understand your fears, and to release any anger or resentment you've been carrying. Our bodies are extremely wise and will give us the signs we need. A better life is waiting if we are willing and brave enough to explore the meaning behind the symptoms, and that exploration can begin with the chakras.

Are you ready to be self-realized, empowered, and more at home than ever before in your own body, mind, and spirit? Are you ready to integrate all the parts of yourself into one amazing whole? Then you are ready to start working with your chakras. So, grab the wheel, and get ready to start driving your own life. You've got an exciting journey ahead, and we'll be right there with you.

About This Book

Chakra Healing is divided into five parts that cover everything you need to know to explore and balance your own chakras.

In **Part 1, Awaken to Chakras' Healing Power**, we introduce you to the whole chakra concept, from a brief explanation of each chakra, where it is, and what it means, to a fun history lesson about chakras and an explanation about how they actually work in the body and in conjunction with the entire network of life force energy.

In **Part 2, Dynamics of Chakra Energy**, we explore all the many symbolic examples of chakras, from the tiniest atom to the largest galaxy. In this part, you'll learn about the notorious *Kundalini* energy, so critical to understanding chakra awakening, and you'll also learn how to work with your actual chakras, including how to measure them.

Part 3, Healing Chakras: Root to Crown, is the heart of the book. We spend a chapter on each of the seven chakras, telling you everything you need to know about what each one means, what happens when it gets blocked or overloaded with energy, and how to heal and balance it.

In **Part 4, High Octane Healing Bliss … No Caffeine Necessary!**, we get serious about actually integrating chakra work into real life, with chapters on using chakras to feel better every day, using your own voice to increase chakra vibration, how chakras can enhance your love life, and how to use meditation techniques for greater chakra awareness.

Part 5, Relax, Release, Restore, Renew, covers more advanced techniques for working with the chakras, from partner exercises for releasing chakra blocks to guided visualizations and an exploration of the astral and causal bodies.

Acknowledgments

Betsy: Thanks to Eve Adamson for being my experienced, wise, and grounded guide who journeyed with me on this amazing chakra trip! Thanks to Dr. Candida Maurer and Dr. Michael Santangelo, who first opened my eyes to the world of energy, chakras, Reiki, and healing—your wisdom and guidance have been priceless. Thanks to Marsha Nieland, my *Anusara* teacher and mentor, for changing my life by your strong practice, exceptional teaching, open heart, playfulness, generosity, and dedication to the *kula*. Thanks to all the exceptional teachers who work with me at Heartland Yoga—this studio would not be thriving without your talents and enthusiasm. Thanks to my boys: Pieter, for constant comic relief, grounding, and reminding me of what is truly important in life; and Jack, my steady, stable, and blissful baby boy who epitomizes open-heartedness. Finally, this book is dedicated to my dear husband, Jon, who always lends his support and believes in me, no matter what adventure I'm navigating.

Eve: Thank you to my fantastic, loving, open-hearted co-author, Dr. Betsy Rippentrop, whose beautiful spirit and trusty expertise trickle down through every page of this book. Thanks to my BFF and fellow yogi Rachel Klapper, who was a behind-the-scenes source of help, information, and moral support during the writing of this book. Thanks to Lee Ann Chearneyi at Amararanth@LuminAreStudio.com for bringing me this wonderful project, which I enjoyed so much. Thanks to my youngest son, Emmett, who patiently let me measure his chakras and test visualizations and meditations on him. He's a wise spirit filled with love and compassion. He has a magnificent Heart chakra. And as always, thanks to Ben, for listening, for keeping the kids out of the office when I was under deadline, for letting the dogs out so I wouldn't have to break my train of thought, and for making sure there was food on the table (even if it was meat) when I was unable to do even one more thing. I couldn't do it without you, babe!

About Amaranth

Amaranth@LuminAreStudio.com enjoys more than 20 years as a leading producer of health, nutrition, women's interest, and wellness/lifestyles books for publishers in print and digital media. Creative director Lee Ann Chearneyi uses her talent as a published author and her experience as a career editor and former trade publisher to inform and craft innovative creative content.

A special thanks from Amaranth to professional astrologer and Tarot reader, Arlene Tognetti of Mellinetti's, who assisted with Michelle Obama's birth chart chakra reading in Appendix A. Find Arlene on Facebook or email her at arlene@mellinetti.com. Arlene is the author of several books on the intuitive arts including *The Complete Idiot's Guide to Tarot, Second Edition.*

Trademarks

All terms mentioned in this book that are known to be or are suspected of being trademarks or service marks have been appropriately capitalized. Alpha Books and Penguin Random House LLC cannot attest to the accuracy of this information. Use of a term in this book should not be regarded as affecting the validity of any trademark or service mark.

PART 1

AWAKEN TO
CHAKRAS' HEALING POWER

You've heard about chakras. You've seen diagrams. Maybe you've even felt them in yoga class or during meditation. But just what *are* your chakras, where are they, and what do they mean for you and your life? Here, we start you on a healing journey to look for all the answers. You'll find an at-a-glance chart along with introductory information about each chakra and how it influences your body, mind, and spirit. Learn about chakra history—painless, we promise! Next, you'll discover a whole new way of looking at your own anatomy. You will move beyond bones, muscles, and internal organs to examine *prana*, *chi*, *nadis*, and the way energy moves in, out, and through your body and its chakra energy centers.

Chapter
1

Where Are Your Chakras?

Do you ever wonder why on some days, you feel safe, secure, and calm, as if all is right with your world, whereas on other days you feel jittery and anxious, as if someone is about to pull the rug out from under you?

Do you ever notice how on some days, you feel so emotional that you can hardly keep yourself from giggling aloud or bursting into tears, whereas on other days you frankly don't care … about anything?

Have you ever thought of someone just before they happen to text you or tag you in a photo on social media? Have you ever started singing a popular song just before it comes up on a streaming playlist?

And whether or not you consider yourself a spiritual or religious person, do you ever wonder why you have those occasional uplifting moments of realization—those *a-ha* moments that make you feel like you just might be directly connected to some higher, healing power?

All those feelings are natural, normal, and part of being human, but they also come from somewhere. They come straight out of your body, mind, and spirit. To be more precise, they flow from your very own energy—infused, rainbow-hued, and spinning healing *chakras*.

How You've Already Touched Your Chakras

You might already assume you have chakras, and you might even know they are stacked up in line with your backbone, from the base of your spine to the crown of your head. You might have heard that you have five, or seven, or eight, or even hundreds of chakras. Or maybe you have no idea how many might be spinning around inside you. Have you heard that chakras spin?

The word *chakra* means "wheel" in Sanskrit, and that's exactly what these energy vortexes are: spinning wheels of energy—*your* energy. According to ancient Indian wisdom, chakras (pronounced cha-kra, with a hard "ch" like in "chair") are spinning energy centers in the body that lie along the body's many energy pathways. While chakras correspond to certain glands, nerve centers, and organs in the body, they are part of the subtle energy body, not the physical body, so they cannot be detected by standard medical equipment, such as X-rays or MRIs. Chakras also correspond to various aspects of the body's physical, psychological, emotional, and spiritual state.

Even if you don't know much about chakras, we can guarantee you have already felt them. A nervous stomach when you have to do something brave is your third chakra talking. The lump in your throat when you have something important to say but have trouble getting it out is your fifth chakra in action. Those lower-down butterflies you get when you see, touch, or even think about your romantic partner live in your second chakra. That constipation you get when you are traveling far from home is your first chakra getting protective. The stabbing pain you feel in your heart when someone has broken it? That's your injured and throbbing fourth chakra.

You might have also been aware of your chakras while engaging in some of the holistic practices that tap into them, such as yoga, energy healing (like Reiki), massage, or acupuncture. Or you might have heard astrologers talk about the chakra energy of the zodiac signs. So, while a doctor can't pinpoint a chakra on a scan, that doesn't mean you don't feel your heart opening up when you do a deep backbend; feel calm and grounded after a massage; or have a sudden insight after an energy healer has set your *prana* or your *chi* (Indian Sanskrit words for your life force energy) flowing more freely again.

But so what if you have chakras, and so what if you feel them? What does it mean for you? It can mean plenty if you learn to read your own chakras. Chakras can tell you a lot about who you are and how you can increase your health, balance your emotions, clear your mind, improve your relationships, feel more powerful, and even have a more fulfilling spiritual life. Understanding your chakras can greatly increase the speed of your personal evolution because they increase your self-awareness and ability to grow and change in positive ways. You'll "get" yourself better than ever before. You might even feel more comfortable about your spirituality—your place in the Universe. So what are you waiting for?

The Wheels Are Turning

Chakras are amazing tools in your own body, to help you get to know and understand yourself better. They are like barometers for your internal weather—a measure of who you are at any given moment.

Chakras provide a template for your entire life, with each chakra governing major aspects of who you are (your first chakra), how you feel (your second chakra), what you do (your third chakra), how you love (your fourth chakra), what you say (your fifth chakra), what you know (your sixth chakra), and how you perceive your connection with the Universe or a Higher Power (your seventh chakra).

Throughout this book, we'll explore each chakra and how you can learn about and use yours. To get you started thinking about your own chakra healing, check out the following table to see a brief description of what each chakra does.

Chakra	Common name	Sanskrit Name	Location	Associated Color	Element	Associated physiology	Influences/Energy
First chakra	Root chakra	Muladhara (meaning "root")	Base of the spine	Red	Earth	Feet, legs, hips, bones, joints, sacrum, coccygeal nerve plexus, lower intestine, and waste removal system	Security, safety, survival, basic needs (food and shelter), grounding, family and tribe, and health
Second chakra	Sacral chakra	Svadhisthana (meaning "dwelling place of the self" or "sweetness")	Just below the navel	Orange	Water	Reproductive organs, sacral nerve plexus, lower back, pelvis, abdomen, and bladder	Emotions, movement, feelings, pleasure, sexuality, fertility, and creativity
Third chakra	Solar Plexus chakra	Manipura (meaning "dwelling place for the jewel" or "city of the jewel")	At the base of the rib cage, on the solar plexus	Yellow	Fire	Stomach, digestive organs, adrenal glands, liver, kidney, spleen, pancreas, middle back, and solar nerve plexus	Power, energy, self-esteem, will, ego/sense of self, taking action, and making things happen
Fourth chakra	Heart chakra	Anahata (meaning "intact" or "unstruck"—the place that sings without being played)	Behind the heart	Green	Air	Thymus gland, cardiac nerve plexus, heart, lungs, shoulders, arms, and breasts	Love, compassion, empathy, kindness, balance, quest for peace, and love of self
Fifth chakra	Throat chakra	Vissudha (meaning "purity")	Behind the throat, at the base of the neck	Bright blue	Sound	Throat, trachea, neck, thyroid gland, pharyngeal nerve plexus, and mouth	Communication, speaking the truth, listening, hearing the truth, metaphorical thinking, and manifesting creativity

Chakra	Common name	Sanskrit Name	Location	Associated Color	Element	Associated physiology	Influences/Energy
Sixth chakra	Third Eye chakra	Ajna (meaning "understanding" or "commanding")	On the forehead, about an inch above the brow line	Deep indigo	Light	Pituitary and pineal glands and carotid nerve plexus	Intuition, imagination, perception, dreams, symbolic thinking, inner wisdom, and psychic vision
Seventh chakra	Crown chakra	Sahasrara (meaning "thousand")	At the crown of the head	Purple	Thought	Brain, nervous system, pituitary and pineal glands, and cerebral cortex	Spirituality, intelligence, connection to a Higher Power, broad-mindedness, divinity, union, and seeing the "big picture"

Your Body, Your Chakras

If you were to look back into the history of Indian philosophy and theology for information on the chakras, you would find it proliferating on the internet—but some information would contradict other information you might find. Some traditions say the chakras are five regions of the body. Some systems pinpoint hundreds of chakras. Although many different subtraditions have evaluated and interpreted the chakras in different ways, for the purposes of this book, we use the model most commonly accepted today: the seven-chakra system. This system says we have seven energy centers that run along the midline of the body, from the base of the spine to the crown of the head. We acknowledge that there are other smaller chakras in other parts of the body, most notably in the hands and feet. Sometimes, we make note of those, especially in the way the foot chakras can help ground you via your first chakra and the way the hand chakras can help heal you via the fourth chakra. However, we get into all that later.

For now, let's take a brief look at the seven primary chakras, where they are on your body, and what they mean for you. Consider what follows to be a formal introduction to your own chakra system. We cover each chakra in more detail in Part 3.

The First Chakra

First chakra, the Root chakra.

Call it the Root chakra, the Earth chakra, or the Foundation chakra, or use the official Sanskrit term: *Muladhara chakra*. The first chakra is located at the base of your spine, in front of your tailbone. Its symbolic color is red, and its symbolic element is Earth. This chakra is also the center for your feelings of safety, survival, and security, and it is the very root and foundation of your physical body. It all starts here.

When your first chakra is healthy and open, you feel a sense of connection to the ground under your feet, you feel comfortable in your own body, and you feel safe. You feel physically healthy, financially secure, and you have a strong sense of self. You know who you are and where you belong. You feel solid in your body as you walk and experience the grounded strength of your physical being as it moves in alignment with the Earth.

If your first chakra is too tightly closed, you feel flighty and untethered. You are too much in your head or too swayed by your emotions. You aren't sure what home is, or you feel lost. You sometimes feel like you might just float away into the sky because you don't really feel like you belong anywhere. You might have trouble managing your money or practicing good health habits. You might even get so distracted by your thoughts, strong feelings, or even by spiritual practices like meditation or prayer that you forget to do basic survival things like pay your bills, brush your teeth, or eat your dinner. You might have trouble looking up from your smartphone and lose your balance as you attempt to text and walk. (Don't text and drive!) You might tend to trip a lot, have trouble balancing in yoga poses, twist your ankles, or have chronic foot or hip pain.

On the other hand, if your first chakra is too wide open, you might be sluggish, have trouble moving very much, feel heavy and Earthbound, or have a hard time getting things done. You might be a homebody to your own detriment, refusing to leave home or take any risks that involve change and movement. (The Japanese call this "stay at home syndrome" or *hikikomori*, where young people will refuse to leave their parents' houses and only engage with society through the internet and social media from their rooms.) You might also feel ruled by your basic instincts, rather than being in charge of them; your hunger, thirst, desire for sleep, or need to exercise might be so strong that they keep you from getting other things done or prevent you from interacting with other people in real life. Sometimes, people who overeat, sleep too much, or are addicted to exercise have first-chakra issues, though those problems can also be related to other chakras. (Most issues people have do involve more than one chakra, but we get into that more later on.)

Our goal is to get your first chakra up and running, strong, healthy, and balanced with the other chakras. The Root chakra is an important one because all the others stand on top of it. While some people think spiritual pursuits are somehow "higher" or "better" than physical pursuits, we argue that without a strong foundation in the first chakra, it is hard to develop the higher chakras. Right now, you live in the world, in a body, and your job is to do that as well as you can. Your first chakra gives you the power and the resources to do that.

The Second Chakra

Second chakra, the Sacral chakra.

The second chakra is sometimes called the Sacral chakra, Sex chakra, or Emotion chakra. The Sanskrit term for this chakra is *Svadhisthana*. Its symbolic color is orange; its symbolic element is Water; and it is the center of emotions, feelings, creativity, movement, and sexuality. While feelings of love and compassion originate in the fourth chakra, or Heart chakra, the second chakra is the source of passion, desire, sexual attraction, and sexual relationships. Your creativity comes from here, and for women, you create *life* here because the second chakra is also the seat of your fertility.

When you have a strong, healthy, open second chakra, you are comfortable with your emotions and can feel them strongly without letting them take over. (A strong first chakra will help, too.) Your creativity flows, and you have the ability to get things done, make things happen, and accept changes in life with grace and ease. A strong second chakra also fuels a healthy sex life and helps you feel sexy, desirable, and satisfied. You aren't afraid to feel things. When you get butterflies in your stomach, you are feeling your second chakra. This is your pleasure center.

On the other hand, if your second chakra is closed, your emotions might feel cut off or blocked. You might appear cold or unfeeling to others, even though on the inside, your emotions are a mix of depression and frustration. Physically, people with closed second chakras might experience infertility, sexual problems, chronic pelvic pain, gynecological problems (such as endometriosis), and prostate problems. If you have trouble finishing things, fear progress, feel disconnected from your creativity, or have trouble enjoying sex, you might have a second chakra block. Your second chakra might also be closed if you don't or can't feel intimately bonded with your romantic partner. (Although the problem might be related to your partner's second chakra issues, in most cases, both second chakras are involved when a couple has intimacy issues or doesn't feel emotionally bonded.) To protect or guard a sensitive and closed second chakra, some people also gain excess weight in their abdomens.

If your second chakra is too open, you are ruled by your emotions, and they sometimes keep you from getting anything done. Your feelings are too strong, so that they become incapacitating. Sexual addiction can also be related to a second chakra that is too open. (Ironically, if you are addicted to sex without emotional involvement, this sexual dysfunction can be related to a second chakra that is too close.) An overly large second chakra can also result in addictions and hedonism without discipline or structure.

Ideally, you can balance your second chakra with your first chakra. If you have a strong, grounded foundation, then you will feel more able to experience your emotions and explore your sexuality safely and freely. Some experts feel an overexposure to online porn has created distorted views of sexuality and sexual expectations while providing an escape from real-life experiences with a living, breathing partner. Aligning the first and second chakras can help to reconnect partners to real-life experiences of shared intimacy.

The Third Chakra

Third chakra, the Solar Plexus chakra.

The third chakra, sometimes called the Solar Plexus chakra, Power chakra, or in Sanskrit, *Manipura,* is the seat of your personal power. Its color is sunny yellow, and its element is Fire. Confident people radiate like the sun from the third chakra, projecting their energy in front of them from this spot over the solar plexus. This chakra is also linked with your digestion and the transformation of food to energy. What you take in here, you radiate out to the world.

If your third chakra is too closed, you will tend to feel powerless, as if you are at the mercy of fate (or other people) and have no control over what happens to you. Weak third chakras often result in victim mentality, lack of willpower, and an inability to be effective. Digestive problems also originate here, such as irritable bowel syndrome, indigestion, and constipation. A poor appetite, unbalanced gut microbiome, and disinterest in food might also be related to the third chakra. Weight gain might also be related, as if your body is trying to pad and protect your third chakra with body fat. (This can also happen when your body tries to protect your sensitive second chakra.)

A too-open third chakra can be related to overaggressiveness, bossiness, self-centeredness (narcissism), and being overly strict, both with yourself and with others. Very dominant, loud people with huge energy who take over a room often have third chakras that are too open. They might get things done, but it is at the expense of others, especially if they have closed fourth chakras at the same time. Sometimes, it can feel like these people are shooting others down with the intense power of their third chakras.

When you balance your third chakra with your other chakras, you can radiate your personal power and have a strong, confident sense of who you are without stepping on others or ignoring your own feelings and intuitions. A balanced third chakra is effectively powerful and courageous with a healthy dose of humility.

The Fourth Chakra

Fourth chakra, the Heart chakra.

The fourth chakra is usually known as the Heart chakra. In Sanskrit, it is called *Anahata*. This chakra's color is green, and its element is Air. The Heart chakra is just what it sounds like it: the place from which you love. This is also the middle chakra. The three chakras below it are generally considered to be the earthly chakras, and the three chakras above it are generally considered to be the spiritual chakras. The heart links both and anchors them into *you*. Your heart keeps your physical earthly qualities in balance with your spiritual more ethereal qualities, so that you can have both a spiritual life and an earthly body. It all hangs together because of love, which is the very fuel for existence, according to chakra philosophy.

When your fourth chakra is closed, you have a hard time loving. You might feel like you've never really been in love or that your love relationships feel shallow. You might have trouble sympathizing with others or feeling empathy. You might also have difficulty loving yourself. If your third chakra (just below the fourth) is simultaneously too open, you might be more concerned with power, success, and yourself than you are with others. If your fifth chakra (just above the fourth) is simultaneously too open, you might be more interested in intellectual talking than in actual compassion for what's going on right in front of you. Because the fourth chakra is *so essential* for linking body, mind, and spirit into an integrated whole, many yoga poses are intensely focused on opening the Heart chakra, often through backbends. Closed fourth chakras can also be related to actual heart disease, specifically heart attacks, angina, and other conditions related to clogged and blocked arteries to the heart.

When the fourth chakra is too open, you might be letting others into your heart to the detriment of your own health; you might feel so compelled to help others and sacrifice your own needs for the needs of humanity that you neglect yourself completely. You might lose your grounding or your sense of personal power because all you care about is giving yourself away. You might also feel such strong empathy for the feelings of others that you mistake those feelings for your own and lose your sense of identity. You might be too inclined to take on the pain and suffering of others without regard for your own heart.

When you learn to balance your fourth chakra with the other chakras, you can love fully, openly, and sincerely. You also feel comfortable accepting the sense of deep inner peace that true compassion and the ability to connect through love can bring to your body, mind, and spirit. You learn to love without losing yourself. Your fourth chakra serves as an anchor for all the other chakras, yoking them together like a strong central link in a long chain.

The Fifth Chakra

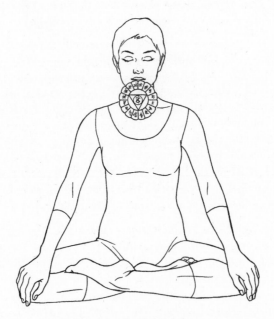

Fifth chakra, the Throat chakra.

The fifth chakra, or Throat chakra, is called *Vishuddha* in Sanskrit. Its color is a bright sapphire blue, and its element is Sound. The fifth chakra produces your voice and is the center for creative expression. The impulse to talk, write, draw, or paint comes from here; it is the place that compels you to communicate your ideas about the world. The fifth chakra is also the truth center. From here, you can speak the truth, and you can also learn to hear the truth from others, rather than deluding yourself about what is happening.

A closed fifth chakra can result in difficulty communicating. You might stumble over words, stutter, or tend to be silent, even when it would be appropriate to speak. You might know exactly what you want to say but just can't get the words out. Often, you fear telling people what you really believe and become good at literally "swallowing" your words. You might also have a compulsion toward self-delusion. A closed fifth chakra also makes it difficult to hear the truth, especially the truth beyond the actual words someone else might be saying. You might experience creative blocks or feel as if you can't find inspiration. When you are having trouble getting to the core issue of a problem or discovering the truth of a situation, try writing your random thoughts or even drawing a picture. The answer might pop out and surprise you, courtesy of your fifth chakra. Physically, you might experience sore throats, laryngitis, neck pain, vocal cord problems, and ear infections. Most of us have felt a temporarily closed fifth chakra in the form of a lump in the throat when we are trying not to say something or trying to repress a strong emotion that wants to come out in words or sobbing.

Often, people with fifth chakras that are too open tend to talk too much, yammering on and oversharing long after it is time to listen. Being in a relationship with someone like this can be exhausting because they don't stop talking and they rarely listen. Although such people might be prolific creators, they might be so intellectually stimulated that they lose sight of other people's feelings or needs. Your fifth chakra is probably too open if you attack others with words, argue incessantly, dominate conversations or online comments, always have to prove your point to be right, or are so focused on what to say next instead of actually listening.

A balanced fifth chakra taps into the heart below and the intuition above to speak and hear the truth in just the right measure. This allows you to be creatively charged but also socially sensitive.

The Sixth Chakra

Sixth chakra, the Third Eye chakra.

The sixth chakra is the Third Eye chakra or *Ajna* in Sanskrit. Its color is a deep indigo or, according to some systems, a deep royal purple, and its element is Light. The sixth chakra is the center of your intuition—that feeling you get when you just *know* something is true, even though you have no physical evidence. Your sixth chakra picks up on cues your conscious mind doesn't necessarily detect. It governs your inner knowledge of both yourself and the world. Some people attribute clairvoyance or psychic "seeing" to this chakra, while others believe clairvoyance is just a more refined and sensitive ability to see. This is the place to cultivate that skill.

If you have a closed sixth chakra, you are more likely to be oblivious to your own inner wisdom. You ignore—or don't even hear—those prodding urges that tell you to cross to the other side of the street or accept an offer or ask a friend if something is wrong. You might live too much in your body and be too entrenched in your physical life to spend much time on inner contemplation and the cultivation of your sixth sense; this is especially true if you have an overly open first chakra. If you have an overly open second or fourth chakra, your own emotions or the emotions and needs of others might cloud your inner judgment and ability to see the big picture. People with closed sixth chakras also might experience sinus headaches, tension headaches, sinus infections, nearsightedness, and other vision problems.

Having a sixth chakra that is too open can make you feel ungrounded in reality. People with sixth chakras that are too open tend to be too much in their head, overly intellectual, and likely to overthink everything. If your sixth chakra is too open, you may also confuse your dreams with your waking reality or even see visions and be unsure whether they are real. Such people often are so caught up in spiritual pursuits or psychic "seeing" that they forget they are in human bodies, living human lives. They might become overly obsessive about diet and exercise and might experience eating disorders or a distorted body image.

If you think you have psychic abilities, see ghosts, and/or spend a lot of time meditating or obsessing over food and body issues, you need to be particularly careful to nurture and strengthen your lower chakras. A balanced sixth chakra enables you to tap into inner knowing and wisdom—both in the world and within yourself—while also remaining grounded in the world and in your body. This balance also enables you to temper your strong intellect with emotion and heart.

The Seventh Chakra

Seventh chakra, the Crown chakra.

The seventh chakra, sometimes called the Crown chakra or the Thousand-Petaled Lotus chakra, is called *Sahasrara* in Sanskrit. Its color is purple, or according to some systems, pure white. Its element is Thought. The Crown chakra is the seat of pure consciousness, wisdom, and enlightenment. Here lies your universal self, the self that is greater than the individual you. A healthy seventh chakra indicates a healthy spiritual life and the awareness that you are connected with all things. Some of you exists in everyone and everything else, and some of everyone and everything else in you. Spirit, divinity, God, Goddess, or whatever you consider to be the source of all creation and the key to enlightenment, speaks to you through this chakra, and it lives inside you through this chakra.

People with closed seventh chakras have no interest in spiritual pursuits and make priorities of materialism and their own needs. People with closed seventh chakras probably would never seek out holistic healers, nor would they be likely to pick up this book, so chances are, you do not have this problem. However, sometimes the seventh chakra can shut down temporarily in response to a spiritual crisis, depression, feelings of isolation, or a personal tragedy, such as the death of a loved one.

People with seventh chakras that are too open relish the idea of a solitary life pursuing spiritual practices. They would do just fine living on mountaintops in the Himalayas or in monasteries or caves. In the real world, however, spiritual seventh chakras should be balanced, particularly with Earthly first chakras. This balance results in the ideal for life in the world—grounded in the now, but with a blissful sense of spiritual connectedness to all things in the Universe.

Unspinning the Myths

Now that you know what chakras are, let's talk about what they *aren't*. Some people think the chakras are the solution to all problems—fix the chakra and fix your life. Not exactly. Chakras reflect what is going on in our bodies, minds, and spirits. They are a little bit like mirrors or instrument panels that allow us to read ourselves better. But the chakras don't *cause* the problems. Life brings us problems, and the decisions we make and the attitudes we foster either solve problems or create more. Don't blame your first chakra if you are feeling ungrounded, your fourth chakra for being too trusting, or your sixth chakra for that bad dream that came true. Your chakras just help you understand yourself, so you can make choices that create your best life.

However, that being said, tuning in to and even healing the chakras can help urge your body, mind, feelings, and spiritual life back onto the right path. They go hand in hand with who you are, so if you work on the whole package at once, you will have quicker results. Ground yourself by healing your first chakra (you learn how in Chapter 7) and by eating more protein, getting your finances in order, or visiting home if you've been away for a while. (Texts and social media are great facilitators, but they are no substitute for the joy of seeing you in person, in real life.) Throughout this book, we talk about a lot of other ways to get yourself back in alignment when your chakras reveal that things are askew, but the point here is that your chakras are there for you to read. They are not the original cause of anything.

Another myth about the chakras is that they are gateways to potentially dangerous *Kundalini* energy. Maybe you've heard rumors about the *Kundalini*, or serpent power, and how it can transform you in positive and negative ways. Actually, negative press about *Kundalini* is less of a myth than a misunderstanding. We talk more about *Kundalini* energy in Chapter 5, but for now, rest easy knowing that your chakras are your protection against this intense energy surge, not a facilitator. When you are ready for *Kundalini* energy, your chakras open up and let it through. If you aren't ready, your chakras close like valves. (There are some exceptions to this, when people purposefully open their chakras to release *Kundalini*, but again, we talk about that in more detail in Chapter 5.)

Finally, people sometimes misunderstand what each chakra represents. Just to clear the air right now, we will tell you the following:

- The first chakra is not your animal side. You don't have to worry that tapping into this chakra will make you so instinct-based that you will be ruled by your basest instincts, resort to violence, or lose control of all your good sense. This chakra is grounding, not wild.

- The second chakra is not *only* the sex chakra. It is also about pleasure, passion, creativity, and everything you love to do. It is about moving and doing more than it is about sexual obsession. Sexuality is just one small part of this chakra.

- The third chakra is not the "bad" chakra. Power can be a positive thing for building self-esteem, getting things done in the world, and knowing who you are. Reclaim your third chakra and don't be ashamed of it!

- The fourth chakra is not only about loving others. It is also about loving and *healing* yourself, so don't focus all that energy outside toward others. If you save energy for yourself, you'll be a much more open and giving person because you have the inner resources.

- The fifth chakra isn't just about communicating to the world. It is also about listening to the world communicate to you, and discerning the true parts. This is an important power in our world where the line between what is true and what is untrue, or "fake," has blurred, so don't underestimate the importance of this chakra. Your neck might be hurting for a very good reason. Are you facing the truth?

- The sixth chakra is not just associated with psychic powers. While psychic powers can be part of this chakra, for most people, this is irrelevant. The sixth chakra isn't there just so you can become a clairvoyant and have your own podcast. The sixth chakra is about intuition and learning to listen to your own inner voice. It is an inward-turning chakra that can lead you to deep wisdom and the answers you desire.

- The seventh chakra isn't necessarily about God. You don't have to believe in any particular god to tap into the power of this chakra. Instead, it is your connection to the eternal, the Universe, the life force, or a Higher Power, depending on who you are and what makes sense to you.

Spinning the Chakra Wheels

We want you to use this book as an instruction manual for operating your own chakras in a way that can make a difference in your life. You can learn to see them, measure them, understand them, and even change them. Their condition reflects who you are at any given moment, so it only makes sense that you should learn everything you can about them. Are you ready to spin the chakra energy wheels?

Whether you are new to chakra healing energy or you want to learn more, begin by introducing yourself to your chakras, one at a time, as they are right now.

1. Sit comfortably with good posture in a straight-backed chair with your hands on your knees.

2. Slowly and consciously breathe in and out; concentrate on following your breath.

3. Beginning with the first chakra, the Root chakra, place a hand on that chakra and breathe deeply into it. Let yourself feel your breath moving into the chakra and filling it up.

4. Hold your breath and while doing so, feel yourself holding your chakra with nurturing care.

5. Pay attention to the thoughts that arise in your mind.

6. Release the breath and with it the chakra.

7. Return your hand to your knee.

8. Take a few centering breaths in and out and repeat the process for each chakra, culminating in the seventh chakra, the Crown chakra.

What did you feel? How did you feel? Did you notice your thoughts? You've begun your healing chakra journey.

Chapter
2

Chakra *Shakti:* The Power Tradition

Chakras? Who ever thought of such a thing? And how did anyone ever figure out what and where they were? The concept of spinning energy centers in the body has an ancient Eastern feel, and indeed, the chakra concept has been around for many thousands of years. It is integral to many different branches of yoga, and ideas about chakras have evolved and changed (along with yoga itself) over the last 20 centuries or so. We promise not to bore you with a lot of history or technical detail, but let's take a brief look at how chakras originated and what they mean in context. In this chapter, you not only find out why chakras have such staying power but also the ways you might be most comfortable thinking about and working with them now in daily practice.

Chakras' Origins: On the Wheels of Chariots

The first written texts in India are called the *Vedas*, a huge body of literature that probably dates as far back as 2000 B.C.E. Before the *Vedas*, knowledge was passed along orally, and the *Vedas* probably include information that had been a part of Indian culture long before anyone thought to write down any of it. The *Vedas* are considered sacred texts in the Hindu religion, and they were written in *Sanskrit*, one of the ancient languages of India. The *Vedas* consist of several different works, including hymns, chants, stories, prophecies, poems, and more. They are long, so unless you decide to become a Hindu scholar, you probably won't get around to reading them … even in translation! In orthodox Hinduism, however, the *Vedas* are sacred, considered passed down by God, and not something people just wrote down without any divine guidance.

The *Vedas* are the first place where the chakras are mentioned, and because the *Vedas* are the oldest written text in India and among the oldest of written texts in the world, that means people have been talking about, thinking about, and writing about chakras for a lot longer than they have been talking, thinking, and writing about a lot of things.

According to chakra expert Anodea Judith, part of the *Vedas* contains the story of the Indo-European invasion when the Aryans stormed into India on wheeled chariots. The wheels of those chariots were described as *cakras*. The Aryans were also described as *cakravartins*, and the story says that golden wheels of light preceded their chariots. We can only speculate about what these golden disks of light might have been. Gold adornments to their chariots? Weapons? Judith wonders if it might have been the glow of their excessively powerful third chakras, which certainly would have had to be pretty fired up to conquer another race.

Judith also writes that the chakras were mentioned around 600 C.E in the *Upanishads*—Hindu scriptures, sacred to the Vendanta branch of Hinduism. They are also briefly mentioned in the *Yoga Sutras*, a collection of aphorisms defining yoga, written by the Hindu sage *Patanjali* in the second century, even though they are in no way central to that famous collection of aphorisms still often quoted today in yoga classes.

Chakras and Yoga: A Match Made in Heaven

Yoga is the practice of yoking the body, mind, and spirit (to put it in very simple terms). Chakras are energy centers that also serve to link these different levels of the self, and the concept of chakras has been an integral part of yogic philosophy for thousands of years. However, not every branch of yoga emphasizes or even mentions chakras. The concept caught on and became a more central part of yoga with the development of *Tantra*.

Tantra is a branch of yoga that developed in the seventh century as a response to the previous notion (which many yogis still embrace) that we should rise above our physical lives, desires, and senses, to touch a higher plane of existence. According to Tantra, our physical lives, desires, and senses are grounded in the Earthly world and are worth embracing because they are the physical manifestation of Divine energy. To live in the physical world and accept both its light and dark aspects is to worship God. This is also a central concept when working with chakras, as each chakra encompasses both the light and dark sides of the human body, mind, and spirit.

Tantra was widespread and took many forms, including *Kashmir Shavism*, a Shiva-worshipping form that originated in the eighth and ninth centuries and spawned the notion of *Kundalini* energy, which we talk about more in Chapter 5. *Kundalini* energy—the female aspect of the Divine, or feminine energy—lies coiled around the first chakra like a sleeping serpent. As each chakra is energized, she rises up, piercing each one in succession and progressing on toward the Crown chakra where she can finally unite with her beloved, the god Shiva, also known as the masculine principle of the Divine. This can result in enlightenment, even if it only lasts for a little while. According to many sources, it can also result in mental problems and hallucinations for people who are not ready to experience the serpent power. (Don't worry. We talk you through this in Chapter 5.)

Westerners first heard about the chakras through a book published in 1919 called *The Serpent Power*, in which an Englishman named Arthur Avalon translated older *Hindu* texts and explained concepts like tantra, *kundalini*, and the chakras. This is only one of many interpretations, however. As any well-versed scholar will tell you, different schools of thought and various Hindu texts throughout history describe the chakras in different ways. Hinduism is the predominant religion of India (where the religion began). Hindus have numerous diverse beliefs, but many embrace the concepts of a Supreme Being and of reincarnation. Some Hindu texts describe hundreds or even thousands of chakras. Some say there are eight chakras, or seven, or only five. Some say the chakras are energy centers, and others say they are regions in the body. But Avalon's translation isn't a scholarly text, so we'll work to simplify as easily as we can and distill what we and others have learned about the chakras into information that will be useful to you in your daily life. If you want more scholarly information, historical context, or anything else beyond the scope of this book, we encourage you to continue your studies by researching the history and origins of chakra practice.

Chakras and the Eightfold Path

We mostly think of chakras in terms of yoga, but remember that Buddhism began in India, too, even though it is now more widespread in Asia. Buddhism is a religion that began in India more than 2,000 years ago when Siddhartha Gautama, became enlightened and is now known as the Buddha. Today, millions of people all over the world practice several branches of Buddhism.

The idea of chakras isn't central to Buddhism, but the *Noble Eightfold Path* of Buddhism is often depicted as a spinning wheel with eight spokes that represent the eight aspects of the *Noble Eightfold Path*. The *Noble Eightfold Path* is the fourth of the Four Noble Truths of Buddhism.

It consists of guidelines for living that help increase knowledge and maximize the chances for enlightenment. The eight paths are as follows:

Right understanding

Right thought

Right speech

Right action

Right livelihood

Right effort

Right mindfulness

Right concentration

The *Noble Eightfold Path* is often represented by a chakra called the *dharma wheel* or *dharmachakra* in Sanskrit. This is a symbol of a wheel with eight spokes each of which represents a limb of the *Noble Eightfold Path*.

Because Hinduism and Buddhism both began in India, the Eightfold Path of Buddhism is probably related at its beginnings to the Eight Limbs of Yoga, which Patanjali wrote about in the *Yoga Sutras*. These aren't the same eight limbs as the limbs of the *Noble Eightfold Path*, but the idea is the same: to offer guidelines for living that will maximize physical and spiritual development.

The Eight Limbs of Yoga aren't directly related to the chakras, except that if you are practicing yoga, you should be aware of them because they are so essential to yogic thought. Unlike the Eightfold Path of Buddhism, the Eight Limbs of Yoga aren't typically depicted as chakras. However, practicing these eight limbs is energizing and balancing for all the chakras, so we go over them briefly:

o The *Yamas:* five positive practices to help you resist negative things like violence and lying. They are *ahimsa,* nonviolence; *satya,* telling the truth; *asteya,* not stealing; *brahmacharya,* abstaining from sexual misconduct; and *aparigraha,* not being jealous or coveting what others have. Practicing the *yamas* are particularly helpful for energizing the bottom four chakras—Root, Sacral, Solar Plexus, and Heart.

o The *Niyamas:* five observances, or things to practice to enhance your life. They are *shaucha,* being pure by practicing cleanliness (in body and mind); *santosha,* being content or satisfied; *tapas,* being self-disciplined; *svadhyaya,* studying both the self and sacred texts; and *ishvarapranidhana,* worshipping God or surrendering to a Higher Power. Practicing the *niyamas* are particularly helpful for energizing the top three chakras—Throat, Third Eye, and Crown.

- *Asana:* disciplining the body through yoga poses. Note that this is just one of the Eight Limbs of Yoga, even though many people today think of *Asana* as the entirety of yoga. As you can see throughout this book, there are *Asanas* that are particularly good for each of the seven chakras.

- *Pranayama:* breath control through specific breathing exercises. Depending on which type of breathing exercise you do, *Pranayama* is good for all the chakras, but it is particularly energizing for the fourth chakra, or Heart chakra.

- *Pratyahara:* the purposeful withdrawal of the senses for greater control over the mind. This is an excellent exercise for unblocking and energizing the sixth chakra, or Third Eye chakra.

- *Dharana:* concentration for mastery of the mind. This is particularly helpful for energizing and unblocking the sixth or Third Eye and seventh or Crown chakras.

- *Dhyana:* meditation, which is good for all the chakras, but it is particularly good for the province of the seventh chakra, or Crown chakra.

- *Samadhi:* the experience of the unity of all things. When all your chakras are energized and awakened, you might have beautiful flashes of *Samadhi.*

The Eight Limbs of Yoga aren't just similar to the Eightfold Path of Buddhism. They also sound a little bit like the Ten Commandments (for those of you who paid attention in your Sunday School classes). In other words, they are good advice and they promote physical, mental, and spiritual health. Those are all good for your chakras, so if you've been looking for some lifestyle guidance, there you have it!

Chakra Mind, Chakra Matters

Now that we are smack in the middle of the internet age, facilitating the instant transmission of knowledge from anywhere to anywhere else on the globe, millions of people know about chakras, yoga, Patanjali, Buddhism, Sanskrit, and all the other things we've talked about in this chapter. They don't all know how each of these things originated or what they mean in their historical context, but they know the words and many of us use those words often. We think about what they mean for us, in our twenty-first century lives. Considering the ancient history of these ideas, that's amazing.

Today, people use the concept of chakras in all sorts of contexts that they were never originally intended. But who says that's not okay? Chakras have followed us into the twenty-first century, and they still spin, open and close, and work inside our bodies, so why shouldn't we adapt our thinking about them to match our lives? Of course, we should.

One of the most common ways people work with chakras today is through *meditation* because the calm and stillness of mind you gain from meditation can help you tune in to how each chakra feels. Meditation techniques can also help you access your chakras in other ways, as you'll see throughout this book.

Meditation is defined in many ways by different people and traditions, and if you read about meditation, you can find numerous techniques, from slow counting or focusing on the breath to repeating a *mantra*; staring at and contemplating a *mandala*; considering illogical puzzles that push the mind beyond its logical limitations; and the practice of *zazen*, or "just sitting," to let all fluctuations of thought dissipate until the mind becomes like still water with no ripples.

Entering a labyrinth like this one from the Chartres cathedral in France can be like entering spinning chakra energy only to travel to rest at the divine center of being.

To some, meditation is good for stress relief, relaxation, or to work out problems and find solutions. To others, it is mental exercise that is the brain's equivalent to the body's yoga practice of the *asanas*. To still others, the point is to experience only the present moment with no journeys to the past or future. Many use meditation as a form of prayer or communion with God, the Divine spirit, Higher Powers, or universal energy.

Meditation is also an integral part of the yogic path. The physical practice of yoga, the *asanas*, were developed to prepare the body for seated meditation. Meditation allows the mind to quiet and achieve such one-pointed concentration that you can perceive and actually experience the oneness of all things. Yogic meditation is the path to ultimate unity with all living things, during which the person meditating understands that all is one.

This is also the goal of *Kundalini* during her journey from the Root chakra to the Crown: to merge with Shiva in ultimate union, symbolizing the great unity of all life. Therefore, it makes logical sense that meditation and the chakras go together.

In the previous chapter, we included an exercise that introduced you to your chakras. Now, to begin meditating on your own chakras, sit quietly and repeat the exercise. This time begin to concentrate your focus on each chakra, one at a time. Try to connect your mind with your chakra as you feel its energy center in your body. If you are new to chakra healing, don't worry about "getting it right." Just focus your attention at the locus of each chakra and let yourself have an experience. As you connect with each chakra, make mental notes about that experience.

Do this chakra meditation without judgment—let your breath guide you to steady your mind, body, and spirit in the energy of each chakra as you move from the Root chakra to the Crown.

Begin with the first chakra, or Root chakra, at the base of the spine. Visualize its color (red), try to feel it spinning, and imagine what it looks like. Is it round? Crooked? Does it have any dents or dark spots? Is it in line with your spine? Which way is it turning? Imagine filling it with color and light to energize and balance it. Then, move on to the second chakra, or Sacral chakra, just above the navel.

Proceed in the same way for the third chakra at the Solar Plexus, the fourth chakra at the Heart, the fifth chakra in the Throat, the sixth chakra in the Third Eye, and the seventh chakra at the Crown of the head. Checking in each day with a meditative look at your own chakras can tell you a lot about what you need at any given moment, such as what your current strengths are and where you need a little more loving care.

Consider keeping a chakra journal filled with descriptive text or drawings—whichever method corresponds to the way you record your experiences during chakra meditation—to chronicle your healing chakra journey. If you already keep a journal of any kind, whether a cycling log or a gardener's plant list or a reader's booklist, you know how useful it can be to keep a record of dates and details and descriptions of what happened. Your healing chakra journal can serve a similar function, helping you to track your discovery and understanding of how your chakras are flowing the life force energy through your body.

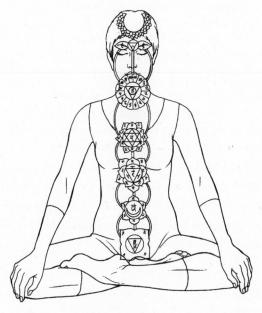

Meditate on the chakras.

Owning the Chakras

Remember that although many great scholars and wise people have written about the chakras throughout history, your chakras belong to you—right here and right now. The point of this book is not to school you on chakra philosophy; instead, this book is designed to help you own your chakras, work with them, balance them, heal them, and become a better, more fully realized person because of that inner work.

Maybe you'll find the best way to work with your own chakras will be through the poses of Hatha yoga, through mindful meditation, or through reading translations of some of the ancient sacred texts of yoga. Maybe you prefer the Tantric approach of embracing the physical world, or maybe you are more comfortable with a prayer-like communion with Spirit or a Higher Power to help balance your chakras.

Whatever way you choose to work with your chakras, this book can help you through it. If you love learning (your seventh chakra does!), the next chapter introduces you to chakra correspondences in the world. You learn how to tune in to the spinning wheels that make up our bodies, our cultures, and even our Universe—from the atoms that comprise us to the solar systems that carry us through space. But if you want to get right down to working with your chakras, skip to Chapter 4, where we help you tune in to and even measure yours. Remember, they are *your* chakras, so forge your own path. We are right there with you.

Chapter
3

Prana and *Nadis* and *Chi*

Chakras are only a part of a complex, esoteric Eastern view of the body your Western medical doctor never encountered during medical school. It's a different way of thinking about reality itself and a product of a different culture than ours. But that doesn't mean it isn't worth consideration because the anatomical and spiritual view of the body so familiar to those growing up in India is not just well-established but time-honored and enduring in many other countries around the world. You already know this isn't a book about esoteric Indian health practices, Chinese medicine, or Eastern theology. This is a book about *you* and the energy flow inside your own body. That means we are going to have to simplify things a bit. However, we don't want you to miss out on any of the good stuff, so in this chapter, we'll talk about the Indian view of anatomy, and what it means to you.

For now, we draw this picture in broad strokes, so you get all the information you need without a lot of unnecessary extras. This chapter gives you the tools to understand your energy body and see what it's doing, so you can begin to understand how your chakras work in conjunction with everything else.

Get *Prana*

First, let's talk about what moves you. Or, more precisely, let's talk about the energy that flows through you. Let's talk about *prana*.

As we explained in Chapter 1, *prana* is the Sanskrit term for life force energy. Technically, there are several levels of *prana*, but for now, let's just talk about *prana* as the energy that flows in and out of the body and in and out of all living things. Sometimes, the word *prana* is used as a synonym for the breath, but *prana* is not the same as the breath. The breath is actually a vehicle to carry *prana* in and out of the body. *Prana* rides on and infuses the breath, but is not the breath.

Prana is a key element in Ayurveda, the ancient Indian science of health and longevity that emphasizes a whole-life approach to health and life extension, including physical and breathing exercises, diet, massage, herbal medicine, and meditation. According to Ayurveda, a body with free-flowing *prana* will be healthy. Blocks and overloads in the *prana* can lead to illness and disease. Ayurveda takes a holistic approach to health. By balancing *prana* through exercise, breathing, good hygiene, diet, massage, herbal medicine, and other specific practices, *prana* will become balanced, and the body will heal itself. This healing allows the full expression of life: an integrated body, mind, and spirit.

This view of health and healing, along with the idea of *prana*, is an ancient one, and it is not unique to India. You might have heard about *chi* or *qi,* the word for life force energy that comes from China and is so often used in discussions of acupuncture, *Shiatsu* massage, Traditional Chinese Medicine (TCM), and *Tai Chi Chuan* or *Chi Kung* (sometimes called *Qi Gong*).

Acupuncture is a Chinese healing technique for freeing the flow of *chi* in the body by piercing energy centers with thin needles. Acupuncture relieves pain and promotes healing. Shiatsu massage is a Chinese healing technique in which the massage therapist uses manual pressure on acupressure points to correct energy imbalances. Traditional Chinese Medicine (TCM) is a system of healing techniques based on traditional Chinese health practices. These may include acupuncture, herbal and other remedies, and special exercises and massage designed to correct energy imbalances. *Tai Chi Chuan* is a form of Chinese martial arts related to *Chi Kung*, primarily practiced today as a meditative moving exercise to balance life force energy. *Chi Kung*, also called *Qi Gong*, is the art and practice of manipulating *chi* through movement and breath control.

Chi is essentially the same thing as *prana*, though they go by different names because they come from different languages. Because the word *chakra* is a Sanskrit word, in this book, we generally use the term *prana* instead of *chi* when talking about this life force energy. It is called *ki* in Japanese, *khi* in Vietnamese, and *gi* in Korean. In essence, these other systems of healing in other countries are the same as Ayurveda. They all perceive that blocked, overloaded, or imbalanced life force energy leads to ill health and disease. Balanced, free-flowing energy leads to vibrant health and an integrated body, mind, and spirit. As opposed to Western medicine, which seeks to treat specific symptoms or physical abnormalities, these energy-based healing systems see the body in a more holistic way. Correct the body's energy, and the body will take care of the rest.

Nadi or Nice?

Prana flows in and out of the body; but how does it do that? Just as water flows over the planet or electricity flows through a power plant, *prana* moves through the body via certain channels or meridians of energy. In Sanskrit, these channels are called *nadis.* In Chinese medicine, they are called meridians or channels. Again, however, the concept is basically the same.

Technically, *nadi* comes from the Sanskrit root *nad,* which means "movement." The word has been used in many ways in ancient yogic texts and Hindu scriptures. You could say that every blood vessel, artery, nerve, and breathing tube in your body is a *nadi* because *nadis* are basically passages through which something moves. In yoga, however, *nadis* generally refer specifically to the channels that carry life force energy, or *prana.*

Healers who are schooled in the subtleties of *nadis* or energy meridians use this knowledge in their practices. For example, according to Dr. Richard Gerber in his book *A Practical Guide to Vibrational Medicine,* knowing that a particular meridian passes through both the stomach and the knee joint can explain why people with knee arthritis or bursitis might also suffer from stomach problems. He writes, "It is not unusual for people to experience pain along a meridian pathway if there are physical problems affecting the corresponding meridian-linked organ."

For most of us, however, we don't have the time or resources to study every single meridian and its course through the body. We leave that to our healing professionals. Your body contains thousands of *nadis,* and it would take a long time and a lot of training to master them all. However, you can learn about three important ones that are directly related to your chakras. These are *nadis* you can influence through your own breathwork, movement, and even thought. They are *sushumna nadi, ida nadi,* and *pingala nadi.*

Sushumna nadi is a large central energy channel that runs along the spinal column from the base of the spine to the crown of the head. *Ida nadi* is the energy channel that carries feminine energy from the base of the spine to the left of *sushumna nadi,* coiling around the spine in opposition to *pingala nadi* and ending at the left nostril. *Pingala nadi* is the energy channel that carries masculine energy from the base of the spine to the right of *sushumna nadi,* coiling around the spine in opposition to *ida nadi* and ending at the right nostril.

Sushumna Nadi

One of the most important *nadis* in your body is *sushumna nadi.* This is the central *nadi* that runs along the midline of your body, right along your spinal column. It isn't your spinal column, but it coincides with your spinal column.

Sushumna begins at your first chakra or Root chakra, and ends at your seventh chakra or Crown chakra, piercing the center of each chakra. Somewhere around the sixth chakra, or Third Eye chakra, behind your forehead, the *sushumna nadi* divides into two, like a fork in the road. The front side moves straight up to the seventh chakra at the crown of the head. The back side curves around the back side of your brain and meets the front side at the seventh chakra.

Sushumna nadi is important because this is the channel that carries *Kundalini* energy from the base of the spine to the crown of the head. In his book *Light on Pranayama*, B.K.S. Iyengar writes: "Through the discipline of yoga, the direction of the mouth of the coiled serpentine energy is made to turn upwards. It rises like steam through the *sushumna* … till it reaches the *sahasrara*." That serpentine energy is *Kundalini*. We talk more about that in Chapter 5, but for now, just remember that *sushumna nadi* is *Kundalini's* private highway.

To ascend through the *sushumna nadi, Kundalini* must move through each of the primary seven chakras along the spine. For that to happen, those chakras must be open, healthy, and free-flowing.

Ida and *Pingala Nadis*

Wrapped around *sushumna* are two other important *nadis* that cross and recross each other at each chakra. These are the *ida* and *pingala nadis*. *Ida* and *pingala nadis* begin at the base of the spine, to the left and right (respectively) of *sushumna nadi*. (Some texts say they begin higher up, around the second chakra, or Sacral chakra.) *Ida* and *pingala* coil around *sushumna nadi* in a sort of double-helix pattern, intertwining and crossing each other at each chakra point. Some people compare this structure to a strand of DNA, or to the Greek *caduceus* symbol of two snakes entwined around a staff. Indeed, the staff is like *sushumna nadi*, and the two snakes are like *ida* and *pingala*, so this is an appropriate way to think about it.

The caduceus is a Greek symbol used today to represent the practice of medicine. It depicts a staff with two snakes entwining around it from bottom to top. This symbol is often used to describe the way in which the masculine and feminine energy channels or nadis coil around a central energy channel in the body called sushumna nadi *which runs along the spinal column.*

Like the Chinese concept of *yin* and *yang* energy, *ida* and *pingala* each carry a different kind of energy. *Ida* transports lunar, female energy. It is a calm, cooling, meditative, receptive, and centered energy that is good to channel during meditation. *Pingala* energy is active, energetic, heating, and forceful energy that is good to channel when you need to get things done. When you breathe out of your left nostril, you tap into *ida's* energy. When you breathe out of your right nostril, you channel *pingala* energy.

According to ancient Chinese philosophy, yin and yang are terms for opposite but balancing forces. All things have yin and yang energy. Yin energy is lunar, feminine, cooling, and receptive energy. Yang energy is solar, masculine, heating, and forceful energy. Yin energy is equivalent to the energy that moves through ida nadi. Yang energy is equivalent to the energy that moves through pingala nadi.

According to yogic belief, at certain times of the day, we all tend to breathe primarily out of one nostril and then out of the other nostril. The nostril that is dominant at any given moment is the energy that is flowing, either through *ida* or *pingala*. For a few breaths each hour, when our breath is shifting from one nostril to the other, we breathe out of both nostrils at the same time, activating the *sushumna nadi*.

Pranayama exercises, which are meant to train and channel the breath to infuse our bodies with *prana*, can also influence the channels we use. In particular, *nadi shodhana*, or alternate nostril breathing, helps balance our *prana* along both *ida* and *pingala* by purposefully inhaling through one nostril while holding the other closed, then switching nostrils and exhaling out of the opposite nostril, then inhaling and switching again.

Ida and *pingala* are important to understand when working with the chakras because they can be helpful, depending on which chakra you are working on and whether that chakra is blocked or overloaded. *Ida* energy can help calm and dissipate an overloaded chakra, while *pingala* energy can help energize and open a blocked chakra. *Ida* energy is good for meditation, while *pingala* energy is good for invigorating exercise. Learn how to use these energies to your own benefit, and you'll have another powerful tool for working with your chakras.

Chakras: Traffic Circles, Energy Transformers, Cosmic Vortices

Now, imagine energy, or *prana,* flowing through your body and coursing through thousands of channels like a network of rivers and streams running through every inch from torso to fingertips and from the bottoms of your toes to the top of your head. *Nadis* run up and down your body, not just *sushumna, ida,* and *pingala,* but a lot of smaller ones. For example, *nadis* connect your left ear to your right big toe (that one is called *yashasvini*), and *nadis* connect your right ear to your left big toe (that one is called *pusha*). *Nadis* connect your eyes to your feet, your throat to your genitals, and your hands to your heart. You've got thousands of *nadis* splitting into thousands more smaller *nadis,* and all of them are filled with moving and flowing energy. This is a road map of you.

Imagine those spots in this vast system of energy flow that are like whirlpools or vortices of energy, where big groups of rivers and streams come together into a swirling central area and then flow back out to other rivers and streams. They collect along your spine, in the palms of your hands, and in the soles of your feet. These are your chakras.

If you read a lot about chakras, you read a lot of metaphors. Call them whirlpools in your network of rivers and streams; traffic circles on the interstate highway system that is you; energy transformers in the vast power plant of your body; or cosmic vortices in your individual manifestation of universal energy. What you call them doesn't matter so much as how you use them.

Because chakras are energy centers where *prana* collects as it travels through the *nadis* of your body, these are energy-intensive spots with a lot of power. That power is yours, swirling there inside for you to read, feel, contemplate, and *use.* This energy belongs to you. It *is* you. So, you might as well start tapping into its healing power.

Feeling the Energy

Now that you have a general idea of the network of energy running through your body, we would like you to start feeling it.

Of course, you already feel your own energy flow all the time as you go through your daily life. Whenever you get a surge of energy or good feeling or when you feel blocked, low on energy, or depressed, you are perceiving your own energy flow. Excitement, fright, anxiety, nervousness, and contentment all reflect what your energy is doing at any given moment. However, feeling your energy and really focusing in on your energy are two different things.

Feel the energy of your fourth chakra, or Heart chakra.

Any physical exercise can help get *prana* or *chi* moving in your body, but *Chi Kung*, the art and practice of manipulating *chi* in the body, consists of different exercises that specifically move and intensify your inner *chi*. The *Chi Kung* windmill exercise is particularly good for drawing in and strengthening inner *chi*. Some say that with the regular practice of this exercise, you can build such inner strength that you can break a board without ever doing any other muscle-strengthening exercises.

Chi Kung Windmill

This exercise is adapted from an exercise that Gene Wong taught to David Carradine, as described in his book *Introduction to Chi Kung*.

1. Stand with your feet a little wider than shoulder-width apart and your toes pointed forward. Settle your weight into your heels and bend your knees just slightly but not so much that they extend past the feet. Tuck your tailbone in, pull your chin slightly in, and lift up at the crown of your head. Broaden your upper and middle back and imagine sending energy forward from the area just over your navel. This is the appropriate stance for many *Chi Kung* exercises.

2. Hold your left palm facing up against your abdomen. Raise your right hand in front of you, palm facing out, and look at the back of your hand. Slowly and with control, move your palm up, keeping your elbow slightly bent. Move your arm in a big circle, like a windmill blade, back behind you and around, following the back of your hand with your eyes.

3. Bring your right hand, palm up, against your abdomen, and rotate your left arm in a big circle, following the back of your hand with your eyes.

4. Repeat several times with both arms.

Do this exercise every day and enjoy dramatic energy reserves. This exercise is also particularly energizing for the third chakra, or Solar Plexus chakra.

Now that we've got those spinning chakra wheels into perspective, let's go deeper. Circles, after all, penetrate our culture, our biology, and our Universe. Keep reading to find out how.

PART 2

Dynamics of Chakra Energy

Chakra means "wheel," and here, you'll learn about how those inner chakra wheels actually work: how they turn, how they manipulate and dispense energy, and exactly what they do. We explore the notorious *Kundalini* energy that lies coiled around your first chakra, waiting to be awakened. We talk about myths and truths associated with *Kundalini* and how you can energize yours. Finally, we show you how to tune in to your chakras, measure them, and diagnose your own chakra blockages and overloads for better health, mental clarity, emotional balance—and who knows?—maybe even spiritual enlightenment.

Chapter
4

Wheels of Life

From an atom to a galaxy, the physical world is filled with spinning wheels. Chakras—those spinning wheels of life force energy within us—might not be visible with medical imaging equipment, but they mirror the physical world in its countless manifestations of the same shape and movement. The wheel, circle, spiral, double helix, vortex—the concepts are practically motifs for physical reality. In this chapter, we explore what it means to be going around in circles.

Spinning Wheels of Life Force Energy

Think about an atom, the smallest possible piece of something that still has the chemical properties of that thing. Atoms make up all matter in the Universe. You can't see them because light particles are too large to illuminate them. Traditionally, atoms have always been depicted as a central nucleus made of protons and neutrons surrounded by orbiting electrons. Now, scientists think that the electrons around an atom's nucleus are probably moving more randomly in a cloud around the nucleus; but nevertheless, the shape is probably round, with particles surrounding a center.

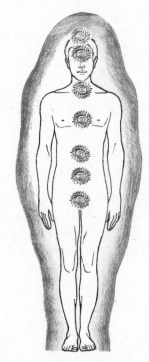

Chakras are spinning life force energy.

But let's get bigger. Nature is filled with circles, spirals, and wheels, which chakras resemble. Look at the center of a flower with its petals curling around the bud. Consider the shape of a raindrop as it splashes onto the pavement or the ripples that move out over the stillness of a pond when you skip a stone across its surface. Look into the eyes of a person, an animal, or even an insect and see the circles within the circles. Our fingerprints contain circles and spirals. So do snail shells and so many other things!

Let's think even bigger. Tornadoes, hurricanes, waterspouts, and whirlpools all move in circles and spin like wheels. Planets, moons, and suns are spheres, with moons moving in orbit around planets and planets moving in orbits around suns. Entire galaxies full of millions of stars and solar systems move in elliptic circles around a center or a source.

Back on Earth, humans like to make circles, too. Not only did we invent the wheel, but we also invented clocks, compasses, rings, crowns, cymbals, hula hoops, doorknobs, plates and saucers, labyrinths, Frisbees, fidget spinners, motors, and fans, not to mention computer drives that spin and store information much like chakras do. We have circles of friends and spheres of influence. We hold sewing circles and prayer circles. We use circles to unpuzzle geometry problems, and we engage in circular reasoning. We use magnets to create spinning energy fields that give rise to electricity. Our culture has ideas about flying saucers and crop circles and ancient circular formations such as Stonehenge (or the Scottish stone circles of *Outlander*). We judge artistic skill by the ability to draft a perfect circle.

Our blood vessels circulate through our bodies, air circulates through our lungs, and our heads spin with thoughts and feelings. It's no wonder our chakras spin, too. The more we reflect on circles and wheels being a part of human existence in the Universe, the more it makes perfect sense that our energy flows through us and collects in powerful circles of healing energy.

Chakra Correspondences

Our culture is full of circle and wheel symbols, but each chakra also has its own slew of associations. Depending on what book you read, what website you surf, or what teacher, yogi, astrologer, or healer you hear expounding on the chakras, you can find lists of correspondences. In addition to associations between colors, body systems, and elements, you can find chakra associations with planets, hand positions, numbers, zodiac signs, sections on the palms of the hands, key words, and types of people. Each chakra also has a seed sound, and when chanted, that sound is thought to awaken the chakra. Each of these correspondences might suggest new ways of looking at, experiencing, and doing healing work with your own chakras.

People often wonder why things like Tarot suits, Zodiac signs, or musical notes relate to each chakra. Actually, different traditions and even different individuals emphasize different interpretations about what corresponds to each chakra. However, most of the correspondences are based not just in someone's intuition but grounded in thousands of years of study of ancient texts, spiritual contemplation, and plain old similarity. People have likened the placement and spin of the chakras to many other aspects of human knowledge and consciousness, including the placement and spin of planets, the healing power of gemstones and crystals, the traditional aspects of life governed by various goddesses and gods, and a more scientific analysis of sound waves and light spectrums. In this chapter, we've listed some of the correspondences familiar to us, but there are others out there, and you might discover still more useful ones using your intuition about your *own* chakras. That's all part of the fun! Here are just a few of the many chakra correspondences we've uncovered through our own research.

First Chakra, or Root Chakra (*Muludhara*)

The first chakra, also called the Root chakra or *Muludhara*, is identified with the following correspondences:

- **Animal:** Snake, elephant, bull, or ox
- **Archangel:** Auriel or Michael
- **Body:** Physical
- **Color:** Red
- **Element:** Earth
- **Food:** All food, but especially proteins like meat
- **Gemstone or crystal:** Ruby, cinnabar, bloodstone, garnet, or other red stones
- **Goddesses and gods:** Atlas, Brahma, Demeter and Persephone, Gaia, or Ganesha
- **Herbs/spices:** Ashwangandha
- **Incense:** Cedar
- **Keyword:** Security
- **Kinds of people:** Family members, including ancestors
- **Metal:** Lead
- **Musical note:** C
- **Number of lotus petals:** Four
- **Plane of existence:** Physical or material plane
- **Ruling planet:** Saturn ♄ (also Uranus ♅)
- **Seed sound:** LANG
- **Sense:** Smell
- **Sense organ:** Nose
- **Shape:** Square
- **Tarot suit:** Pentacles
- **Verb:** To have
- **Vowel or vibration:** U (as in "you") or OH (as in "rope")
- **Yoga path:** *Hatha* yoga
- **Zodiac sign:** Capricorn ♑ and Aquarius ♒

Second Chakra, or Sacral Chakra (*Svadhisthana*)

The second chakra, also called the Sacral chakra or *Svadhisthana*, is identified with the following correspondences:

- **Animal:** Fish and other sea creatures
- **Archangel:** Gabriel or Metatron
- **Body:** Emotional
- **Color:** Orange
- **Element:** Water
- **Food:** Sweet fruit such as melons, strawberries, mangoes, and coconut; honey; nuts; spices such as vanilla, carob, and cinnamon
- **Gemstone or crystal:** Carnelian, coral, amber, or other orange stones
- **Goddesses and gods:** Diana, Dionysius, Indra, Pan, Rakini, Varuna, or Vishnu
- **Herbs/spices:** Coriander or fennel
- **Incense:** Gardenia
- **Keyword:** Feeling
- **Kinds of people:** Children or romantic partners
- **Metal:** Tin
- **Musical note:** D
- **Number of lotus petals:** Six
- **Plane of existence:** Astral plane
- **Ruling planet:** Jupiter ♃ (also Neptune ♆)
- **Seed sound:** VANG
- **Sense:** Taste
- **Sense organ:** Tongue
- **Shape:** Teardrop
- **Tarot suit:** Cups
- **Verb:** To feel
- **Vowel or vibration:** OH (as in "home") or OO (as in "due")
- **Yoga path:** Tantra yoga
- **Zodiac sign:** Sagittarius ♐ and Pisces ♓

Third Chakra, or Solar Plexus Chakra (*Manipura*)

The third chakra, also called the Solar Plexus chakra or *Manipura,* is identified with the following correspondences:

- **Animal:** Birds or the ram
- **Archangel:** Michael or Uriel
- **Body:** Mental
- **Color:** Yellow
- **Element:** Fire
- **Food:** Grains such as pasta, bread, rice, and cereal; seeds such as sunflower seeds, sesame seeds, and flaxseeds; dairy products such as milk, cheese, and yogurt; mint; spices such as turmeric, ginger, and cumin
- **Gemstone or crystal:** Amber, topaz, citrine, gold, or other yellow or gold stones
- **Goddesses and gods:** Agni, Athena, Helios, Lakini, Rudra, Surya
- **Herbs/spices:** Goldenseal or lemon balm
- **Incense:** Cinnamon, Dragon's blood, or ginger
- **Keyword:** Opinion
- **Kinds of people:** Friends or colleagues
- **Metal:** Iron
- **Musical note:** E
- **Number of lotus petals:** Ten
- **Plane of existence:** Celestial plane
- **Ruling planet:** Mars ♂ (also Pluto ♀)
- **Seed sound:** RANG
- **Sense:** Sight
- **Sense organ:** Eyes
- **Shape:** Downward-pointing triangle
- **Tarot suit:** Wands
- **Verb:** To do
- **Vowel or vibration:** O (as in "top") or AH (as in "father")
- **Yoga path:** Power yoga (a contemporary form of yoga that combines traditional poses with challenging and dynamic movements for a more intense physical workout)
- **Zodiac sign:** Aries ♈ and Scorpio ♏

Fourth Chakra, or Heart Chakra (*Anahata*)

The fourth chakra, also called the Heart chakra or *Anahata,* is identified with the following correspondences:

- **Animal:** Antelopes, doves, or mammals with four legs
- **Archangel:** Raphael or Chamuel
- **Body:** Astral
- **Color:** Green
- **Element:** Air
- **Food:** Leafy green vegetables like kale, spinach, and lettuce; broccoli; celery; cabbage; squash; greens
- **Herbs/spices:** Basil, thyme, cilantro, and parsley; green tea
- **Gemstone or crystal:** Emerald, jade, malachite, green tourmaline, or other green stones
- **Goddesses and gods:** Aphrodite, Eros, Jesus Christ, Krishna, or Lakshmi
- **Herbs/spices:** Rue or saffron
- **Incense:** Lavender or jasmine
- **Keyword:** Love
- **Kinds of people:** Teachers, *boddhisatvas* (people who delay their own enlightenment to help others reach enlightenment)
- **Metal:** Copper
- **Musical note:** F
- **Number of lotus petals:** Twelve
- **Plane of existence:** Balance plane
- **Ruling planet:** Venus ♀
- **Seed sound:** YANG
- **Sense:** Touch
- **Sense organ:** Skin
- **Shape:** Hexagram
- **Tarot suit:** Swords
- **Verb:** To love
- **Vowel sound:** AH (as in "far") or AY (as in "play")

- **Yoga path:** *Bhakti* yoga (the yoga of devotion, involves the practice and expression of the emotional connection with a Higher Power, universal spirit, or ultimate reality through chanting and worship rituals)
- **Zodiac sign:** Taurus ♉ and Libra ♎

Fifth Chakra, or Throat Chakra (*Vishuddha*)

The fifth chakra, also called the Throat chakra or *Vishuddha*, is identified with the following correspondences:

- **Animal:** Humans, elephants, bulls, or lions
- **Archangel:** Michael or Gabriel
- **Body:** Etheric
- **Color:** Blue
- **Element:** Ether or space
- **Food:** Fruit (especially tart fruits like citrus), fruit juice, herbal tea, salt
- **Gemstone or crystal:** Sapphire, lapis lazuli, turquoise, blue sapphire, sodalite, aquamarine, abalone, or other blue stones
- **Goddesses and gods:** Apollo, Brigit, Ganga (the river goddess), or Sarasvati
- **Herbs/spices:** Cloves or vervain
- **Incense:** Frankincense or mace
- **Keyword:** Expression
- **Kinds of people:** Teachers and leaders
- **Metal:** Mercury
- **Musical note:** G
- **Number of lotus petals:** Sixteen
- **Plane of existence:** Human
- **Ruling planet:** Mercury ☿
- **Seed sound:** HANG
- **Sense:** Hearing
- **Sense organ:** Ears
- **Shape:** Crescent
- **Tarot suit:** Wands
- **Verb:** To speak

- **Vowel sound:** EH (as in "let") or EE (as in "seen")
- **Yoga path:** *Mantra* yoga (the practice of chanting a *mantra*, a sacred syllable or phrase that is spoken repeatedly to aid in concentration and focus)
- **Zodiac sign:** Gemini ♊ and Virgo ♍

Sixth Chakra, or Third Eye Chakra (*Ajna*)

The sixth chakra, also called the Third Eye chakra or *Ajna*, is identified with the following correspondences:

- **Animal:** Archetypes (first defined by psychologist Carl Jung, archetypes are powerful inner patterns of behavior, or universal roles) and owls
- **Archangel:** Raphael
- **Body:** Celestial
- **Color:** Deep indigo or purple
- **Element:** Supreme element, a combination of all the other elements.
- **Food:** Blackberries, blueberries, purple grapes, poppy seeds, any food/substance that affects perception and intuition, including red wine
- **Gemstone or crystal:** Amethyst, alexandrite, azurite, fluorite, star sapphire, or other deep blue or purple stones
- **Goddesses and gods:** Apollo, Hecate, Isis, Krishna, Paramasiva (form of Shiva), or Shakti Hakini
- **Herbs/spices:** Sandalwood
- **Incense:** Star anise or acacia
- **Keyword:** Insight
- **Kinds of people:** Spiritual friends, the people it seems like you've "always known"
- **Metal:** Silver
- **Musical note:** A
- **Number of lotus petals:** Two
- **Plane of existence:** Austerity
- **Ruling planet:** Sun ☉ and Moon ☽
- **Seed sound:** AUM
- **Sense:** Intuition
- **Sense organ:** Third Eye

- **Shape:** A circle with two petals
- **Tarot suit:** Swords
- **Verb:** To see
- **Vowel or vibration:** EE (as in "me") or MM
- **Yoga path:** *Yantra* yoga (Tibetan form of yoga similar to Hatha yoga that combines poses with breathing exercises and meditation to increase life force energy)
- **Zodiac sign:** Leo ♌ and Cancer ♋

Seventh Chakra, or Crown Chakra (*Sahasrara*)

The seventh chakra, also called the Crown chakra or *Sahasrara,* is identified with the following correspondences:

- **Animal:** Spirits of the deceased, especially ancestral spirits
- **Archangel:** Jophiel
- **Body:** Causal or auric
- **Color:** Purple or white
- **Element:** Thought or Goddess/God
- **Food:** None (fasting), or dark-blue grapes, blackberries, or garlic
- **Gemstone or crystal:** Diamond, amethyst, or quartz crystal
- **Goddesses and gods:** Allah, Ama-kala, Inanna, Nut, Odin, Shiva, or Varuna
- **Herbs/spices:** Gotu kola or nutmeg
- **Incense:** Lotus or gotu kola
- **Keyword:** Freedom
- **Kinds of people:** Saints, prophets, or true gurus
- **Metal:** gold
- **Musical note:** B
- **Number of lotus petals:** 1,000
- **Plane of existence:** Reality
- **Ruling planet:** Ketu, the South Node of the Moon in Vedic astrology. (In Western astrology, the Crown chakra has no planet but represents the Universe, the Source of Enlightenment.)
- **Seed sound:** Universal vibration making the sound of AUM
- **Sense:** Perception of Goddess/God

- **Sense organ:** Brain
- **Shape:** Circle
- **Tarot suit:** The entire Major Arcana (the 22 dominant Tarot cards in a standard deck)
- **Verb:** To know
- **Vowel or vibration:** AUM or OM (as in "ah-oo-oh-m") or Ngngng (as in "sing")
- **Yoga path:** *Jnana* yoga (the yoga of knowledge, practiced by meditating on the self and studying spiritual texts)
- **Zodiac sign:** None (Crown chakra energy is of Spirit and beyond the material realm, and as such, it is beyond our body but within reach of our enlightenment.)

Inside the Chakras

Each chakra has plenty of symbolic connections and correspondences, but what's going on inside those spinning energy circles we call the chakras? In the previous chapter, we explained how life force energy moves in and out and through the body via meridians or channels, which are called *nadis* in yoga. Inside the chakras, energy also moves in and out in a lot of different ways, depending on what's going on with you.

If you could see your own chakras (which some people can, through meditation techniques), you might see transparent-colored wheels of energy turning clockwise. Or, you might see some disturbances. From moment to moment, a lot of things can happen to a chakra. Our chakras change size, shape, and speed of spin throughout the day. They are taking in *prana*, processing it so the body can use it, and releasing it back into the system, like energy transformers.

However, sometimes things go awry. A temporary change in a chakra isn't a big deal, but chronic changes can indicate a problem. Chakras don't cause problems; instead, chakras *reflect* problems in your body, mind, or spirit. In Chapter 6, we show you how to measure your own chakras and give you the opportunity to feel your own chakras through a simple exercise. In Chapter 19, we walk you through a meditative exercise to help you see your own chakras; but for now, let's talk about what they are doing, regardless of whether you can see them.

Healthy Chakras

Healthy chakras are the ideal, and chances are, most of your chakras are doing pretty well most of the time. A healthy chakra takes in *prana*, spins it around, and shoots it out again. Healthy chakras appear round with solid borders, bright colors, and a clockwise spin.

Connecting with Your Core

Here, we're going to look into the centering power of your Solar Plexus chakra, using a few of the correspondences identified with it.

Find an open space and stand tall in yoga's Mountain pose, as shown in the following illustration. Take a few calming and centering breaths to allow your body to align and relax into the strength of the pose, lowering your shoulders as your fingertips lengthen toward the Earth and the crown of your head lifts to float easily above your body. As you do this, you will begin to see your third chakra spinning in your solar plexus and to feel its energy build and radiate your surrounding aura.

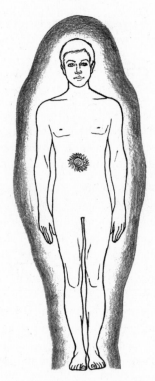

The spinning energy of a healthy third chakra, or Solar Plexus chakra (Manipura).

Use your breath to begin to connect to your chakra's healing energy. Let your breaths become slow and rhythmic. When you are relaxed and fully attentive to the moment, look within your body to see the spinning chakra energy glow yellow as the Sun shining strong and bright. With each breath, see the Sun's light shine with a brightness that brings focusing clarity to your eyesight. After a while, when you feel the energy rising, solid and strong at your core of being, begin to vocalize the sound of "AH" on each exhale; feel the vibration enter the yellow light shining from your third chakra to illuminate your aura. If you are musical, create the vibrating sound on the musical note "E." Take your time. Stand in the golden glow of the light spinning in your solar plexus. Feel its warmth and power. See it radiate strength. Return to the world with new confidence and warmth as you move through your day.

Now you can see how you can use the chakra correspondences to focus in on the energy associated with each one. Consider these correspondences more than simply descriptions of a chakra's nature. See them as talismans of each chakra's energy, tools you can use to draw upon the chakra you are working with. Recognize how much healing potential you can gain from standing quietly and simply *seeing* each chakra.

Look through the correspondences for the third chakra to find other ways of seeing its energy. For example, you can take the Wand suit out of your favorite Tarot deck and do daily three-card readings to explore what the Tarot reveals about your third chakra. Or, you can look at the planets and signs associated with the third chakra in your astrological birth chart. Wear gold jewelry. Become aware of the birds you encounter when you are out and about in your hometown environment. There are many, many ways to see the energy of each chakra and explore what it reveals to *you* about *you*.

Before we move on to doing healing work with your chakras, we have one more interesting aspect of the chakra system to discover: the mysterious, notorious, and much-misunderstood *Kundalini*. Check out the next chapter to learn more about your own personal serpent power.

Chapter
5

Kundalini: Be a Snake Charmer

Perhaps no yoga concept is more misunderstood, feared, maligned, and sought after than the concept of *Kundalini.* Yet no book about the chakras could be complete without it because *Kundalini* is an integral part of the entire chakra system. *Kundalini* has been discussed, debated, analyzed, and experienced by people practicing and studying yoga for thousands of years, but the secrets of *Kundalini* were always passed orally from guru to student. The student had to prove purity and discipline before learning the secrets. That is until *Kundalini* master Yogi Bhajan came to the United States and began to lecture publicly about *Kundalini,* beginning in 1969.

Since then, *Kundalini* yoga has become a widely practiced form of yoga, emphasizing awareness and the mobilization of the life force. Yogi Bhajan famously once said, "If flexibility of the body is the only yoga, then clowns in the circus are the best yogis." In other words, *Kundalini* yoga (indeed, all true yoga) is much more than poses or *asanas.* In many traditions, that "much more" part has a lot to do with *Kundalini.*

As with any esoteric yoga concept that has been around for a while, different ancient and modern scholarly and popular texts discuss *Kundalini* in many different ways. Some directly contradict each other, and some are so steeped in the culture of India that they can be difficult for Westerners to comprehend. In this chapter, however, we're going to minimize the esoteric part and get right down to what you really want to know: What is your own *Kundalini* energy all about, and how can you make it work for you?

What *Kundalini* Is

Kundalini is a Sanskrit term meaning (approximately) "coiled one." *Kundalini* is also an ancient esoteric yoga concept that feminine energy lies coiled like a serpent at the base of the spine inside the first chakra. As *Kundalini* energy is awakened through spiritual practices like yoga, she desires to merge with masculine energy (sometimes represented as the Hindu god Shiva), so she rises up through each chakra as it opens, energizing and activating that chakra. The result is gradual awakening leading to enlightenment, and the intense activation of creative energy and spiritual awareness in the body. But if snakes freak you out, you don't have to think of *Kundalini* in this way. *Kundalini* isn't some foreign presence in your body. It is part of you.

Kundalini is divine power within you, which is separate from (and incomplete without) the divine power of the Universe. *Kundalini* yoga is a form of yoga that seeks to awaken and utilize *Kundalini* energy through poses, meditation, chanting, breathing exercises, and other techniques with the ultimate goal of realizing the individual's inner divinity and oneness with God and all creation. It seeks to join the two, so you can realize and truly comprehend your own inner divinity and your connection with God, universal energy, or whatever the external, sacred force of life is to you.

When these two are yoked—your own divinity and universal divinity—through *Kundalini*-arousing techniques—you reach a new level of understanding, a sort of spiritual evolutionary leap forward. It isn't necessarily a permanent leap; instead, it's more often a glimpse of (or a temporary immersion into) your highest self.

Can you perceive, believe in, and awaken *Kundalini* without believing in any particular God? What if you aren't sure about the whole Higher Power concept at all? No problem. *Kundalini* is the source of divinity within you. It is yours, and it is the catalyst for connecting to all life. But that can mean different things to different people. We can describe *Kundalini* only in mere words, which pale in comparison to the actual experience of it. This is about a universal quest for meaning, so rather than abandoning that quest over semantics, let that quest take you in a direction that makes sense for *you*.

Because *Kundalini* is a difficult concept to grasp, people often explain it using metaphors. One of the most common is that *Kundalini* is a goddess who seeks her male counterpart, Shiva. When aroused, she rises through the chakras to reach Shiva at the Crown chakra, where they merge in holy union. Remember, this is a metaphor, and it's one that makes sense to people in India who are familiar with Shiva and the idea of other gods and goddesses.

But this metaphor might not work so well for you. After all, your spinal column isn't a celestial hook-up spot. The idea of a union between *Kundalini* and Shiva simply represents the union of your consciousness with universal consciousness. It is a glimpse into the divine spark within you. To put it in more Western terms, *Kundalini* rising is like experiencing your own perfection by finally seeing your place in the universal scheme of things. This is the answer to "Who am I and what does it all mean?" When *Kundalini* reaches your seventh chakra, you know the answer to that question.

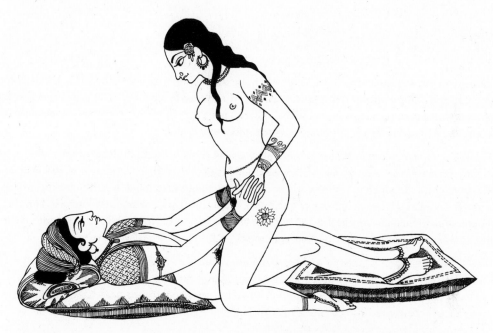

In Kama Sutra, this position arouses Kundalini *and is called Shakti Expressing Her Energy with Shiva.*

No, we can't just tell you the answer to save time. Each person is a unique manifestation of divine energy. You are the only *you* in the Universe, and when you recognize yourself at last, that recognition will be entirely unique. According to yoga philosophy, we are all one, and we are one with the divine universal presence. However, at the same time, we are all different, too. During our time on Earth living in these bodies, we perceive our immense diversity. And yet, we also have the capacity to understand our ultimate unity. Pretty cool, right?

But it isn't easy. You can't just kick *Kundalini* awake and sit back waiting for the ecstasy to start rolling in. Awakening *Kundalini* for ultimate universal fusion takes time, preparation, and commitment (like any good relationship). *Kundalini* is one of the gifts we get in this life, along with our bodies, minds, and spirits. We can waste it, or we can use it to become better, happier, clearer, healthier, and more at peace.

What *Kundalini* Isn't

You might be wondering about some of the things you've heard about *Kundalini*. If you read about *Kundalini*, you might run across references to the dangers of prematurely awakening the "serpent power." Maybe you've read that when *Kundalini* moves, you can experience weird bodily sensations like intense heat or cold in the spinal column, feelings of fluttering or slithering, spontaneous movements of your body, and even hearing voices or hallucinating. We've even read about violent reactions to *Kundalini* awakenings, complete psychotic breaks, and death. That sounds pretty scary, doesn't it?

Okay, you can stop worrying now. There are quite a lot of theories about the so-called dangers of awakening *Kundalini*, but the simple truth is that *Kundalini* is part of you, and inner awakening doesn't hurt you. In many cases, people who have violent psychopathic episodes associated with supposed *Kundalini* awakenings already suffer from mental illness.

In other cases, people were so immersed in hours and hours of meditation that they threw themselves out of balance. When accompanied by fasting (on purpose or just because someone forgets to eat), the problem can be compounded through dehydration. Humans have incredibly complex minds and are susceptible to suggestion. Emotional and mental problems are fairly common in the human species, and sometimes these go hand in hand with the quest for religious experience or understanding of the self.

If you have emotional or mental problems, intense immersion into the quest for awakening *Kundalini* could result in some psychological issues, but it isn't the *Kundalini* doing it. It is an imbalance within you, and that means you need to seek help from a professional who understands the context of your problems. We urge you to seek help from a counselor or therapist if you are suffering from an imbalance.

If you have physical, emotional, mental, or spiritual issues, *your chakras won't be healthy, balanced, and open.* And that means *Kundalini* won't rise. This is your body's own internal security system. If, on the other hand, you are a sound, healthy person who is balanced and primed for a spiritual experience, you are ready for *Kundalini* to rise. You aren't going to suffer a mental breakdown or drop dead because you practiced the *Kundalini*-awakening exercises in this book. We promise. When you are in an unhealthy state and you have a physical or emotional issue or episode, *it is not Kundalini*. It is something that needs to be addressed by a medical or mental health professional. If you find you are distressed by physical or emotional issues you've not been able to resolve on your own, please do seek care as soon as possible from a health professional.

Kundalini is a powerful internal force, for sure, but it's *your* power. To repeat: If your chakras aren't open and ready (meaning you are not open and ready), *Kundalini* can't move up through them. They will keep *Kundalini* down by closing like little round doors. If your chakras *are* open and ready because you are physically, mentally, and spiritually balanced and strong, then you are ready for the transformative energy of *Kundalini*.

In Betsy's practice, she has not encountered anyone experiencing the rise of Kundalini. She believes this is because people typically come to her when they feel out of balance, physically and/or emotionally. We've already said this, but we want to emphasize it again: When we are in a state of imbalance, *Kundalini cannot rise*. Betsy also believes that the rising of this intense energy is a fairly rare occurrence. It is hard work to bring awareness and attention to one's own issues, and it's even harder to change those aspects of our lives that are not working. We all have "stuff"— baggage and issues that limit our potential. When we work through one layer of our "stuff," we often discover another layer, and another, and another! This is normal, and part of our contracts as human beings is to work through our issues so that we can be open vessels through which *Kundalini* energy can flow. But this might take a lifetime (or many lifetimes) of work! So stop worrying about *Kundalini*, and start working on paving the way for her future passage.

Preparing the Body for *Kundalini*

One of the ways the practitioner of yoga prepares for spiritual awakening is by practicing the Eight Limbs of Yoga, also called *Ashtanga* yoga. (*Ashtanga* means eight limbs or eight parts.) Most yoga paths mention and recommend following the eight limbs, even though many Western yoga paths mostly emphasize just the third limb—the *asanas* or physical poses. These are important, but they are not the only aspect of yoga.

The purpose of the eight limbs, which we explained in Chapter 2, is to help the individual fully integrate with universal divinity. They are like stepping-stones to make it easier. There have been those few who manage to achieve enlightenment without necessarily following all these steps, but the point of the eight limbs is to prime the body, mind, and spirit. Think of it as taking singing lessons to sing better. Some people have amazing voices without lessons, but most can benefit from some instruction and a lot of practice.

The Eight Limbs of Yoga are all things you can do in your daily life. They comprise a whole-self workout plan, covering the behavior, the body, the breath, the mind, and the spirit. You can look back to Chapter 2 for more detail, but just as a quick review, the eight limbs are:

- The *yamas* (healthy behaviors to practice, like nonviolence, truthfulness, and not stealing)
- The *niyamas* (things to observe, like cleanliness, inner contentment, and self-discipline)
- The *asanas* (the yoga poses)
- *Pranayama* (breathing exercises)
- *Pratyahara* (sensory withdrawal)
- *Dharana* (concentration)
- *Dhyana* (meditation)
- *Samadhi* (union with divine energy)

These are all goals to work toward, but this is good physical, mental, and spiritual work. The peripheral benefits of practicing the Eight Limbs of Yoga are amazing. You get physically and mentally stronger, calmer, more content, and more centered. The healthy open state of your chakras proves it. Regular practice of the eight limbs also primes your body, mind, and spirit for *Kundalini* to wake up and get moving.

But even then, *Kundalini* isn't going to just suddenly zip up your spine and turn you into some levitating guru right in the middle of your dinner meeting. You have to be working on it, and if you are working on it, you will be ready for it. (And even when it happens, we're sorry to say that you probably will not levitate.)

Getting *Kundalini* to rise is a long process of preparation. You might hear stories about people who experienced spontaneous *Kundalini* rising, but we believe that when this happens, it isn't as spontaneous as it might seem. Those people really were ready. Or, it wasn't *Kundalini* rising at all. It was something else. Rest assured that a focus on a healthy body and mind, which are reflected in strong, balanced, and open chakras, is a safe, sound, and ultimately rewarding path.

How *Kundalini* Moves

Kundalini might begin to stir when you get to that strong, balanced, healthy point (maybe you are already there), and you are practicing yoga or exercising regularly, eating a pure healthy diet, and spending time each day meditating or praying. It might happen during a yoga practice or especially if you are meditating.

When *Kundalini* begins to move, it feels like different things to different people. Some people experience a feeling of movement at the base of the spine, like a creeping or jumping feeling. Some feel heat in the spine. Others experience a flutter or the sensation of cold in the lower back. Sometimes, the feeling is dramatic, like your mind suddenly popping open. Sometimes, the feeling is subtle, as if *Kundalini* has moved just a little. You might feel a rising sensation at the base and moving up your spine, or you might not feel much movement at all. The way *Kundalini* manifests for you depends on who you are, the state of your body and mind, and what you are prepared to experience.

Betsy has a friend who slowly began to notice snakes everywhere in her environment—not only real snakes, but also pictures, cartoons, TV commercials, and books about snakes. Her friend was in the midst of deep spiritual work and took these signs as proof that *Kundalini* was rising.

Whether the sensation is dramatic doesn't really matter. If you get too attached to the idea of making *Kundalini* move, you can throw yourself out of balance again. Remember, Kundalini is just you waking up. When that happens, you will enjoy a creative surge like you've never experienced before. You might feel suddenly filled with love, or you might feel deeply connected to everyone around you. The feeling might last for a while, or it might be fleeting. Let yourself feel it and see where it takes you.

When *Kundalini* moves, it can feel exciting, serene, or just interesting, but it's not going to change your personality. What it can do is show you the best aspects of your personality that you might not have been allowing full expression. Just remember, *Kundalini* is part of you. Work on yourself, and allow your best self to emerge. That's what it's really all about.

No matter how often we tell people not to worry about *Kundalini,* some people still do. They worry about feeling something foreign or scary or going to a mental or spiritual place they can't handle. The human mind is highly suggestible, but an authentic *Kundalini* experience is a beautiful thing. Personally, we believe that bad *Kundalini* experiences aren't *Kundalini* experiences, but not everybody agrees with us on this point. In any case, if you ever experience disturbing physical sensations, thoughts, or feelings that are violent, self-destructive, or frightening to you, don't try to deal with them alone. There are many wonderful, experienced therapists and health practitioners out there who can help you sort out what's going on.

Kundalini Transformation

People often wonder what happens to them *after Kundalini* wakes up. Will they be the same? Will they be normal? Or will they become all weird and nobody will be able to relate to them anymore? Fear not. Those who engage in serious spiritual work and finally do experience *Kundalini* awakening report surges of creativity, brilliance, engagement in the world, an ability to help others, and other wonderful results. Some people believe that *Kundalini* awakenings are the source of great artistic ability and genius. Many also believe that as more people experience *Kundalini* awakening, the human race will take an evolutionary leap forward.

Perhaps *Kundalini* is a catalyst for activating our higher selves. We see the world changing around us every day in amazing and transformative ways. As the great teacher and peace activist, India's Father, Gandhi said, "Be the change you wish to see in the world." Those words have resounded throughout the world. As you awaken through the help of your own *Kundalini* energy, you will have the energy, the vision, and the inspiration to be that change.

Getting Started with *Kundalini*

In addition to practicing the Eight Limbs of Yoga, there are some specific exercises you can do that tone your chakras and manipulate your *prana* in a way that can encourage *Kundalini* to awaken. You can do this in many ways, including the following two exercises.

Cobra Pose (*Bhujangasana*)

Yoga's Cobra pose evokes serpent power.

The Cobra pose is a simple yoga pose that actually imitates the shape and movement of a snake—an apt pose for awakening the serpent power. Because *Kundalini* starts in your first chakra, this pose is effective because it concentrates energy in that first chakra. Here's how to do it:

1. Lie on your stomach on a yoga mat or a folded blanket. Place your hands on either side of you, palms on the floor, at the level of your chest. Keep your elbows hugging into the sides of your body. Stretch your legs out behind you and click your toenails into the mat.

2. Visualize your first chakra at the base of your spine. Press this area into the floor, along with the tops of your thighs, your knees, and the tops of your feet so that your entire lower body feels rooted to the ground. Keep your tailbone tucked in to prevent low back pain. Everything from the hips down should be pressing into the floor, but you should especially feel the area around the first chakra at the base of your tailbone rooting down into the ground.

3. Inhale and begin to lift your chest off the floor. Gradually rise up, using your arms for support without putting any pressure on your back. Your lower back moves inward and up.

4. Press your hands firmly into the mat, and imagine your hands moving back toward your hips as your heart and chest open, expanding forward. Breathe normally and hold this position for 10 to 30 seconds or as long as feels comfortable and energizing.

5. Exhale and slowly lower your chest and head back to the floor. Rest your forehead on the floor and breathe. Feel the energy accumulating in your first chakra. Repeat one or two more times.

Mula Bandha

Bandha is the Sanskrit word for lock, and *bandhas* are muscular contractions (locks) inside the body that seal off the *nadis* to concentrate *prana*. The three primary locks used in yoga practice and *Kundalini* work are:

- *Mula bandha* (or Root lock—a lock at the first chakra)
- *Uddiyana bandha* (or Abdominal lock—a lock at the third chakra)
- *Jalandhara bandha* (or Throat lock—a lock at the fifth chakra)

The *bandhas* are key for energizing the chakras and awakening *Kundalini*. To understand how this works, it helps to understand that within the body, there are different kinds of *prana*.

Without getting too technical, a kind of sub-*prana* moves upward through the *sushumna nadi* when you inhale, and another type of *prana*, called *apana* (a type of sub-*prana*), moves downward through the *sushumna nadi* when you exhale. One of its functions is to move spent energy out of the body. When *prana* and *apana* meet, they create a spark, which can awaken *Kundalini*. Getting them to meet means infusing the body with *prana* and holding it inside.

Mula bandha, or Root lock, is one of three primary *bandhas*. This one involves a muscular contraction of the pelvic floor, at the first chakra. Normally, *apana* moves downward, but with the first chakra locked, it gets trapped and moves back up, where it meets and mingles with *prana*. This causes a sort of combustion, an inner spark that can help to nudge *Kundalini* awake.

Regular practice of *mula bandha* can help your awareness expand beyond the boundaries of the physical world and material concerns, to a higher awareness. It's a powerful exercise, but it's not hard to do. Here's how to do it.

1. Sit comfortably on the floor on a folded blanket with your legs crossed and your spine straight. Breathe normally.

2. Focus your attention on the first chakra, at the base of your spine. Feel the muscles on your pelvic floor all around the area where your body touches the blanket. Try to contract these muscles as if pulling the first chakra inward and upward. Relax. Do this a few times to get the feel of it. We don't want to offend anybody, but for the sake of being clear, this contraction is what you would do if you were urinating and wanted to stop the flow while contracting the muscles around your anus at the same time. (If you've ever been instructed on how to do Kegel exercises, do that. It's the same idea.) The movement is actually to contract and raise the entire pelvic floor so your internal energy moves up instead of down.

3. Now, take a long, slow, and gentle breath in. When you have filled up your lungs, hold your breath and engage those first chakra muscles. Hold your breath for 5 to 10 seconds, and then gently exhale. Release the lock. Repeat. For maximum effect, do this a few times every day.

As you've learned from reading this chapter and doing the exercises, *Kundalini* serpent power is an energy most profoundly nurtured by someone who has worked through a deep spiritual practice. If you understand the strength and purpose of each chakra and embark on a journey to release the healing power of the chakras in your life, then rousing *Kundalini* power might become possible for you. As in *mula bandha*, you may begin to feel your *Kundalini* energy coiled and waiting.

Be Mindful of Your Chakras

"I think, therefore I am," wrote Descartes, the seventeenth-century French philosopher. Most of us have been raised to believe that we are our thoughts, for how can we ever separate ourselves from them? With social media, we're constantly posting and commenting on all manner of experience and opinion. Our thoughts are everywhere. And yet, according to yoga philosophy, *we are not our thoughts.* Thoughts are something we have, like hands or hair or clothing or a smart phone, but they are not *us.* They are not *you,* or at least, your thoughts do not define you. They are not the *whole* you.

But it probably will be difficult for you to recognize the truth of this unless you practice *mindfulness.* Mindfulness is the act of paying attention without engaging in what you are paying attention to. In other words, mindfulness is awareness, pure and simple. It is not thought, but it is aware of thought. It is not feelings, but it is aware of feelings. It is not your physical body, but it is aware of your physical body. It is the ability to perceive yourself and all your qualities without making the mistake that you *are* any of your qualities. It is the you that transcends qualities. *Mindfulness meditation* is a specific technique to cultivate mindfulness, but you can be mindful anytime, anywhere. You just have to stop your chattering brain, take a deep breath, and *be.*

The Benefits of Mindfulness

Mindfulness isn't just helpful for meditation. It has tangible physical benefits. Many doctors, psychologists, and healthcare facilities teach and employ mindfulness techniques because of their proven stress-reducing effects. Mindfulness techniques, including mindfulness meditation, can significantly reduce blood pressure as well as muscle tension and stressful feelings, including anxiety.

Mindfulness can also improve your performance in all aspects of your life. If you are exercising, including doing yoga, mindfulness can reduce the risk of injury because you will be so keenly aware of your body and how it feels as you move it. In your work, mindfulness can aid your concentration and improve the efficiency and quality of what you are doing. Your mind won't be wandering off to what you will do next or what you did before. Instead, you can experience total absorption in your task through mindfulness.

Why do we bring up mindfulness now? Because mindfulness is a key element in healing your own chakras. It's easy to imagine what your chakras might be doing, but through mindfulness, you can gain a more clear, unadorned perception of your chakras. Through mindfulness techniques, you can learn to feel your chakras, assess their current qualities, and even fix them.

If you ever eat while watching television, watch television while surfing the Internet, or surf the Internet while talking to your kids, you know about multitasking. However, you might not know much about mindfulness. Beginning to eat a bag of chips and then suddenly realizing the entire bag of chips is gone is eating *without* mindfulness. Listening *without* mindfulness occurs when someone is talking to you and you suddenly realize your mind has wandered , and you haven't heard anything that person said to you. Multitasking is anti-mindfulness, so give yourself a break from it once in a while. When you need to do something, eat something, or listen to something, do that one thing and nothing else. Try it. You'll instantly get better at whatever you are doing.

Pay No Mind

Mindfulness takes some practice because most of us aren't used to paying attention to the present moment without letting our brains simultaneously wander elsewhere. Daily mindfulness practice helps to train your mind into increased awareness, and what better way to practice than by meeting and greeting your own chakras?

You don't have to get all meditative about mindfulness. You can have mindfulness moments throughout the day, whenever you choose to have them. Just stop what you are doing, disengage from your thoughts, and expand your awareness so that you look *at* your thoughts, feelings, and sensory perceptions without letting them rule you.

You can tune in to your chakras in this way throughout the day, too, especially if you notice a physical sensation in the area of a particular chakra. Do you have a sore throat, butterflies in your stomach, chest pain, or an ache in your lower back? Bring your awareness to that area and without judgment, see if you can notice anything going on in your chakra.

But wait—tuning in to your chakras is pretty challenging work if you aren't even used to tuning in to your physical body. Chakras are part of your *energy body,* so they require even more finely honed perceptive powers. Your energy body is part of you, not part of your physical body. Your energy body is the layer of you consisting of the energy that flows in and around your body and through your *nadis,* and it concentrates in your chakras.

Mindful Matters

This mindfulness exercise can be challenging, but we're confident you can give it a try. You might have a hard time the first time, but every time you practice this exercise, it will get easier. It's like a workout for your brain, and you get in better shape the more you practice.

1. Sit comfortably on a folded blanket or even in a chair; just make sure you are sitting upright and your spine is straight.

2. Lower your eyes to approximately a 45-degree angle and soften your gaze so you aren't looking at anything. Keep your eyes open; closing your eyes makes it easier for your mind to wander.

3. Withdraw your awareness from your thoughts. In other words, step back mentally from your thoughts and look at them, as if they belonged to someone else. Don't expect them to stop because they won't. Just look at them. For example, you might notice you are thinking about whether you can do this exercise or not. That's a thought. Visualize wrapping it up inside a bubble and labeling it as *thought.*

4. Now, expand your awareness to your physical body. Notice how it feels, as if someone else were telling you about it. For example, "That person's knee itches"; "That person's shoulders are rolling forward"; or "That person is hungry." You can scratch your itches or adjust your posture if you want to. (Hold off on getting up to get something to eat for the moment!). Notice how it feels to do those things. Visualize wrapping every physical sensation you notice in a bubble and labeling it. For example, "itch," "shoulder roll," or "hunger."

5. Now, expand your awareness to the room around you. What do you hear? How does the air feel on your skin, and how does the blanket feel underneath you? Do you smell anything? Notice what your senses perceive, but again, notice them as if they belong to someone else. Visualize wrapping every sensation you have in a bubble and labeling it, such as "cold," "soft," "radiator noise," or "burnt toast."

6. Now, expand your attention to include your awareness—be aware of your awareness. Has it shrunk to the size of a thought? Step back again out of your thoughts and your sensory perceptions. Mentally look at them all as if they belonged to someone else. Now, try looking away from them. What is left to perceive that is not thought or sensory perception?

7. Stay there as long as you can. When you get caught up in a thought or a feeling and it sweeps you away, notice it happening, and then step back off the ride, wrap it in a bubble, and label it. Then turn back around and step back into your unbridled awareness.

8. Try to stick with this for about five minutes. Repeat once or twice a day and see if you can work up to 20 minutes.

Your chakras tend to be open and strong after a yoga class, a massage, or energy work. When you are feeling particularly anxious or stressed, or you just experienced something traumatic, your chakras tend to close temporarily. Chakras can change from day to day and moment to moment. Long-term patterns are more significant than a chakra's condition at any given moment.

Hello, Chakras!

After you have the concept of mindfulness in your head, you don't have to master it to start checking out your own chakras. Go ahead and try this exercise, even if the previous exercise was challenging.

We go into more detail about actually visualizing your chakras in Chapter 19. For now, we just want you to focus on your perceptions. Let your mind be open and unengaged, and see what happens when you focus your awareness on your chakras. Mindfulness is a process, not a goal, and this chakra introduction exercise is part of that process.

1. Place a yoga mat or folded blanket on the floor and lie on your back. Tuck your shoulder blades under you so your chest feels broad and your heart opens. Stretch your legs out as far as you can and then relax them. Adjust your arms so they are about a foot from the sides of your body and rest your hands with the palms facing up.

2. Take a moment to step into mindfulness mode. Disengage from your thoughts. Don't try to banish them; just step back out your thoughts and look at them. Look at your physical sensations. Look at your sensory perceptions. Let them be, disengage, and avoid any judgments you might feel toward yourself.

3. When you feel like you have stepped back from your thoughts and sensory perceptions, bring awareness to the base of your spine and into your first chakra. Theoretically, you know this chakra should be round, red, and turning like a wheel, but rather than just imagining it, try to feel and perceive it with your awareness.

4. As you bring your awareness to your chakra, continue to let your thoughts come and go as they will, but let your chakra be the focus of your concentration. Let images, feelings, and other sensory perceptions come to you. Don't judge what happens or try to control it. Remember, you are standing back and being mindful; you are not immersing yourself in thoughts or feelings right now. Just *notice*. You might get some images or feelings, or maybe you won't. Just let whatever happens, happen.

5. Now, shift your awareness to your second chakra. You know it should be round, orange, and turning like a wheel; again, rather than imagining how it should look, try to feel and perceive what is really going on in there, just behind your navel. Mentally record your perceptions.

6. Move your awareness to each chakra, in order:

    To your yellow third chakra under your rib cage

    To your green fourth chakra at your heart

    To your blue fifth chakra in your throat

    To your indigo/purple sixth chakra in your forehead

    To your purple or white seventh chakra at the crown of your head

7. Spend some time contemplating each one without judgment. Just perceive.

8. After you've finished perceiving each chakra with awareness, slowly wiggle your fingers and toes, bringing your awareness back to your physical body. Roll to your right side, and when you are ready, sit up.

Write down your perceptions about your chakras right away before you forget. If you've already forgotten, that's okay. The exercise is the important part right now. (However, next time, you can also get up and write down what you perceive after each chakra, instead of waiting until the end if you really want a written record of the experience.) Record any sensory perceptions or thoughts you had about each chakra. Your perceptions are unique to you, so don't worry about what they are supposed to be. Just consider what they *are*. Writing your perceptions by hand engages a different part of the brain than typing or dictating by voice, and it aids in enhancing understanding and memory.

Repeat this exercise at least once a week, so you can begin to perceive patterns in your chakras, such as which ones tend to be more noticeable to you and which ones you have a hard time perceiving.

Some people find mindfulness exercises easy, but for others, they are incredibly challenging, especially when attempting to perceive subtle nonphysical phenomena like the chakras. If you try the chakra mindfulness exercise in this chapter and you don't feel, see, or perceive anything, don't worry. Try again later. The more you get comfortable with the notion of mindfulness and perceiving your own chakras, the easier the perceptions will come. Massage therapists and energy workers often have the ability to tune in to your energy and provide feedback about the health of your chakras. You might also consider enlisting a particularly intuitive friend who might be able to meditate on and perceive qualities of your chakras for you. Later, as you hone your mindfulness skills, you can return the favor.

Measure for Measure

After you start tuning in to your own chakras, things start to get interesting. Suddenly, you have a tool for determining what aspects of your life are working well and which ones need more attention (or less attention). Here's another tool for you: you can actually measure your own chakras.

When you measure your chakras, you can see exactly how big they are, what shape they are, and which direction they are spinning. Betsy frequently measures her clients' chakras, taking a baseline measurement at the beginning of therapy and then repeats the measurement on a periodic basis, such as weekly or monthly, to see what changes. Betsy explains that a single reading isn't necessarily significant. Chakras change from day to day, even from moment to moment. Depending on what you are thinking, feeling, and experiencing at any given moment, your chakras can open and close, widen and narrow, change shape or position or direction of spin, then change back again.

However, regular measuring can reveal more overarching patterns. For instance, a closed fourth chakra during a single measuring session doesn't necessarily mean that person is having heart issues. However, a fourth chakra that is persistently closed session after session is more telling. Perhaps that person has closed herself off from feeling love and compassion for others or refuses to take care of herself.

To measure your chakras, you need just two things: a pendulum and a partner. A pendulum is an object hanging from a chain, cord, or other similar apparatus, which can swing freely. Pendulums can be used as tools for measuring the chakras because they swing freely and can therefore be influenced by the chakra's energy; this is similar to the way a wind chime or mobile is affected by air currents. You can buy pendulums, but you can also use a necklace with a weighty pendant on it. A tiny charm probably isn't heavy enough. The pendant should weigh more than the chain or cord on which it hangs.

Your partner should be a relatively disinterested person. In other words, he or she should not care what your chakras are like. If you have an emotional relationship with someone, especially if that person has strong opinions about which of your chakras will probably be open or closed, then that person is not a good choice for this exercise. Choose someone who is open to the idea of measuring your chakras but has no stake in the information.

Grounding Your Partner

Before you and your partner begin the chakra-measuring process, your partner must get grounded and separate her energy from yours. This is how Betsy suggests you can accomplish this:

1. You lie down on your back on a bed or on the floor (on a yoga mat or a folded blanket). Ask your partner to stand or kneel beside you.

2. Your partner can now close her eyes and imagine her own energy rooting her down into the ground. She can visualize roots coming out of her feet or legs and anchoring her to the earth.

3. Next, your partner can open her eyes but visualize a heavy curtain of energy falling between the two of you. She can put her hand through it, but the rest of her body must stay on one side of the curtain while your body stays on the other side. Mentally, your partner can say to herself, "I am detached from outcomes. What is hers is hers, what is mine is mine, and nothing crosses the curtain. My stuff stays on my side, and her stuff stays on her side." This separates your energy so the pendulum can read your energy and not your partner's energy.

Some people wonder if chakras can pour out enough energy to influence a pendulum, why would you need another person to hold the pendulum? It's true that if you were to hang a pendulum from an inanimate object over someone's chakra, it would not spin. The pendulum must be in contact with energy to conduct energy. A wire can't transfer electricity unless it is connected on both ends, and although *prana* is a little bit different than electrical energy, the concept is similar. (For example, the pendulum doesn't have to touch you to pick up your chakra energy pattern.) Your partner is the energizing force that powers the pendulum to be able to pick up your chakra's energy flow pattern.

How to Measure Your Chakras

When your partner is grounded, it's your turn to relax. Lie back and let the weight of the bed or floor support you. Breathe normally and close your eyes. Then follow these steps to measure your chakras:

○ With the pendulum in her dominant hand, your partner can now hold the pendulum by its cord about two feet above your body, which will be above your energy field. Your partner then moves the pendulum above your first chakra (at the base of your spine) and lowers it straight down to about two to three inches above your first chakra, which should bring the pendulum into the energy field of that chakra. Your partner should try to keep her hand as steady as possible and hold the pendulum with a loose grip rather than with a firm and rigid hold, which could prevent the pendulum from spinning in response to the chakra energy. Have your friend concentrate on keeping her own energy to herself so she doesn't influence the pendulum. You want your own chakra energy to get it spinning, not hers.

○ In most cases, the pendulum starts to swing. The shape of the swing and the direction indicate the shape and direction of your chakra's energy flow. You can both look at it, but try to stay still and centered. If the pendulum does not move, try moving it closer to your body. If the pendulum still doesn't move, the chakra you are measuring might be closed. Remember, the pendulum not moving might be just a momentary reaction. Sometimes people get nervous about having their chakras measured, and all the chakras clamp shut. Try to relax. This is supposed to be fun!

Using a pendulum to measure the fourth chakra, the Heart chakra.

○ After you have determined the general state of your first chakra, your partner should lift the pendulum up about 2 feet, back out of the energy field, and with her other hand, stop the swing. Now, she can bring it over the second chakra, around the navel area, and again, lower it straight down to about 2 to 3 inches over the chakra. Wait for the pendulum to start swinging.

○ Repeat this process over each of the other chakras:

- The third chakra at the solar plexus.
- The fourth chakra at the heart.
- The fifth chakra at the throat.
- The sixth chakra at the forehead.

- The seventh chakra about 2 inches above the crown of the head. (The pendulum will not actually be over your body; instead, it will be 2 inches higher than the top of your head.)

  ○ *Now it is your partner's turn. You try it on her.*

What Do the Measurements Mean?

Now that you've watched the pendulum swinging in response to your energy fields and your friend's, you can interpret the results. Here are some guidelines to help you understand what your measurements mean:

  ○ *Movement:* Once the pendulum is brought into the energy field of the chakra, the pendulum will start to move if the chakra is open. If there is no movement of the pendulum and it is about 1 to 2 inches above the body, this likely means that the chakra is blocked or closed.

  ○ *Direction:* A healthy chakra should spin in a clockwise direction. If the pendulum is going back and forth, it may mean the chakra is skewed in an oblong shape, which could mean the chakra is taking in energy sporadically. A right-left swing could mean that chakra is more skewed toward its physical aspects. An up-down swing could indicate that chakra is more skewed toward its psychological or spiritual aspects. (See Chapters 7 through 13 for more on the physical and psychological/ spiritual aspects of each chakra.) If the pendulum goes counter-clockwise, it could mean that chakra is closed or that chakra is releasing energy instead of taking it in.

  ○ *Diameter:* Ideally, all your chakras are spinning in the same direction with the same diameter. This indicates balance. In general, the diameter or distance across the circle created by the pendulum's spin should be about 4 to 6 inches. If it is less than this, it might mean the chakra is open but weak. If the diameter is greater than 6 inches, this usually signifies an excessive chakra that is overloaded with energy. You might find that if one of your chakras is excessive, the chakras on either side of it will measure a bit deficient or small.

Remember, a single measurement doesn't mean much. Measuring your chakras is best for establishing long-term patterns. However, a single measurement can be good at helping you to assess your mood or feelings at the moment. Maybe your second chakra is temporarily huge, and this helps you realize you are being overly emotional about something. Or maybe your first chakra is closed, and this helps you recognize that you are feeling insecure or unsafe about something.

Mindful attention to your chakras is fun, interesting, and helpful in so many ways that we think it is well worth a few minutes out of your day. Tune in and see where you are. You'll begin to achieve a whole new level of self-awareness. Writing your chakra perceptions in a journal dedicated to this practice can help you recognize patterns and identify which chakras you want to focus on and work with specifically. You'll find that healing your chakras is whole-body healing that can open your life in so many beneficial ways.

PART 3

HEALING CHAKRAS: ROOT TO CROWN

This part is the heart of *Chakra Healing*. We begin at the bottom with the first chakra and work our way up, chapter by chapter, through each chakra. We'll travel from the Root chakra at the base of your spine, where your survival instincts and sense of security sit, all the way up to your Crown chakra at the crown of your head, where you connect with a healing force greater than yourself. You learn what's going on inside each chakra, gaining a more intimate knowledge of your own physical and psychological issues. You'll gain the tools you need to awaken, align, energize, and heal your chakras, one by one.

Chapter
7

Root Chakra (*Muladhara*): Sleeping Power

They say every story has a beginning, a middle, and an end. For you and your story, your first chakra, or Root chakra, is your personal beginning. This is the place where you commence as an individual, and this chakra begins to form while you are still in the womb, not long before birth. Here lies your sense of security, belonging, well-being, physical health, and prosperity. This is where you become grounded, and everything that happens in your body, your mind, and your spirit finds its source here.

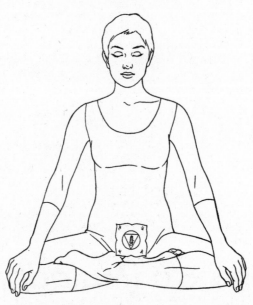

The first chakra, or Root chakra (Muladhara), is the seat of security and physical health.

Although the higher chakras are more spiritual, we would argue that in many ways, the Root chakra is the most important of all the chakras because without a strong, healthy Root chakra, it is difficult to maximize your potential in any area of your life. It is nearly impossible to achieve spiritual enlightenment without the steady, stable energy of your first chakra. A tree can't thrive, live, or even stay upright without roots, and that's exactly what your first chakra is for you: your roots. Without a strong and open first chakra, the first storm to come along would uproot and topple you.

Root Chakra 101

Whether you notice it, work with it, or ignore it, your first chakra is always right there at the base of your spine, spinning its energy and trying to keep you grounded. Sometimes, this chakra might grow larger with excessive energy, and sometimes it might grow smaller or even close down for a while. However, it is consistently the root of your energy body—the sleeping spot for your *Kundalini* energy—and the measure of your sense of security, physical sensations, and place in the world.

The first chakra, also called the Root chakra or Earth chakra, is called *Muladhara* in traditional Sanskrit, which means root or base support. It is associated with the Earth element because it represents the actual, physical connection to Earth and physical incarnation in a body. Its symbolic color is red, and the traditional lotus symbol depicting this chakra has four petals. The sound associated with this chakra is the seed sound *LANG* (rhymes with "song"). Chanting this sound helps to activate the first chakra.

This chakra is located at the base of your spine in the area of your perineum. It is associated with several physical structures in the body: the coccygeal nerve plexus, the adrenal glands, the sacrum, and the organs that govern the elimination of waste from the body, particularly the anus.

Your Root chakra governs several very important aspects of your life, so let's look at them one at a time.

Security, Safety, and Survival

We all come into this world in a vulnerable state and totally dependent on others for survival. This is where our quest for security begins—a quest that will last a lifetime and originates in the Root chakra. Some people simply feel safe in the world and feel as though they belong, no matter what happens to them. Others always seem to have a gnawing sense of impending doom and might even want to escape from life.

These feelings are reflected in the state of your Root chakra, revealing how secure you feel in your life and even in your body. Are you safe? Do you have the basic requirements for survival, such as food and shelter? You probably do, and you might know this rationally, but you might not always trust or believe that you do. This is a first chakra issue.

First chakra security issues often stem from childhood experiences. If you didn't feel protected or were mistreated as a child, you probably have first chakra issues now. Birth trauma or a lack of good bonding with a mother figure in the early months of your life can wreak serious damage to a first chakra. If your parents didn't feel safe or secure while you were growing up, you might have inherited that internal sense of unease. On the other hand, if you felt safe and sheltered as a child and all your needs were met—from food and shelter to love and attention— you are more likely to have a strong and open first chakra as an adult.

Grounded for Life

Betsy encounters many clients in her practice with grounding issues, so this is something she often focuses on in treatment. Being grounded means feeling connected to the Earth, comfortable in your body, and present in your physical surroundings—all signs of a healthy Root chakra. People who are grounded recognize that they live in bodies and that they have to take care of those bodies, as well as their homes, their cars, their bank accounts, and all the other aspects of life in the physical world. Being grounded gives you a firm foundation on which to build a life. The most spiritual person in the world won't get very far without also being grounded. The reality is that we might be spiritual beings, but we exist in human bodies and we need to care for them.

One of Betsy's clients, a young woman with an amazing talent for writing, was full of creative ideas but couldn't ever seem to manifest them. She lived in her own creative world in her head, but she had difficulty managing finances, remembering to eat, or putting her brilliant ideas onto paper. During therapy, Betsy asked her client to take off her shoes, put her feet on the ground, and describe how the floor felt against the soles of her feet. With her bare feet on the floor, the client admitted that she couldn't feel the floor at all. This was a sure sign that her first chakra needed work!

People who aren't grounded tend to be flighty, anxious, detached, and have little sense of their own bodies or how best to function in the physical world. Some of the most effective first chakra healing exercises have to do with grounding. We talk about those later in this chapter.

Family Matters

An important part of each person's sense of belonging in the world is directly related to family and also to what author and *medical intuitive* Caroline Myss refers to as "tribe." Medical intuitives are people with the ability to use their own intuition to determine specific physical, emotional, or psychological illnesses or imbalances in other people. Sometimes, medical intuitives "see" a specific problem, such as a cancerous tumor in a particular place or the settling of a pernicious infection in the lungs. Sometimes, intuitives simply get a sense of what the problem is or even feel the same pain, such as arthritis or migraine, in their own bodies.

Your family is your tribe (like it or not), but you might have other tribes as well, such as your friends, the people you work with, your fellow students, your social media followers, or other groups who share common interests or life experiences with you. Your country can be your tribe, generating feelings of patriotism and civic duty. Your ethnic group, your gender, your neighborhood, or that tight-knit group of friends you've known since high school are all examples of different tribes you might claim as your own. When your tribe changes because of a move, a divorce, or a new job, you might encounter a period of first chakra upheaval until you settle into a new tribe and can establish new roots.

Your feelings about your place in your own family and your own tribe are reflected in your Root chakra and can include feelings like and loyalty. Do you know that feeling you get when someone insults one of your family members or friends? That feeling of anger that says, "Nobody better say anything against my mother, father, brother, sister, colleague, friend, partner, mentor, husband, wife, child, dog, cat, town, ethnic group, religion, or country?"

That instinctual reaction and that connection through loyalty comes from the first chakra.

Boundaries

The first chakra not only reflects your feelings of belonging in a group, but it also sets boundaries that separate you from the other members of the group. You know where you end and others begin. First chakra problems are often related to boundary issues, which occur when people are too open with others at their own expense or are so closed off from people that they never develop genuine and close relationships.

Prosperity Starts Here

How you handle your finances, pay your bills, and save for the future are all aspects tied to your first chakra. People with strong first chakras tend to have a good grasp of what money represents (security and the ability to meet basic needs), and they handle their finances in an organized and rational way. People with constant financial worries and irresponsible financial behavior often have blocked first chakras, whereas people who hoard money or are obsessed with material gain tend to have overloaded first chakras.

Getting control of your financial life isn't quite as easy as opening your first chakra. Keep making the same mistakes, and your first chakra will keep closing again. Instead, think about the ideas you have—perhaps inherited from your parents or related to impressions from childhood—that make you feel like you can't control your money or that having enough money is somehow a bad thing. Examine these ideas and what you *think* about money versus what you actually know to be *true* about money. Have your ideas about money been negatively affecting your financial life? Consider whether those ideas might be misconceptions.

Your Body and Your Health

The first chakra represents the physical aspect of you—your body. That means the condition of your body, your body image, your physical health, and your weight are directly tied to your Root chakra. When you are healthy and fit, you are in a better position to feel safe and secure and to meet your own basic needs. When you are ill or unfit, you might feel less secure and less able to master your own survival needs.

Root Chakra Correspondences

You've already learned that each of your chakras corresponds to a particular color and sound and that each chakra also corresponds to a part of your body, a part of your mind, and a part of your emotional life. We'll go into more detail throughout this chapter about the many ways your first chakra speaks to you, but the following chart will lay it all out for you in a nutshell.

First Chakra	Correspondence
Sanskrit name	Muladhara (Root or base support)
Element	Earth
Color	Red
Seed sound	LANG
Location	At the base of the spine
Associated cultural phrases	"You have your two feet on the ground."
	"I'm putting my foot down."
	"Stand your ground!"
	"Take a stand."
	"I can't stand that."
	"What do you stand for?"
	"I understand."
Associated anatomy	Sacrum, coccygeal nerve plexus, adrenal glands, feet, legs, hips, bones, large intestine, anus, and skin
Associated psychological and life issues	Security, safety, survival, being grounded, family and tribe (patriotism, loyalty), financial issues, health, body image, and weight
Physical issues related to a blocked first chakra	Constantly getting sick, insomnia, endless dieting, anorexia nervosa, constipation, any disorders of the large intestine or problems related to the bowels, pain in the feet or legs, hip pain, any disorders of the bones, skin problems such as lesions or breakouts
Psychological issues related to a blocked first chakra	Fear, insecurity, flightiness, anxiety, inability to focus, disorganization, poor self-discipline, poor boundaries, poor sense of self, financial problems, separation or dissociation from the body
Physical issues related to an overloaded first chakra	Obesity, overeating, addictions, sleeping too much, fatigue, low energy, inability to move gracefully, plodding movements, and heavy feet
Psychological issues related to an overloaded first chakra	Greed, materialism, obsession with money, inability to be generous, hoarding, workaholism, obsession with routines and security, fear of change, and overly strict boundaries/refusal to be open to others
First chakra therapy	Eating protein and root vegetables
	Sleeping enough but not too much
	Massage
	Physical exercise
	Going barefoot
	Being outdoors
	Lying on the ground
	Yoga poses that emphasize a firm base

Awakening the Root Chakra

Before you open any of your other chakras, you must open this one, the place where your *Kundalini* energy lies sleeping. Awakening the Root chakra is easy to do. Vibration, movement, touch, exercise—anything physical awakens this grounded, centering chakra. Healing the first chakra will increase vitality and general energy, and it will help you feel more secure as well as less anxious.

To awaken your Root chakra, try this exercise:

1. Sit on the floor, legs crossed, seat firmly planted on the floor. Feel your pelvic bones and imagine roots anchoring those bones to the earth.

2. Take several long, slow, and deep breaths as you visualize your deep red spinning first chakra that is open and healthy at the base of your spine.

3. Imagine your chakra radiating a wide red beam of light from the base of your spine down into the floor, down into the Earth, and all the way to the center of the planet.

4. Imagine slowly dropping an anchor from the center of your first chakra into the center of the planet and anchoring your body there.

5. Take a deep breath, and in a low resonating tone, say the word: *LANG*, holding the "A" sound (pronounced "ah"; the word rhymes with "song"). Imagine the planet's energy beaming back up into your first chakra in a mutual exchange of energy that ignites your first chakra, so that it glows gently as it spins.

6. As you imagine your first chakra heating up, continue to connect to the Earth's center, and let yourself relax into a feeling of safety and security.

Aligning the Root Chakra

Crooked roots grow a crooked tree, so try this exercise to make sure your Root chakra is properly aligned:

1. Stand in bare feet with your feet about hip-width apart. Feel the soles of your feet against the ground, and imagine them rooting you firmly to the ground as if they are magnetized.

2. Imagine your first chakra at the base of your spine, and try to feel it spinning. Imagine a ray of light emanating downward from your first chakra through the floor. Imagine the same ray of light radiating upward, straight through the crown of your head, and pulling all your other chakras in line with this central column of light.

3. Lift your arms straight up overhead and imagine the red light pulsing upward and downward, reaching to the center of the Earth and all the way to the sky. Your chakra should now be aligned. Let it ground and support you.

Blocks in the Root Chakra

As we mentioned earlier, Betsy encounters many clients with underactive or blocked first chakras. You might be able to spot this type of person on the street. They are the ones with darting eyes, uneven movements, and who appear detached from this world. They are so in their heads that they might walk across a street, oblivious to the honking car racing toward them.

Childhood trauma or abuse is a common cause of first chakra blockage. Being neglected or lacking a strong bond with a parental figure early in life can also block a first chakra. If you didn't feel safe as you were growing up, it is difficult to feel safe as an adult without some help. However, even if you weren't abused as a child, you might feel insecure in your first chakra, especially if you've had some financial, housing, health, or family problems.

Any one of these events can trigger the beginning of a series of events that can cascade into an energy imbalance that is reflected in a first chakra that closes up defensively. When your first chakra stops the flow of energy right at the root of your body, you can experience a whole host of physical and psychological issues.

Blocked Root Chakra Health Issues

In particular, first chakra physical problems can be tied to the feet, legs, hips, and bones—the skeleton that supports you. Arthritis, osteoporosis, diabetic nerve pain in the feet, and even some therapeutic drugs, such as aromatase inhibitors for cancer, give rise to bone pain and complications. Conditions that involve tightness are usually associated with the first chakra and include lower back problems, constipation, and difficulty having an orgasm. People who get sick all the time and generally have low energy often have first chakra blocks. Also, people with eating disorders, excessive weight loss, and anxiety often have first chakra blocks. Insomnia is generally caused by stress and tension, and those who suffer from it are prone to lying in bed caught in their heads, thinking of everything that happened that day and everything that needs to be completed tomorrow. If an insomniac can work on becoming grounded into their first chakra while lying in bed, sweet sleep often follows.

Sometimes, your first chakra will close temporarily in an unsecure situation, such as when you are traveling. This is why so many people experience constipation when they leave home. Their first chakras close tightly as if to say, "Nothing's coming out of this end. We're all sealed up and safe, thanks." In these cases, be sure you are still taking care of your basic needs and spend some extra time getting exercise. Even if you aren't home, you can still focus on being in your body with both feet on the ground.

To alleviate temporary first chakra blocks while traveling, take a few minutes to meditate on how your body feels. Are you holding tension in your shoulders? Furrowing your brow? Is your neck stiff from a long plane ride? Have you spent all day on your feet? Lie on the floor for a few minutes and concentrate on relaxing anxious muscles and focusing on the feel of the Earth's depths beneath you. No matter where you are, you are always connected to our planet Earth.

Blocked Root Chakra Psychological Issues

Psychologically, people with a blocked first chakra might be anxious, "wound tight," or might even feel a desire to detach completely from life. Detaching might mean avoiding friends, missing deadlines, or losing track of possessions; or it can be even more serious such that people feel like they literally float away and leave their bodies. This type of detachment is often called dissociation, which is a disruption in a person's memory, identity, or perception of that person's environment. Dissociation usually warrants treatment by a mental health professional.

Food addictions, alcoholism, and even workaholism are all complicated problems that involve multiple chakras; however, the first chakra is always a part of the equation. Addictions enable people to detach from a part of their lives that is difficult or uncomfortable. Many people with an addiction admit that drinking, eating, or drugs help numb and disconnect them from who they truly are.

Other issues related to first chakra blocks can include problems meeting your own basic needs, getting along with family members, and paying bills. It is very important for people with blocked first chakras to pay attention to basic self-care, such as personal hygiene, decluttering the house, paying the bills, and taking care of the work of daily life in the world. People with first chakra blocks have a hard time doing these things and might need to ask for help from a grounded friend to get organized. Getting into regular routines can make a big difference.

Healing a Blocked Root Chakra

To heal and strengthen a blocked Root chakra, Betsy always encourages her clients to feel the floor. Take off your shoes and touch your feet to the ground. You can do this outside (weather permitting), but even bare feet on the floor of your home can be very grounding. Pay attention to how your feet feel against the floor. Walk on different surfaces and tune in to the varying sensations. Stand still and imagine roots growing down from your feet. Squat down if you feel steadier that way, and imagine heavy weights in your feet or magnets holding you to the surface of the Earth.

Physical activity of any kind is also great for unblocking the first chakra. Anything that gets you out of your head and back into your body will help strengthen your foundation:

o Eating, especially protein and root vegetables like potatoes, carrots, sweet potatoes, onions, and radishes; red foods like meat, beets, grapes, strawberries, and cherries also support a healthy first chakra.

o Sleeping more—reading print books and magazines is encouraged. (However, don't use screens in bed; reserve the bed for rest and sleep, not browsing social media and reading the news.)

o Getting a massage.

o Taking a long, hot bath; washing your hair; washing your feet.

o Being outdoors in nature; connecting with the ground by walking in a forest; being barefoot on the beach; collecting pieces of nature to bring inside such as shells, leaves, and flowers.

o Exercising, including dancing, yoga, lifting weights, or just walking—anything that forces you to focus on being present in your own body.

o Consciously keeping both feet on the floor, preferably barefooted. (If it's cold, put on some socks.) Press both feet into the floor to strengthen your connection with the ground. Imagine you are trying to part the floorboards with your feet to nestle as a seed would in the rich nurturing soil, or imagine the floor is made of sand and you are digging in before the gentle wave washes the shoreline.

o Using mantras to help train your mind and allow you to become more grounded into your first chakra. Mantras work best when repeated out loud prior to falling asleep and when first awakening. Examples of first chakra mantras:

- *My feet are firmly rooted to the Earth.*
- *My body is well cared for and appreciated.*
- *The energy of the Universe nurtures me.*
- *I feel at home in my body.*
- *My life is abundant.*
- *I am safe, strong, and alive.*

An easy way to tune up your first chakra is to pay attention to your physical environment. What do you detect through your five senses? Stay quiet for a few minutes and note what you see, hear, smell, taste, and feel in your actual immediate surroundings—the right here, right now.

Overload in the Root Chakra

While first chakra blocks might be more common than first chakra overloads, the first chakra can certainly be prone to excess. First chakra overloads can be caused by too much routine, too little flexibility, too little change, boundaries that are too stiff, or a life void of spontaneity.

For some people, this pattern started in childhood. Maybe your upbringing was so rigid and rule-oriented that you aren't sure how to live any other way. Or maybe you had so few rules growing up that you overreacted by imposing extremely rigid rules and boundaries for yourself in your daily life, and you are afraid to be too lax because that doesn't feel safe.

Overloaded Root Chakra Health Issues

The most common physical sign of an overloaded first chakra is obesity. Eating strengthens the first chakra, but some people go overboard and eat too much to feel heavier, more substantial, and thus more secure. For these people, losing weight isn't just a health issue; it feels like a threat to their own safety. They *want* to feel heavy and take up a lot of space, as a confirmation of their existence and place in the world. If you are very overweight, you might think you want to lose weight because, well … doesn't everyone? However, if you have an overloaded first chakra, you might not want to admit that being overweight really does feel safer to you.

Not all overloaded first chakra people are overweight, however. Some hyperfocus on their bodies to such an extent that they completely ignore other aspects of life, such as cultivating relationships or spirituality. These people tend to approach exercise and other physical pursuits in an extremely regimented fashion and can't go a day without exercising. They tend to have highly developed muscles and may be very physically healthy but are not balanced in other aspects of their lives.

Other more typical overloaded first chakra physical issues can include stiff ankles, knees, and hip joints; excessive fatigue; sluggishness; a heavy plodding gait; foot pain such as plantar fasciitis; and the feeling that you just can't get moving.

If you are overweight, don't blame your first chakra. It reflects the imbalance that exists in your own energy field. To help repair your overloaded chakra, try moving more. Moving gets stagnant, pooled energy circulating through your body, which can make you feel better and set you on the right course for rebalancing your first chakra to be strong and healthy. Any movement is good movement, whether you are walking around your living room, walking in your neighborhood with your child, or going out in nature for day hikes. Use an app on your smart phone to track your steps and watch the numbers go up the more you engage the world and move about it.

Overloaded Root Chakra Psychological Issues

Overloaded first chakras often result in people who hoard. They may overeat and become overweight, which is a form of hoarding food, but they may also hoard possessions and money, focusing so intensely on accumulating material wealth that they don't know how to give to others.

Overloaded first chakra people also tend to have a rigid sense of rules and boundaries, rarely allowing themselves to be vulnerable to other people or to act spontaneously. This extreme control keeps them feeling safe but prevents them from experiencing genuine and open relationships, which leads to loneliness and discontent.

A lack of spiritual beliefs or a sense of disconnection from anything "otherworldly" is often a hallmark of people with overloaded first chakras. They tend to be so concrete in their thinking that they have a hard time connecting with an energy force larger than their own, such as a Higher Power.

Healing an Overloaded Root Chakra

Healing an overloaded Root chakra means draining some of that excessive physical energy to make room for other kinds of energy, such as emotional and spiritual energy. Some of these strategies are the same as those needed to heal a blocked chakra, but the most important is to *move* the physical body because particularly earthbound people tend to have a hard time with movement and flexibility. Try these activities:

- Exercises that increase heart rate, such as walking, running, or dancing.
- Jumping up and down, paying attention to the feel of your feet hitting the Earth and how that balances with the feel of freedom from the Earth when you grab some air.
- Flowing styles of yoga such as *vinyasa*—a Sanskrit word commonly used to describe a style of Hatha yoga that links sequences of poses together in a flowing motion, rather than holding poses for long periods. Yoga's Sun Salutations are a form of *vinyasa*.
- Stretching exercises, to increase range of motion in muscles and joints.
- Massage, including foot massage, which can get energy moving and flowing out.
- Eating lighter, airier foods such as leafy greens and fruits.

Yoga Poses to Balance the Root Chakra

The best yoga poses for balancing both blocked and overloaded Root chakras are those poses that help encourage your connection with the Earth in addition to your flexibility above it. These poses encourage you not only to be rooted, but also to grow up and out from those roots into your full flowering.

Mountain Pose (*Tadasana*)

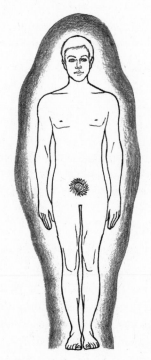

The Root chakra in Mountain pose (Tadasana).

Mountain pose is one of the simplest and most effective Root chakra balancing poses. Just as the first chakra is the foundation of the body's energy system, *Tadasana*, or Mountain pose, is the foundation of all the other yoga standing poses, no matter how advanced. Here's how to do it:

1. Stand in bare feet with your feet hip-width apart. Inhale and feel your muscles soften as you open your mind and heart to grace.

2. Place your feet parallel. Imagine a line running from the center of your ankle to your second toe, on each foot, and make sure these two lines are parallel. Lift and spread your toes, and experience muscular energy in your legs. Feel all four corners of your feet touching the ground: the top outside corner, the outside heel, the top inside corner (the ball of your foot), and the inside heel. Evenly press all parts of your feet into the surface of the floor.

3. Inhale and move your upper inner thighs back and apart while scooping your tailbone down and forward while drawing your lower belly in and up toward your navel.

4. Imagine the crown of your head rising straight up to the sky and your spine lengthening as the muscular energy in your legs powers down into the Earth.

5. Breathe slowly and evenly as you imagine your feet sinking deeply into the Earth and becoming part of the ground as you stand as firm and strong as a mountain.

Tree Pose (*Vrksasana*)

Tree pose is meant to represent a tree with roots deep in the soil and branches outstretched in air, bringing perfect balance to the body and mind. Of course, to balance in this pose, you need a solid and open first chakra. You might need to do this pose while holding on to the wall or a chair at first, but if you work on it regularly, you will probably be able to balance on one foot in the full pose without assistance. Practice hones the first chakra as well as the pose itself.

1. Stand in *Tadasana* (described above). Take a deep breath and allow your mind and body to relax.

2. Shift your weight to your left foot and imagine your left foot sprouting roots that grow deep down into the floor below you. Concentrate on feeling all four corners of your foot against the floor. If your foot turns in, try lifting up the arch of your foot for a more stable foundation.

3. Breathe in and lift your right foot off the floor. Take hold of it with your right hand. If you have trouble standing on one foot (a common problem for people with blocked first chakras), you can hold on to a wall or a chair with your other hand to support yourself.

Moving into Tree pose is a rooting first chakra experience.

4. Put the sole of your right foot against the inside of your upper left thigh. If you can't quite reach your thigh, rest the sole of your foot against the inside of your left calf muscle. Don't rest your foot on your knee, which can put pressure on this sensitive joint. Note: this is easier if your legs and feet are bare. Fabric can make your leg too slippery. This pose is also easier if you angle your heel slightly forward, which might give your foot a better grip. If you can't keep your foot against your leg without help, you can hold your foot in place with your right hand.

5. To counteract the push of your right foot against your left leg, subtly shift your left hip toward the midline of your body so you are standing with hips level. Firmly push your right foot into your upper left thigh, as your upper left thigh also pushes firmly into your right foot to provide stability.

6. Put your hands, palms together, in front of your heart. Breathe. If you can, slowly raise your hands up, separate your palms, and balance with both arms raised straight up overhead like the branches of a tree.

7. Lower slowly as you exhale. Repeat on the other side.

Corpse Pose (*Savasana*)

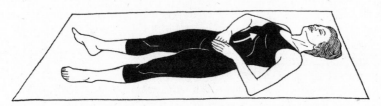

As you breathe out, feel your first chakra ground and root you. Still, you are alive.

Savasana, meant to imitate the utter stillness of a corpse, is traditional for rejuvenating the body after a rigorous yoga pose or practice, but you can practice it any time you need to get back in touch with the Earth. This pose is excellent for grounding the first chakra because so much of your body literally touches the ground.

1. Lie on your back on the floor or on a yoga mat. If it's more comfortable, you can place a folded blanket under your head and/or cover yourself with a blanket.

2. Stretch both legs out as far as you can and then relax your legs completely.

3. Draw your shoulder blades onto your back, almost as if they are cradling your heart. Lift your chest as your heart center shines out in gratitude for this opportunity to rest deeply. Rotate your arms so your palms face the ceiling.

4. Adjust your head so it feels centered and comfortable.

5. While breathing slowly and in a relaxed, unforced way, close your eyes and concentrate on relaxing every part of your body, letting it melt down into the ground. Imagine the Earth is holding you, supporting you, and keeping you safe. Let your brow, temples, jaw, and even your scalp relax. Your eyelids feel heavy. Relax the muscles in your chest, stomach, arms, pelvis, and legs. Feel your entire back body sink into the yoga mat, making deep contact with the Earth.

6. Imagine your first chakra glowing a deep red, slowly turning, and expanding as you let the Earth's energy support you and flow into you. Hold the position for as long as you are comfortable, preferably for at least five minutes.

Partner *Savasana*

Enlist a partner or friend to help you experience even deeper levels of relaxation in *Savasana*. In this pose, a partner helps you move your thighs back to give you a deep sense of being grounded to the Earth. When we are stressed, we unconsciously move our thighs forward. If our thighs can move into the back plane of the body, the entire body relaxes more deeply.

1. Set up in *Savasana* (as described previously).

2. Your partner stands above you with their feet straddling either side of your legs. With fingers spread and arms straight, your partner places their hands on your upper thighs and begins to push your legs down more toward the mat. Your partner can put substantial weight and pressure on your upper thighs to help them move into the back plane.

3. If you want more grounding, you can have your partner "surf" on your upper thighs. The person in *Savasana* draws their arms into a 90-degree angle, with triceps pushing into the mat and palms facing up toward the ceiling. The partner places one foot on your upper thigh, close to where the leg meets the pelvis. The partner then places their hands on your hands, and steps the other foot up onto the other upper inner thigh. By continuing to hold your hands, the partner can balance or "surf" on your thighs. The additional weight of the partner on your upper thighs grounds them down, and you might experience a deep wave of relaxation. Hold the pose as long as you like or as long as your partner can balance.

4. To get out of Partner *Savasana*, your partner continues holding your hands and gently jumps both feet back to the floor at the same time.

Regular maintenance of your first chakra is incredibly important, not only for balance but also to maintain your health and to keep you focused on the task of being in your body and taking care of life's work. You'll have plenty of time to focus on your other chakras and reap the benefits of balancing those, but until your Root chakra is open, nothing else will work as well as possible. First chakra work is essential to the job of being human, so spend as much time working on this Root chakra as necessary. When *Kundalini* energy can flow cleanly and easily through your first chakra, you are on your way to the next stage of personal development.

Astrology for the Awakened Root Chakra

Now, we're going to look more closely at the astrological correspondences for the first, or Root chakra. In Chapter 4, you learned:

- The planetary rulers of the Root chakra are Saturn ♄ and Uranus ♅.
- The signs for the Root chakra are Capricorn ♑ and Aquarius ♒.

Planetary Ruler	Sign(s) Ruled
Saturn ♄	Capricorn ♑, co-ruler of Aquarius ♒
Uranus ♅	Aquarius ♒

If you are working with the energy of your Root chakra, you will want to discover what kind of energy Saturn ♄ and Uranus ♅ hold and empower. While yoga can help open, heal, and energize the chakras in your body, astrology can help you understand their meaning and learn how to use the chakras with purpose to benefit your life's journey.

You can study the energy of the Root chakra's astrological planetary rulers and their zodiac signs so you'll recognize their influence in your life. Once you do that, you can use the knowledge to heal your Root chakra energy. If you want to do a bit more with chakras and astrology, you can explore the chakras in your birth chart. Plus, you can even look at the effect the transiting planetary energy in astrological cycles has on your chakras.

The Chakras and Your Astrological Birth Chart

Astrology, the ancient practice of reading the Heavens, has gotten a big boost from modern technology. Computers use powerful algorithms to calculate astrological birth charts, bringing astrology's heavenly map of the signs, planets, and houses into your hands in a matter of seconds. An astrological birth chart actually is a map of the Universe at the precise time and place of your birth.

Your birth chart is your astrological signature, unique to you and of the Universe. It reveals the essential nature of your character and your path through life. But remember, astrology only reveals *potentials*. You and you alone make freewill choices, even as you grapple with your karmic challenges. Your chart simply is a tool—a wonderful tool—to help you find your way. Find out more about astrological birth chart basics and how to read the chakras in a birth chart in Appendix A (where we'll look at the chakras in Michelle Obama's birth chart).

How Saturn ♄ Awakens the Root Chakra

Saturn ♄ is one of astrology's *social* planets. Saturn ♄ is the natural ruler of Capricorn ♑ and the tenth house of ethics, reputation, career and social responsibility. Saturn ♄ is the natural co-ruler of Aquarius ♒ (its energy is weaker than the ruler's) and the eleventh house of goals and groups, as well as friends and community. As a social planet, Saturn ♄ governs how you engage (or not) with others in your community, in society, and in the world.

Saturn ♄ is the Universe's celestial taskmaster. Saturn is the planner and the regulator of checks and balances. It is the planet of responsibility, achievement, self-discipline, and self-respect. Saturn can stand in for authority figures in your life. This planet makes sure you are always prepared, ever vigilant—ready to meet and conquer all obstacles in your path. Saturn is not a very forgiving planet; it knows your weaknesses and limitations. But it also knows your tenacity and personal strength, your will to meet life's challenges and take on the tasks of your life's work.

Saturn ♄ relates to the groundedness, the Earth-centered stability of the Root chakra. Located near the base of the spine, the Root chakra holds coiled *Kundalini* energy, and Saturn is its gatekeeper. At the fulcrum of the body, where the perineum holds and releases tension and fear, Saturn acts as a stabilizing force to channel safety and security into the spinning Root chakra. Saturn's ambitions will help you figure out what you stand for, show you how to build a solid plan for the future, and awaken your Root chakra—beginning the rise of your *prana* life force that will make it all happen.

How Uranus ♅ Awakens the Root Chakra

Uranus ♅ is one of astrology's *transpersonal* planets. Uranus ♅ is the natural ruler of Aquarius ♒ and the eleventh house of goals and groups, friends and community. As a transpersonal, or outer planet, Uranus ♅ (with its longer orbit) governs astrological cycles influencing whole generations of people.

Uranus ♅ is the planet of sudden or unexpected change; of original, almost radical ideas; and of authenticity. Uranus ♅ holds a "sixth sense" spark of ingenuity that seems to arise out of thin air. The Root chakra feels the influence of Saturn ♄ because it is the weaker co-ruler (with Uranus ♅) of Aquarius ♒. This means that responsible, ambitious Saturn ♄ gives support to the idea-maker, world-changer Uranus ♅ in awakening Root chakra energy. Uranus ♅ can provide the catalyst that gets the *Kundalini* serpent to rouse from sleep and begin to pay attention.

How Capricorn ♑ Awakens the Root Chakra

Capricorn ♑ with its yin, Earth element energy is ruled by planetary taskmaster Saturn ♄. Needless to say, Capricorns are down-to-earth personalities, which suits Root chakra energy just fine. Practical and efficient, able to balance nurturing with responsible effort, Capricorns are sure-footed, patient, and resourceful. The Root chakra harnesses Capricorn reliability to lay a firm foundation to survive and thrive. With Capricorn's influence, awakened *Kundalini* serpent's power in the Root chakra remains channeled responsibly for the best personal good, keeping you on track and in control.

How Aquarius ♒ Awakens the Root Chakra

Aquarius ♒ is ruled by Uranus ♅, with Saturn ♄ as its co-ruler. As the weaker planetary ruler of Aquarius ♒, Saturn's ♄ influence is brought to supplement and give structure to Aquarius's lightning bolts of intuition. Aquarians are progressive, open-minded visionaries that bring innovative and revolutionary ideas that affect generations. In awakening the Root chakra, the Aquarian jolt of electricity is given substance by the tenaciously sure-footed Capricorn ♑ and its Saturn ruler.

Root Chakra Rising

The radical ideas of Aquarius ♒/Uranus ♅ provide the spark to ignite the sleeping *Kundalini* energy coiled at the base of the first chakra. That spark risks flaming out of control without the grounded stability of Capricorn ♑/Saturn ♄ to implement a strategy and find a way forward. To give the Root chakra its proper balance, the energy of both zodiac signs must be present.

As you do healing work with your Root chakra, be aware of the risk for an imbalance and examine the ways in which your big ideas may be ungrounded, or that you might seem to find yourself forever stuck in old patterns and systems. Once you've hit upon the right plan of action to liberate you, the Root chakra will activate. Filled with purpose and securely grounded, your Root chakra spins, providing a safe, solid Earth base for the life force to rise up to meet your passion in the second, or Sacral chakra.

Sacral Chakra (*Svadhisthana*): Creating Passion

Everything you create, from a drawing or a poem to a strong emotion to an actual human being, is generated from energy that starts in your second chakra. As the seat of your passions, the Sacral chakra governs your creativity, sexuality, fertility, and your most intimate relationships. This is where you *feel*. Indian artist and author Harish Johari writes that the second chakra moves "like a butterfly," and indeed, that feeling you get when you have "butterflies in your stomach" is your second chakra spinning with a particularly strong emotion.

When your Root chakra is strong, balanced, and open, your Sacral chakra has the best chance to regulate your passions like a thermostat. Imbalances in the chakras directly below or above your Sacral chakra can sometimes force the nearby chakra to overcompensate, resulting in too much emotion … or not enough. Always get grounded first, but once you have a firm foundation, you can do a lot with the powerful creative force of the Sacral chakra.

Sacral Chakra 101

The second chakra, the Sacral chakra, is also sometimes called the Passion, Sexuality, or Water chakra. The Sacral chakra is called *Svadhisthana* in the traditional Sanskrit. This word is variously translated. Literally, *Svadhisthana* means "dwelling place of the self," but chakra expert Anodea Judith translates the word as "sweetness." The second chakra is associated with the Water element because, in contrast to the first chakra's solid, grounded earthiness, the second chakra is filled with flowing, moving, watery energy, representing your connection with your own emotions and impulses to create. The second chakra's symbolic color is orange, and the traditional lotus symbol depicting this chakra has six petals. The sound associated with this chakra is the seed sound *VANG* (rhymes with "song"). Chanting this sound helps to activate the second chakra.

The Sacral chakra is located just below your belly button and radiates in and around your abdomen and your genitals, including the ovaries and uterus for women. In addition to being associated with the genitals and organs of procreation, this chakra is associated with several other physical structures in the body, including the sacral nerve plexus, lower abdomen, lower back, appendix, bladder, kidneys, and hip areas.

Your Sacral chakra has everything to do with some pretty interesting passionate parts of you, so let's investigate.

Feeling It

Being able to feel emotions without becoming in thrall to those emotions is an important part of psychological health, and that balance happens in the Sacral chakra. In our culture, it's easy to believe you *are* your feelings, but feelings, emotions, and passions are just one part of the being that is you. Recognizing that feelings are something you *experience*, not something you *are*, is the key to emotional balance and a healthy, open second chakra.

Of course, feelings and emotions are an important part of your whole self, but they are also seductive, and some people become addicted to the intensity that these strong emotions can bring. Emotions such as jealousy, admiration, sexual attraction, revulsion, inspiration, or the feeling you get when you experience something pleasurable or painful or beautiful or disturbing, come from the second chakra. Learn to recognize these emotions and sensory feelings for what they are, and you will be on your way to a better healing chakra balance.

Children who don't get enough emotional attention from their parents often have second chakra issues; also, children who get too much emotional attention from parents who are defined by or obsessively interested in their children often have second chakra issues. Second chakra issues also are common in children who were sexually or emotionally abused. Severe pleasure restrictions or not enough control over pleasures can also influence children as their second chakras are developing. Consider how your family handled emotions and love to get an idea of your own second chakra issues. Was emotional expression suppressed or overexpressed in your home when you were growing up? If so, consider how you might be repeating these dysfunctional patterns in your adult life.

The second chakra, or Sacral chakra (Suadhisthana), is the seat of passion and creativity.

The One(s) You Love

The Sacral chakra's passions extend most immediately to those we love the most. The fourth chakra (which we'll talk more about in Chapter 10) is the Heart chakra, sometimes also called the Love chakra. However, our most intimate relationships start lower, at the second chakra. The feelings we get when we are physically, emotionally, and sexually attracted to someone happen here, and sometimes, they radiate through our entire bodies. Have you ever felt weak in the knees when you saw or even thought about the object of your desire? Your Sacral chakra made that happen.

Of course, the natural culmination of sexual desire is sometimes reproduction, and that is a second chakra function, too. Our fertility is rooted in the second chakra, and by association, our deepest feelings for the children we produce come from the second chakra. Your fourth chakra helps you love yourself and the other beings on the planet, but your feelings for those special few that are almost a part of your own body are second chakra territory.

What About the Sex?

The Sacral chakra is often called the Sexuality chakra for good reason. Sexual desire starts here, and so do all the feelings of pleasure that come from that. Even when you are not involved in a meaningful emotional relationship, the second chakra still generates feelings of sexual attraction and pleasure, and that can be a problem for some people who get so addicted to that pleasure they forget about the relationship part and just go for the sexual thrill or a casual hookup. Engaging too much in the hookup culture is one sign of second chakra overload.

On the other hand, blocked second chakras can cause a different kind of sexual problem—*sexual arousal disorder*. Sexual arousal disorder is the inability to become aroused, sustain arousal, or experience orgasm during sexual activity. This can happen to men or women and might have physical or psychological causes. In either case, this disorder is reflected in a blocked second chakra. Ideally, when the second chakra is open and healthy, sexual pleasure becomes one lovely part of a balanced set of passionate emotions.

Fertility

Your Sacral chakra reflects your fertility, and people with infertility problems typically have a blocked second chakra. Working to open the second chakra while in treatment for infertility can help support your efforts to conceive. (See the sections later in this chapter for exercises to open the second chakra.)

Betsy has a female client struggling with infertility, which is generally related to the second chakra where our reproductive organs are housed. As the oldest daughter of a dysfunctional shattered family, Betsy's client felt the responsibility of constantly picking up the pieces. Despite having several siblings, she was the one who planned and hosted the family dinners, took care of her ailing mom and dad, lent money to extended family members, and offered to take in a family member who had recently become homeless. She was constantly giving away her second chakra energy to her family of origin, and they were happy to take it. Because of this, the woman had little energy left in her second chakra to nurture the development of a newborn life to start her own family. Until she could develop better boundaries with her siblings and parents and summon the courage to say "no" to her family of origin, Betsy explained that the woman's beleaguered Sacral chakra would remain weakened, which could be making conception more difficult.

An open Sacral chakra aligned with an open Root chakra will allow for the sense of security and safety that encourages the conditions for fertility and conception to occur. Doing chakra partner work with your sex partner and chakra visualizations (see Chapters 18 and 19) can also help. You can try to facilitate conception by addressing your relationship with your sex partner as expressed through the union of your chakras. Working together to heal second chakra issues can spark the passion between you, and it can spark your shared passion to create a family. That family could be a result of conception, adoption, or the union of you and your life partner.

Your Creative Spark

The second chakra gets a lot of attention for being all about the sex, but another important part of your passionate self exists here, too—your creativity. Everything you create in your own mind comes out of the Sacral chakra. This is the chakra that generates your impulse to make art, discover poetry, write songs and record your own music, dance, design your own website or podcast, decorate your living room, or get crafty with a scrapbook on Pinterest.

Life gets busy, and finding time for creativity can sometimes feel frustratingly elusive. However, exercising your creative impulses is just as important as exercising your body and mind. You don't have to draft the Great American Novel or produce a masterpiece of performance art to stay creatively charged. Something as simple as musing in a journal each night, creating doodles on a digital sketchbook, or using a design app to imagine a blueprint for your dream house will make you a more open, flexible, and well-rounded human being. The second chakra is the gateway to your creative power, as it is the genesis of creation.

A blocked second chakra can result in a creative block, a tsunami of indecision, self-doubt, and procrastination. But a healthy, open Sacral chakra often reflects an open, creative person who can become passionately absorbed in work, hobbies, or whatever other passions inspire the creative flow.

Grace

You can spot a person with a healthy second chakra by the way she moves. Graceful, flowing, sensual bodies almost certainly contain strong, open Sacral chakras. Consider how you move, and what that says about your second chakra. Clumsy, awkward, stiff, stilted movements are often a sign of a closed second chakra, while hyperflexible limbs and a lot of back-and-forth movement while walking might be a sign that your second chakra is too open. Are you graceful or clumsy? Do you float or stomp? Purposefully moving in a more graceful way with full-body awareness will, in turn, help to relax and open a closed second chakra.

Sacral Chakra Correspondences

Your Sacral chakra governs many aspects of your body as well as your mind and feelings. Check out the following chart for a summary of Sacral chakra correspondences, and then read on to find out more detail about the many ways in which your Sacral chakra reflects and influences the passions of your life.

Second Chakra	Correspondence
Sanskrit name	Svadhisthana (dwelling place of the passionate self, sweetness)
Element	Water
Color	Orange
Seed sound	VANG
Location	Just below the bellybutton, in the abdomen
Associated cultural phrases	"Listen to your gut." "I've got butterflies in my stomach!" "I have a funny feeling …."
Associated anatomy	Abdomen, sacral nerve plexus, genitals, reproductive organs, kidneys, and bladder
Associated psychological and life issues	Passion, emotions, sexuality, creativity, intimate relationships, and parenting issues
Physical issues related to second chakra blockage	Fertility problems, sexual arousal disorder, nervous stomach, stiffness, stilted movements, bladder infections, kidney stones, skipped or stopped menstrual periods in women, and lower back pain
Psychological issues related to second chakra blockage	Creative blocks, fear of relationships/commitment issues, emotional coldness, inability to experience pleasure, shallow relationships, and communication problems with children
Physical issues related to second chakra overload	Emotional eating, sexual addiction, substance abuse, frequent urination, heavy menstrual flow and/or PMS in women, and hyperflexibility
Psychological issues related to second chakra overload	Bipolar disorder, panic attacks, excessive emotionality, mood swings, hypersensitivity, addiction to pleasure, emotional dependency, ruled by feelings, and over-association (enmeshment) with children
Second chakra therapy	Drinking more fluids
	Swimming
	Treatment for addictions
	Balancing pleasure activities (increasing or decreasing)
	Counseling for emotional, relationship, and/or sexual problems
	Moving and flowing exercises that increase grace, including ballet, Tai Chi, and flowing vinyasas, such as yoga's Sun Salutation or other flow styles of asanas

Awakening the Sacral Chakra

If your *Kundalini* energy is activated in your first chakra, then you can encourage it to rise up into your second chakra. When you awaken your passionate second chakra, you are likely to experience more vivid and intense emotions, a higher level of creativity, and more intimate relationships. Your potential increases when this chakra is healthy. Awakening the Sacral chakra is easy and pleasurable.

Anything that gets your body moving in a graceful, flowing way or that puts you in direct contact with someone you love, can activate this chakra. Or you can combine the two: try dancing slowly in rhythm with your partner as you both look directly into each other's eyes. This exercise is intense for some people, but it should launch you right into second chakra arousal. Try it in a hot tub and … well, we can't be responsible for what might happen next!

To get more passionate Sacral chakra energy into your environment, highlight the color orange. Wear orange, paint your bedroom orange, or put orange flowers around the house. Just seeing the color can help to awaken this chakra. Also include more Water element influences in your home. Remember lava lamps? Those flowing water lights are not only groovy, they can encourage a more fluid mood. Fill up crystal bowls with water and float flower buds in them, or add a desktop fountain or aquarium to your home. Drink mineral water with orange slices for a refreshing stimulus.

You can also try this exercise for awakening your passions with the Sacral chakra:

1. Sit on the floor with your legs crossed and your seat firmly planted on the floor. Feel your pelvic bones and imagine roots anchoring those bones to the Earth.

2. Take several long, slow, deep breaths, then draw your attention to the area just below your belly button. Imagine your second chakra as a bright fiery orange circle spinning slowly.

3. Imagine your chakra radiating an orange circle of watery light that encompasses your entire abdomen. Feel the warm light pulsing in waves like ripples in a pond that expand outward from your spine, flowing to the front of your body and all the way to the back of your body, as well as out to each side. Feel the warmth in your hips and genitals.

4. Take a deep breath in and in a low, resonating tone, say the word: *VANG,* holding the "A" sound (pronounced "ah"; the word rhymes with "song"). Imagine the orange light filling your entire body with slow, steady waves of warm water.

5. Continue to breathe and let the warm waves of emotion and pleasure continue to radiate from your second chakra as long as you like, allowing yourself to bask in the warm pleasure of the second chakra.

Aligning the Sacral Chakra

When waves hit the beach at a diagonal, the beach erodes. To make sure your Sacral chakra is properly aligned, you can try this exercise:

1. Immerse yourself in warm water, either in a bathtub, hot tub, or even a natural body of water like a lake or the ocean on a warm day, if you are lucky enough to have access.

2. Sitting or standing in water at least up to your waist, imagine your second chakra just below your belly button, and try to feel it spinning. Imagine a ray of orange light emanating down into your first chakra, where it combines with the red light and beams down into the ground. Then, imagine that same ray of orange light radiating upward, straight through the crown of your head, pulling all your other chakras in line with this central column of light.

3. Lift your arms straight up overhead, and imagine the orange light pulsing up and down, radiating to the center of the Earth and all the way to the sky. Your second chakra should now be aligned. How does it feel? Breathe through the chakras and dare to feel the creative power of the second chakra stirring passions within and around you.

Blocks in the Sacral Chakra

Although many people are in tune with their emotions, there are exceptions. If you grew up in an environment where emotional expression or pleasure seeking was discouraged, you might never have learned how to be emotionally open. Or if your upbringing was emotionally overwhelming—maybe one of your parents had emotional issues and subjected you to too much emotional energy—you might react by withdrawing your own emotions to protect yourself.

In turn, that can block your ability to have intimate relationships. It can also block your creativity. People who think they "just aren't creative" are more likely to have blocked second chakras. Believe it or not, everybody is born with creative potential. It's just that we don't all get the chance to nurture this inborn quality.

Your second chakra can get blocked later in life, too. A particularly painful relationship or breakup can cause a temporary or long-term second chakra block, especially if you didn't get support for your feelings or were discouraged from expressing your feelings over the course of a relationship. Sexual rejection or sexual exploitation can cause serious second chakra issues. Naturally sensitive people are also more likely to experience pain (both emotional and physical) associated with feelings, causing a chain reaction of imbalance that can influence future relationships, as well as the ability to experience physical pleasure.

Blocked Sacral Health Issues

Second chakra issues are largely centered around the sexual and reproductive organs. Infertility and sexual arousal disorder in both sexes and skipped menstrual periods in women can all be related to second chakra blocks. Also, a so-called "nervous stomach," stiffness, stilted movements, bladder infections, kidney stones, and lower back pain can be related to second chakra blocks.

Blocked Sacral Chakra Psychological Issues

Emotional blockages are at the heart of a blocked second chakra. Creative blocks, such as writer's block, are also common when this chakra's energy is obstructed. You might have a fear of relationships, commitment issues, and resistance to change. People might see you as emotionally cold, or you might only be able to maintain shallow relationships with other people, without true intimacy. You might also feel like you are unable or unworthy of experiencing pleasure. As a parent, a sign of a second chakra blockage is sometimes an inability or unwillingness to communicate or bond with your children. However, this can also be a sign of second chakra overload, when your overemotional attachment to your children makes *them* withdraw, thus creating the communication problem.

Sometimes a painful emotional experience, such as the loss of a loved one, a breakup, or a big disappointment related to your creativity, can create a temporary second chakra blockage. This is the time to pay extra-special attention to your own emotional needs. There is nothing wrong with allowing yourself a little extra pampering and pleasure to help yourself heal and your second chakra to open again. Take long, warm mineral baths; have some sliced mango sweetened with honey; stay in and read a favorite book; or turn to your trusted art journal, letting your hand take over your mind's eye as you sketch. If you give yourself permission to rest and grieve and you also give yourself permission to feel pleasure in your own way at your own pace, you can help your own second chakra to heal and open up again.

Healing a Blocked Sacral Chakra

To heal and strengthen a blocked Sacral chakra, Betsy encourages her clients to get in touch with their emotions. If it isn't something you typically do, this can be a difficult task. Talking about your feelings with a close friend, confidant, or family member is a good way to release and express yourself. However, people with a blocked second chakra often don't have close relationships because they might have excessively high boundaries and difficulty connecting with others. Working with a trained counselor, therapist, or psychologist might be key to learning the skills of expressing emotions and connecting with others in a healthy and enjoyable way.

Moving in a graceful, flowing style is also great for unblocking the second chakra. Work with a movement therapist or take a private yoga session with a teacher skilled in the connection between mind and body to bring great healing to the Sacral chakra. Anything that gets your energies moving through and out of your body will help strengthen and validate your emotional and creative self, such as …

- Drinking lots of fluids, especially clean pure mineral water.
- Eating orange foods like sweet potatoes, citrus fruits, salmon, papaya, and melon.
- Purposefully doing pleasurable things.
- Swimming, especially in clean natural bodies of water. (But a local community pool is perfectly suitable if that is your most convenient, available choice.)
- Hugging someone who is emotionally open and who cares about you.
- Talking about your feelings with a good listener.
- Creating something: drawing, writing, playing music, building, coding, dancing, or cooking.
- Spending time with your children and focusing on them, rather than being distracted while you are with them.
- Looking at someone who loves you directly in the eyes.
- Having sex with a caring and committed partner who is sensitive and responsive to your feelings.
- Exercising gracefully, including dancing (such as ballet or contemporary) and flowing yoga (such as *vinyasa* style Sun Salutation).
- Movement-based therapy.
- Counseling for emotional, relationship, or sexual problems.
- Therapy for addictions.
- Reciting these mantras:
  - *I am a desirable person.*
  - *My feelings are good.*
  - *It is safe to feel things.*
  - *I create newness in my life.*
  - *I feel pleasure in my relationships.*
  - *I move easily and gracefully through life.*

Overload in the Sacral Chakra

Why are you *so emotional?* Sometimes, life demands an emotional response, but an overloaded second chakra can cause a host of problems, from mood swings and a general overly emotional reaction to things, all the way to full-blown addictions, codependency, or bipolar disorder.

Second chakra overload can happen when a naturally emotional person is encouraged to be that way early in life, by overly emotional or overly unemotional parents. Sometimes, second chakra overload is a temporary response to an emotional situation or simply a poor sense of how to regulate the eternal quest for pleasure. The result is emotion, emotion, emotion, and while overloaded second chakra people might be extra creative, they might also be so controlled by their feelings and passions that they completely lose their common sense.

An easy way to tune up your second chakra is to pay attention to how other people feel. Sometimes, what we see in others is a mirror for ourselves (psychologists call this projection), so tune in to people in your immediate environment. What do you notice about how others appear to feel? Especially notice the things that create an emotional response in you, whether it is sympathy or annoyance. Could that be a clue to how *you* are actually feeling?

Overloaded Sacral Chakra Health Issues

The most common physical signs of an overloaded second chakra are problems related to the sexual and reproductive organs. Heavy menstrual flow and severe PMS symptoms in women (especially mood swings, irritability, bloating, and abdominal cramps) are signs of flooded second chakras. In both sexes, so is a high frequency of sexual arousal, especially coupled with the inability to control sexual conduct. Addictive behavior can be a sign of a second chakra flood, whether the addiction is to sex, food, alcohol, or caffeine.

Although eating is a classic first chakra activity, overloaded second chakra people are prone to emotional eating and often become overweight because of this problem. Bulimia can be reflected in the second chakra, as people eat to dull strong emotions and then feel such strong guilt that they purge by vomiting or by abusing laxatives. Compulsive eating might be a first chakra problem, as people try to get heavier to get grounded. Compulsive eating might be a second chakra problem if the eating is being used for the purpose of squelching strong feelings, while eating too little or being clinically anorexic reflects the desire to control or sublimate emotions.

Other signs of an overloaded second chakra include severe menstrual pain caused by endometriosis in women and urinary problems in men. Hypermobility and/or a wobbly or swaying walk is common with an overloaded second chakra. People with hypermobile joints and uncontrolled body movements are more prone to joint injury and osteoarthritis. This is often reflected in an overly open second chakra.

Overloaded Sacral Chakra Psychological Issues

Overloaded second chakras can result in all kinds of destructive behaviors. This passion and pleasure center is easy to obsess about, and addiction to pleasure is a common problem. Sure, it might be fun to call yourself a hedonist, but if you can't stop a pleasurable behavior or if you gear your entire life around seeking pleasure, you are out of balance. For men especially, the current wave of available online porn makes real-life sexual partnerships more difficult and skews expectations about what the sexual experience should be like. Hookup culture and the popularity of dating apps that encourage casual sexual encounters can turn a one-off release of sexual energy into a flood of indiscriminate and unbalanced Sacral chakra problems leading to a lack of spiritual fulfillment.

According to yoga philosophy, one of the primary reasons why people are hindered in their spiritual progress is through excessive attachment to pleasure. But even if spiritual progress isn't your goal, too much short-term pleasure seeking can seriously hinder your progress toward long-term goals, and it will lead you on a very crooked path to spiritual enlightenment that is full of detours and backtracking. It can also lead to addiction, not to mention the destruction of relationships, the loss of jobs, and even the loss of health.

The other way in which addictive behaviors are linked to overloaded second chakras is that people sometimes engage in these behaviors to mask uncomfortably strong emotions. If you are flooded with feelings and you don't know how to handle them, pleasurable behaviors can help dull the emotional pain. If you can't stop eating, vaping, drinking alcohol, taking recreational drugs, or seeking sex, you probably have a serious overloaded second chakra problem. Issues of addiction typically require professional intervention. A medical doctor, mental health therapist, or counselor can help you get back into balance if you can't stop doing something. There are too many good things in life to waste it all on an overloaded second chakra, so please get help if you can't help yourself.

Overloaded second chakra people also tend to be emotionally clingy, smothering the people they love and often losing them in the process. Balancing your second chakra can help you get a handle on the way you relate to other people, helping you to back off, balance your emotions, and listen a little more closely to your inner logical voice.

You have emotions so you can deepen your relationships, appreciate the good in the world, learn about yourself, be appropriately repulsed by the bad, and exercise your creativity. But you should be able to manage your emotions. They shouldn't manage you. Remember, you are not your feelings. You can set them aside and even discipline them when they get in your way. Remember, astrologically, the Sacral chakra is ruled by the planet Jupiter ♃, the planet of abundance, of "more is more." The Sacral chakra is also influenced by Neptune ♆, the planet of feelings and deep emotional understanding. Check the placement of these planets in your astrological birth chart for clues about how to manage excess second chakra energy in your life.

Healing an Overloaded Sacral Chakra

Healing an overloaded Sacral chakra means draining out some of that excessive passionate, emotional, creative energy, to make room for other kinds of energy, like grounding energy and spiritual energy. Creative, passionate energy is a good thing, of course—but it isn't the only kind of energy you need, so balance is best. Try strategies such as …

- Crafting a routine and sticking to it every day, especially in terms of when you sleep, eat, and bathe.

- Setting limits for yourself, especially regarding those things you like to do a little too much. If this is too difficult, enlist an accountability partner, such as a friend, coworker, or therapist, who checks in with your progress.

- Aerobic dance, such as hip-hop dance, or the calm flow of a ballet barre workout, to burn off extra energy and help you feel pleasure in a healthy way.

- Strength training (lifting weights) to give support to a hyperflexible body.

- Trying hot yoga styles, such as *Bikram* and Barkan, which are great for flushing excess water and emotions out of your body. *Bikram* yoga and other "hot yoga" styles are practiced in a room typically heated to around 100 degrees with high humidity, which is similar to the climate in India where yoga originated. This type of yoga induces sweating to purge toxins from the body. The heat also increases flexibility.

- Spending quiet time alone to meditate on your own creative strengths and passionate Sacral chakra power so you can feel more independent and self-motivated.

- Grounding exercises for the first, or Root chakra, and strengthening exercises for the third, or Solar Plexus chakra. (See Chapters 7 and 9.) These will help align and support the healing of the second, or Sacral chakra.

Yoga Poses to Balance the Sacral Chakra

The best yoga poses for balancing both blocked and overloaded Sacral chakras are those poses that help encourage graceful, flowing movements along with flexibility and strength. The classic moving sequence of poses for warming the body and increasing flexibility is called *Surya Namaskar. Surya Namaskar* is the Sanskrit name for Sun Salutation, which is a sequence of twelve yoga poses (*asanas*) that is ideally practiced in the morning for warming up the body and honoring the rising sun.

Different teachers approach the sequence in different ways. Here is one flowing sequence we particularly like for balancing the second chakra. Once you know the sequence, work on flowing from one pose to the next with as much grace and smoothness as you can. Don't worry about speed. Form is more important. Always move fully and completely through each pose in the sequence. When you've mastered the sequence, you can add speed to the flow of poses to increase your aerobic energy.

Sun Salutations are beneficial to healing all your chakras, but the flow of movement is particularly beneficial to healing the second chakra, or Sacral chakra. Sun Salutations enhance your sense of your body, mind, and spirit interconnectivity and improve concentration and balance. Doing Sun Salutations awakens Sun ☉ yang energy and can help release *Kundalini* spiritual awakening (see Chapter 3) if your chakras are aligned and ready to channel that serpent power.

Yoga's Sun Salutation **vinyasa** *teaches fluid strength with grace for healing second chakra, or Sacral chakra, energy.*

1. Stand in *Tadasana* (read about how to do that pose in Chapter 7), in bare feet with your feet hip-width apart. Experience stability. Bring your palms together in front of your heart, in prayer position. Take a deep breath to center and connect with something greater than yourself.

2. Inhale and bring your arms overhead, extending the spine long as you look up between your hands. Begin to shine your heart center up toward the ceiling as you bend back slightly.

3. Exhale and bend forward at the hips, bringing your hands down toward the floor on either side of your feet. If your hamstrings are tight and you can't touch the floor, either bend your knees so your fingers reach the floor or put something under each hand that you can press into, such as two blocks, piles of books, or boxes.

4. Keeping your hands on the floor or other support, inhale and look up, stretching your spine forward as your chest lifts slightly, while keeping your feet and hands firmly planted. Exhale and return to a forward bend.

5. Inhale and step your right foot back into a lunge. Keep your back thigh lifted as you bend more deeply into your front leg. Your left knee should be centered over your left ankle. Lift your heart, open your chest, and look up.

6. Exhale and step your left foot back into Plank pose, as if you were on the top end of a push-up, fingertips extended, and elbows pointed toward your feet. Inhale, and as you exhale, slowly lower yourself down to the floor with control, keeping your arms close to your body. If you don't have the arm strength yet to lower yourself down, bring your knees to the floor before lowering your chest and head to the floor.

7. Place your hands on the mat in line with your chest, inhale and take the shoulders back, head up, and chest up into a variation of Cobra pose (*Bhujangasana*; see Chapter 5). Curl into a baby backbend. With your tailbone tucked under, extend your spine forward with every inhale. With every exhale, keep your shoulders back and soften your heart center down between the shoulder blades.

8. Exhale, bringing your head and chest back down to the mat. Curl your toes under, and with your next inhale, lift your hips off the floor. Keeping your arms straight, stretch your hips away from your shoulders. Exhale, and relax your head and neck. This is called Downward Facing Dog pose (*Adho Mukha Shvanasana*).

9. Inhale and step your right foot forward into a lunge, keeping your back leg lifting high.

10. Exhale and step forward with your left foot, returning to a forward bend with your hands on the floor (or on another support) beside your feet.

11. Keeping your hands down, move your chest forward and look up as you inhale. Then exhale and bend forward again.

12. Keeping your feet firmly grounded, inhale as you sweep your arms up over your head, returning to a standing position. Bring your palms together in prayer position in line with your heart. Repeat the entire sequence as many times as you like to warm your body, and pay homage to the Sun ☉.

Astrology for the Awakened Sacral Chakra

Now, we're going to look more closely at the astrological correspondences for the second, or Sacral chakra. In Chapter 4, you learned:

- The planetary rulers of the Sacral chakra are Jupiter ♃ and Neptune ♆.
- The signs for the Sacral chakra are Sagittarius ♐ and Pisces ♓.

Planetary Ruler	Sign(s) Ruled
Jupiter ♃	Sagittarius ♐, co-ruler of Pisces ♓
Neptune ♆	Pisces ♓

Knowing the energy of astrology's planets and signs that correspond to the Sacral chakra helps you understand how to bring awakened second chakra passions to life. Yoga's Sun Salutations use movement to stimulate second chakra energy in your body. Astrology gives that spinning life force energy a meaning and a purpose in your life. To go even further and explore chakra energy in your astrological birth chart, see Appendix A, where we'll look at chakra influences in Michelle Obama's chart. The effect of transiting planetary energy on astrological cycles can also change the chakra "flavor" of the time.

How Jupiter ♃ Awakens the Sacral Chakra

Jupiter ♃ is one of astrology's *social* planets. Jupiter ♃ is the natural ruler of Sagittarius ♐ and the ninth house of education and philosophy, spiritual beliefs, law, and travel. Jupiter ♃ is the natural co-ruler of Pisces ♓ (its energy is weaker than the ruler's) and the twelfth house of the subconscious, the unknown, spirituality, and past karma. As a social planet, Jupiter ♃ governs how you engage (or not) with others in your community, in society, and in the world.

Jupiter ♃ believes in the motto "go big or go home." The planet of expansion and abundance, benevolence and generosity, Jupiter invests momentum in your passions. It gives you the confidence you need to know in your gut that you can do it. But too much Jupiter can lead to excess, while bloviated passions go nowhere. Jupiter allows a balanced Sacral chakra to grow larger and spin faster with the promise of your creative passions (grounded by the safety and security of the Root chakra). You are more confident in your core beliefs and your ability to manifest your dreams, whether of family, career, travel, art—whatever it is you *know* you must do.

How Neptune Ψ Awakens the Sacral Chakra

Neptune Ψ is one of astrology's *transpersonal* planets. Neptune is the natural ruler of Pisces ♓ and is the twelfth house of transformation and metamorphosis, the subconscious, spirituality, and past karma. As a transpersonal, or outer planet, Neptune Ψ (with its longer orbit) governs astrological cycles influencing whole generations of people.

Neptune Ψ is the planet of dreams and illusions, mysticism, hypochondria, and spiritual inspiration. Neptune Ψ is the visionary. The Sacral chakra feels the influence of Jupiter ♃ because it is the weaker co-ruler (with Neptune Ψ) of Pisces ♓. This means the dreamy moonglow of Neptune Ψ receives the support of Jupiter's ♃ expansive abundance in awakening Sacral chakra energy. Jupiter can provide the confidence that gets the *Kundalini* serpent to move the Sacral chakra with bold visions and creative passion.

How Sagittarius ♐ Awakens the Sacral Chakra

Sagittarius ♐ with its yang Fire element energy is ruled by the expansive creator Jupiter ♃. Sagittarians, with their need to explore new horizons, suit Sacral chakra's energy perfectly. Always shooting for the stars, Sagittarians are determined, endlessly curious, honest, and direct. The Sacral chakra welcomes the Sagittarian adventurer's quest for evermore experience of the Universe. With Sagittarian's influence, awakened *Kundalini* serpent power in the Sacral chakra is channeled from the Root chakra to spin with passionate purpose.

How Pisces ♓ Awakens the Sacral Chakra

Pisces ♓ is ruled by Neptune Ψ, with Jupiter ♃ as its co-ruler. As the weaker planetary ruler of Pisces ♓, Jupiter's ♃ influence lends a boldness that seeks fruition to Piscean dreamy visionaries. Jupiter helps keep Pisces's transformative notions from fizzling out in the harsh light of the world. In awakening the Sacral chakra's passions, the Piscean's head full of stars is given direction and persistence by adventuresome Sagittarius and its Jupiter ruler.

Sacral Chakra Rising

The heavenly aim of Sagittarius ♐/Jupiter ♃ provides the target to guide rising *Kundalini* energy from the grounded Root chakra to the passions of the Sacral chakra. That target risks missing the mark without the visionary imagination of Pisces ♓/Neptune ♆ to make the target a truly worthy one. To give the Sacral chakra its proper balance, the energy of both zodiac signs must be present.

As you do healing work with your Sacral chakra, be aware of the risk for an imbalance and examine the ways in which your passions may grow too overwhelming or obsessive, or that you might seem to find yourself forever chasing new adventures and never find a true home for your most cherished goal. Once you've hit upon the right quest to liberate you, the Sacral chakra will activate. Filled with creative purpose and passionate direction, your Sacral chakra spins, as the Root chakra provides a safe, solid Earth base. The life force rises to meet your power in the third, or Solar Plexus chakra.

Chapter
9

Solar Plexus Chakra (*Manipura*): Your Core Self

Who are you? Your third chakra knows. Everything that distinguishes you from anybody else lives here in your Solar Plexus chakra—the seat of your individuality, personal power, and sense of self. Your third chakra is proactive. You move, act, and get things done from the third chakra, but you can also sit very still and feel who you are by focusing on this chakra. Writer Harish Johari says the third chakra "behaves like a cobra," and this is an apt metaphor for the power of the Solar Plexus chakra in several ways: the cobra can invoke fear in others and can get what it wants, but it can also harm others or slink back down into its basket if its authority is threatened.

Think of yoga's Cobra pose (*Bhujangasana*) that stretches through your body's center up through its serpent crown. Also, be aware of *Kundalini* serpent power, which is the electric source of spiritual awakening that lies coiled and waiting to rise through the chakras. *Kundalini* energy requires a strongly balanced and aligned third chakra to support and hold its power.

When your Solar Plexus chakra is strong, balanced, and open, you project a confident, reliable, and trustworthy persona to the world. You exude a warmth and friendliness that others find irresistible. At its best, the third chakra projects a sense of humor and personal charisma. However, without a grounded first chakra and an emotionally balanced second chakra, the third chakra can become like a hammer or a gun, subjecting others to the sudden force of its power. If blocked, you can lose your sense of self, confidence, and ability to get anything accomplished. In other words, balancing the Solar Plexus chakra matters a lot in terms of your ability to function fully in the world.

Solar Plexus Chakra 101

The third chakra, the Solar Plexus chakra, is also called the Sun chakra or Power chakra. *Manipura* is the traditional Sanskrit word. This word is usually translated as "dwelling place of the jewel," "city of jewels," or something similar, but the definition always has to do with a jewel. This is a beautiful image because the third chakra is where you open to abundance, prosperity, and opportunities, and you literally accept the jewels of life. Harish Johari says that the body's center of gravity lies in the third chakra. Imagine a big, weighty, brilliant, and priceless jewel right below your rib cage and in the center of your solar plexus at the core of your body. This is where this chakra resides.

The third chakra is associated with the Fire element because in contrast to the first or Root chakra's solid, grounded earthiness and the second or Sacral chakra's watery, flowing movement, the third or Solar Plexus chakra projects heat and energy as if it were the body's own inner Sun ☉. The third chakra's symbolic color is a bright sunny yellow, and the traditional lotus symbol depicting this chakra has 10 petals. The sound associated with this chakra is the seed sound *RANG* (rhymes with "song"). Chanting this sound helps to activate the third chakra.

The Solar Plexus chakra radiates to encompass your stomach, pancreas, gall bladder, and liver. Your strength, as physically manifested in your muscles, is linked to the third chakra. This chakra is also associated with the middle of the back and the upper intestines.

Your Solar Plexus chakra has everything to do with who you are, what you can do, and how you feel about all of that, so let's look more closely at the direct manifestation of your personal power.

When you are born, you don't understand that you and your mother are not the same being. Once you get to be two or three years of age, however, you start to understand that you are *you,* not anyone else. You gain a sense of autonomy. This marks the beginning of your third chakra's development, but it doesn't stop there or even in childhood. Throughout your life, your Solar Plexus chakra reflects your sense of self, your ego, and who you are in your own mind.

The third chakra, or Solar Plexus chakra (Manipura), resides at the core of your body and radiates your personal power.

Understanding and accepting who you are is a lifelong process, but the third chakra can help you move more swiftly and efficiently in the right direction. A strong sense of self frees you up to get things done. It helps you to exercise your personal power in the service of building a better life for yourself. The Solar Plexus chakra has a reputation for being the selfish chakra. Unfortunately, doing good things for oneself has been associated with the idea of being selfish. To truly be helpful, loving, and effective in the world, you must be autonomous; you must be able to function fully as a whole person, you must know and understand yourself, and you must be confident in your power. Self-care and self-development are not selfish; caring for yourself and your development is essential for a healthy third chakra. You can't go through life pretending to be someone else or constantly leaning on others and expect to succeed at it for very long. Writer, teacher, and mythology expert Joseph Campbell once wrote, "The privilege of a lifetime is being who you are." This is the birthright of the Solar Plexus chakra and your birthright. The quest for *you* is not "selfish" in a negative way, but it is selfish … and absolutely essential.

Children who grow up constantly subjected to the will of a powerful parent are likely to develop third chakra issues. If children never get to be who they are while growing up, how can they be expected to know who they are as adults? As a way to strengthen the third chakras of her own children, every night after her children are fast asleep, Betsy whispers in each of their ears, "Become who you are." This ritual symbolizes Betsy's desire to support her children in whatever path they choose in this life, knowing it will be *their* path, not *her* path, which she persuades them to follow.

Self-Esteem

The third chakra is not only the reflection of our senses of self, but it's also our opinion about ourselves. In other words, here lies your self-esteem. How do you feel about yourself? A healthy third chakra reflects a healthy appreciation of self. If you have too much energy here, you might project narcissism and an inflated ego. Narcissism is a psychological term referring to a personality disorder characterized by excessive self-importance and a need for constant admiration to such an extent that the narcissistic person is not able to love or feel empathy for others. The word comes from the Greek myth of Narcissus, who fell in love with his own reflection and died of unrequited love.

If you don't have enough energy spinning through your third chakra, you might dislike yourself, feel shame about who you are, or even feel like you don't have a personality. You might find that you are unable to summon either the mental or physical stamina to power your core being and are left with a pale shadow of your fully powered-up strength and vitality. Look for the placement of the planet Mars ♂ in your astrological birth chart for clues about how to boost your strength and regain the power to act.

Control Issues

In addition to your identity, your third chakra is also directly related to your feelings of personal power over yourself and others. For this reason, control issues have everything to do with the Solar Plexus chakra. The amount of control you exert over your own behavior, as well as the behavior of others, flows from this chakra.

If you are compelled to control everyone and everything in your life and feel uncomfortable when you are out of control (or never let yourself get out of control), you might have an overactive third chakra. If you never feel like you have control over anything or that you are a victim of circumstance, are at the whim of fate, and blame others for your problems, then you might have a blocked third chakra.

Betsy had a client who was a classic example of someone struggling with an overactive third chakra. This man was having difficulty maintaining close relationships. He badly wanted to find a life partner, but instead, he found himself in many short-term relationships that went nowhere. He was extremely successful, had financial stability, and from the outside, looked like the "perfect catch."

Yet, he was also arrogant and put the majority of his time into the development of his business. He would work days at a time without having contact with any friends, including the woman he was dating at the time. He thrived on stress and consistently pushed himself to achieve and find success. He had a hard time understanding why the women he dated couldn't understand his need to throw himself into his work, especially because it resulted in outward results such as money, an environmentally progressive car, and an expensive weekend home. All his energy, however, was focused in the third chakra, which took away from the passion of his second chakra, or Sacral chakra, and the compassion of his fourth chakra, or Heart chakra. The result was an unemotional man who was unable to feel true empathy or intimacy with someone else and who was unable to really give or receive love from a partner.

Willpower

So, you can't stick with that diet? Do you keep procrastinating and can't finish that project? Your third chakra also reflects your willpower and your ability to follow through with your commitments. When you have a strong sense of self and personal power, you can finish what you start and do what you say (and intend). When you aren't confident in your ability to make things happen, you are less likely to have the *will* to access your own *power*. It's not surprising that those who struggle with a low fitness level often express that they have no willpower. It then becomes a vicious circle because the mental and physical weakness lowers self-esteem, which continues to keep that third chakra weak. Core body strength is the engine that powers the body's *chi*. The stronger your core being, the easier it will be to make decisions and to move and do with confidence and vitality. A strong third chakra supports a strong flow of life force energy within and without you, making what once seemed out of reach in your weakened state now appear readily accessible and well within your personal power.

Moving Forward

The third chakra is also about being proactive. Strong, healthy third chakras reflect the ability to make things happen and get things done. The third chakra is the chakra of action, progress, and enacting change in the world. When you are strong here, you can move forward in your life with purpose and power.

If you have trouble getting moving or have low energy, it can help to tap into the power of your third chakra through vigorous exercise. If you like to walk, step up the pace or include short sprints if you are able. To really increase your third chakra power and energy, consider taking a class in the martial arts. Remember that Tai Chi has its roots in the martial arts. Its movements are based on raising optimal flows of life force energy for meeting and countering the approach of another person, whether adversary or partner. Tai Chi movements facilitate and optimize the flow of *chi* in your body, mind, and spirit.

Digestive Fire

The way you process food into energy is also reflected in your third chakra. Powerful third chakra people often have strong digestion and elimination, whereas people with blocked third chakras have trouble digesting many foods and are often constipated or find they are experiencing colitis or other gut problems. Stoking your inner digestive Fire element through third chakra activation can help you feel better, get more energy from the food you eat, and can help you achieve your ideal weight; a healthy inner Fire means a healthy metabolism. You can see the effects of a healthy digestive Fire in people who glow with energy. People who move sluggishly and look pale or pasty tend to have a suppressed inner Fire, which is related to a blocked Solar Plexus chakra.

Solar Plexus Chakra Correspondences

Your Solar Plexus chakra corresponds with certain colors, elements, sounds, and parts of your body, as well as parts of your life crucial to your sense of self and your ability to get things done. Check out this chart for a summary, and then read on to find out how you can use your Solar Plexus chakra to change your life for the better.

Third Chakra	Correspondence
Sanskrit name	Manipura (dwelling place for the jewel, city of jewels)
Element	Fire
Color	Yellow
Seed sound	RANG
Location	Just below the rib cage, at the solar plexus
Associated cultural phrases	"He's a man of action." "Burn the candle at both ends." "Burn the midnight oil." "Crash and burn." "More power to you!" "I have no willpower." "I need a power tie." "This will whet your appetite." "Put yourself out there."
Associated anatomy	Solar plexus, stomach, digestive organs, upper intestines, middle back, liver, pancreas, gall bladder, and muscles
Associated psychological and life issues	Personal power, ego, sense of self, self-esteem, willpower, and ability to get things done
Physical issues related to third chakra blockage	Sluggishness, low energy, low appetite, chronic fatigue, poor digestion, diabetes, gall bladder problems, feeling cold, stiff muscles, poor liver function, bad posture, and weak middle back
Psychological issues related to third chakra blockage	Low self-esteem, lack of willpower, inability to accomplish things or follow through, unreliability, victim mentality/blaming others for problems, and the feeling of having no personality
Physical issues related to third chakra overloading	Hypertension, stress, ulcers, muscle spasms, insomnia due to excess energy, exercise addiction, constant hunger, and physical signs related to extreme stress

Third Chakra	Correspondence
Psychological issues related to third chakra overloading	Anger issues, control issues, obsession with power and outward signs of power such as money and possessions, inability to compromise with others, excessive competition, arrogance, lack of sensitivity, and narcissism
Third chakra therapy	Aerobic exercise to increase third chakra or meditation to calm third chakra, core-strengthening exercises like sit-ups and Pilates, martial arts, and counseling to acknowledge your inner power and potential or to develop sensitivity and respect for others

Awakening the Solar Plexus Chakra

If your *Kundalini* energy is activated in your first (Root) and second (Sacral) chakras, then you can encourage it to rise up into your third chakra, or Solar Plexus chakra. When you awaken your Solar Plexus chakra, you are likely to experience more self-confidence and ability to act, especially if you have problems getting things done. In those with overloaded Solar Plexus chakras, awakening the third chakra can bring your sense of self back into perspective and can help you see what other people need more clearly. Awakening the core-strengthening Solar Plexus chakra is a great way to energize and jump-start your life and increase your productivity, abundance, and self-esteem.

Anything that heats you up and strengthens your core can activate the third chakra. Hot yoga styles such as *Bikram* yoga or core-strengthening exercises such as Pilates are great for third chakra awakening. Pilates develops core awareness while lengthening, toning, and strengthening muscles. Pilates exercises traditionally use a specific machine designed for the purpose, but they can also be adapted for mat exercises without any equipment. Pilates classes are widely available at health clubs, yoga studios, and community centers. Deep relaxation is also effective for stress relief and centering and to put you back in touch with your own sense of "I." Or you can just go on a brisk walk or run, preferably outside on a beautiful day, or even at the gym on a treadmill if that's your only option. Sit in a sauna or in a hot spa bathtub, submerging your solar plexus under the warm jets of water. The point is to stoke your inner Fire element.

To get more powerful Solar Plexus chakra energy into your environment, highlight the color yellow. Wear yellow, paint your office yellow (or just hang a yellow-dominated picture where you can see it while you work), and spend a few minutes each day in the Sun ☉. Seeing the color and feeling its warmth can help to awaken this chakra. Also, be sure to include more warmth in your home. When was the last time you used your fireplace? Wear more gold jewelry or a gemstone of amber or citrine. Remember, the Solar Plexus is the jewel of the chakras, shining bright at your core being and radiating the strength of action.

You can also try this exercise for awakening the jewel of the Solar Plexus chakra:

1. Sit on the floor, legs crossed, seat firmly planted on the floor. Feel your pelvic bones, and imagine roots anchoring those bones to the earth.

2. Take several long, slow, deep breaths, and then draw your attention to the area just below your rib cage. Imagine your third chakra, a bright burning yellow circle spinning slowly, glinting like the facets of a laser-cut gem sending out strength and power with each breath you take.

3. Imagine your third chakra glowing with a yellow circle of warm, energizing light that encompasses your entire chest. Feel the warm light moving into your stomach, and imagine lighting a tiny flame inside yourself, like a pilot light. Feel the warm glow, and picture the translucent golden depths of the chakra shining as a jewel of fire in your chest.

4. Take a deep breath in, and in a low resonating tone, say the word: *RANG,* holding the "A" sound (pronounced "ah"; the word rhymes with "song"). Imagine the yellow light from the jewel filling your entire body with slow, steady beams of inner sunlight.

5. Continue to breathe and let the warm beams fill you with a feeling of benevolent power and confidence, radiating from the golden jewel of your Solar Plexus chakra, as long as you like.

Aligning the Solar Plexus Chakra

Let the power of the Sun ☉ help pull your Solar Plexus chakra into alignment with this exercise:

1. Stand outside on a sunny day. Plant your feet firmly on the ground. Hold your arms out about a foot away from the sides of your body, and rotate your palms to face up. Close your eyes and lift your face to the Sun.

2. Imagine your third chakra, just below your rib cage, and try to feel it spinning. Feel the rays of the Sun beaming straight down into the crown of your head, and imagine them flowing down through your spine to merge with your Solar Plexus chakra.

3. Imagine your Solar Plexus chakra spinning more quickly, adding power, and then beaming yellow Sun energy back up through the crown of your head to merge with the Sun's energy.

4. Lift your arms straight up overhead, and imagine the yellow light pulsing up and down, radiating to the Sun and back again. Your Solar Plexus chakra should now be aligned.

Blocks in the Solar Plexus Chakra

Our culture certainly values power. We see control as a positive quality and being out of control as a distinctly negative quality. We prize people who achieve; make things happen; who move with the decisive action of astrology's planet Mars ♂; and who radiate personal charisma, even if they use that charisma to control others to get ahead.

In many ways, power *is* a positive thing, though even the more idealistic among us tend to associate it across the board with greed. To feel powerless is certainly not healthy. Feeling powerful and knowing you can control your own destiny and influence the events of your own life is a very good thing. Power only turns negative when we use it against others or lack the sensitivity to understand how our actions affect those around us.

But if you have blocked power in your Solar Plexus chakra, carelessly wielding your power is the least of your problems. You tend to feel powerless and out of control. A blocked third chakra often results in low self-esteem and self-destructive behaviors that can lead to victimization by others. If you let other people take advantage of you, you can almost guarantee that they will (especially those people with overloaded third chakras!).

Blocked Solar Plexus Chakra Health Issues

Third chakra issues usually relate to digestion and poor posture. Conditions like diabetes, hypoglycemia, or problems in the gall bladder and liver might be related to the third chakra. Chronic lack of energy, such as chronic fatigue syndrome or fibromyalgia, might be related to the third chakra. People with blocked third chakras also appear collapsed in the middle. Their abdominal and/or lower back muscles tend to be weak, and they slump instead of standing tall and radiating power. They don't feel that power, so they can't send it out—and the result is an inability to even maintain the basic core structure of the body.

Without its power, the body tends to crater at its core in a self-protective, curled-back, round-shouldered posture aimed at guarding this tender underdeveloped third chakra, and the compassion of the fourth chakra, or Heart chakra is guarded as well. Instead of leading up and forward, open-hearted and strong, the body looks down and turns inward, preserves strength and affection, and withdraws from engagement with the world instead of rising to meet and welcome it. You can help bring awareness and relief with careful stretching exercises, *prana* breathing meditations, and conscious posture work to open the chest and heal the third chakra by providing strong diaphragmatic lung support.

Temporary third chakra blocks can sometimes be caused by a professional setback. Many of us tend to identify at a very deep level with the work we do. When that work is questioned or criticized, we take it very personally. If you are experiencing a problem at your job, it is very important to separate that problem from your sense of personal worth. If you don't, you can set yourself up for a continued downward spiral of failure in your work, which continues to feed your eroding sense of self until you aren't able to fix the problem. Instead, if you let work be work and you be you, then you will be more objective about the situation and better able to address the problem, whatever it is, in a more rational (and powerful) way.

Blocked Solar Plexus Chakra Psychological Issues

People with blocked third chakras tend to put themselves down a lot, blame other people for their problems, and complain of low energy. At the heart of a third chakra block is a weak sense of "I." Blocked third chakra people might seem to others to have very little personality, and indeed, that's often how they feel. They often constrict their feelings and refuse to let others see how they really feel. The third chakra reflects your sense of yourself, and if you don't have a clear sense of who you are, or you don't like who you are and try to disengage from it, all the energy that should be channeled into the practice of engaging with the world dissipates.

Healing a Blocked Solar Plexus Chakra

To unblock your third chakra, think about heating your body and strengthening your core. Following are some great ways to do that, as well as some other ideas for healing the blocked power of your Solar Plexus chakra:

- Exercising until you sweat. Running—even short sprints—is a great third chakra exercise.

- Sitting in a sauna or a steam room.

- Doing hot yoga, such as *Bikram* yoga.

- Taking a Pilates class.

- Eating yellow foods, especially when they are spicy or have the strong flavors of ginger, cinnamon, turmeric, and curry.

- Engaging in positive self-talk. Tell yourself you are strong, capable, and active. Saying things repeatedly to yourself can help you begin to believe them.

- Employing mantras such as:

  - *I am strong and powerful.*

  - *I believe in and celebrate myself.*

  - *I open to the prosperity and abundance in the Universe.*

  - *I can accomplish and complete anything I want to do.*

- Finding a task you can finish that will make even a small difference in your environment. For instance, clean out a drawer, load the dishwasher, or make your bed. Go do it, and don't stop until you are finished.

- Consciously lifting and opening your heart to the sky as you inhale deeply. Hold this brave and powerful posture. Exhale and visualize your third chakra being strong and grounded and supporting your open heart and your deep, steady breath. Practice this calming posture to remind yourself of your personal power, and summon the courage to act on your heart's desires.

- Spending time with a friend who genuinely values you and is good at letting you know it. (Remember, we're not talking about flattery here!)

- Getting counseling for self-esteem issues.

An easy way to tune up your third chakra is to listen to your own inner voice. What messages do you tell yourself throughout the day? Do these messages build you up or tear you down? If you are always criticizing yourself for your failures rather than patting yourself on the back for your successes, you are encouraging the block in your third chakra. Work on purposefully stuffing a sock in that negative voice and focusing on your strengths. Let yourself talk to yourself about all your great qualities—because you have a lot of them!

Overloading in the Solar Plexus Chakra

Overloaded third chakras are easy to recognize. These are the loud, steal-all-the-attention-in-the-room, do-it-my-way, I-have-to-have-the-last-word people. Maybe this is you, but even if it isn't, you probably know people like this. An overloaded third chakra makes you arrogant and self-centered. You always think you are right and people who disagree with you are *wrong* (if you even hear their opinion to consider it at all).

If you lived all alone in the world, an overloaded third chakra might not be much of a problem. However, as long as you have to get along with other people—feeling empathy from your second chakra and genuine love and compassion from your Heart chakra—an overloaded third chakra will thwart your attempts at satisfactory relationships, not to mention spiritual progress. If you seek access to a Higher Power, you'll have a lot of trouble seeing around your own inflated ego.

Got stress? Meditation is an excellent way to begin practicing stress relief. Try sitting in a comfortable position and tuning in to your immediate environment or your breath for just five quiet minutes (no phone, no tablet or laptop, no book, and no sound other than soothing music if that helps to relax you). When thoughts come to mind, look at them as if they belonged to someone else and then let them go. You might need to let go of a thousand thoughts over the course of five minutes, and this is perfectly okay and normal. The point is to keep letting thoughts go rather than letting them carry you away. Keep returning to the rhythm of your breathing or the sound of the music in the room. The more you practice, the better you will get. Meditation gives your busy mind a break, which is crucial for people who tend to be overloaded in the third chakra.

Overloaded Solar Plexus Chakra Health Issues

Overloaded third chakra people tend to have very high stress and all the physical problems that go along with that, such as hypertension, tight muscles, and ulcers. Although chronic fatigue is typical of people with blocked third chakras, overloaded third chakra people tend to be so keyed up all the time. At some point, their bodies can't take it anymore, and they collapse from exhaustion. These are the people admitted to the emergency room because they think they are having heart attacks, when in actuality, they are having severe indigestion, possible panic attacks, and total exhaustion. Overloaded third chakra people also tend to overuse pain medications and sedatives in a misguided attempt to calm down. It's hard work carrying around gigantic egos. Those things are heavy!

Overloaded Solar Plexus Chakra Lifestyle Issues

Overloaded third chakra people can come across as arrogant and as just plain mean, especially to people who are particularly sensitive (overloaded in the second or Sacral chakra). Overloaded Solar Plexus chakra people just can't understand why people don't do things their way, which is obviously the right way. When the world doesn't oblige them, they can become snappy, aggressive, and even violent. If you've ever seen an adult throw a temper tantrum, you can bet an overloaded third chakra is involved.

Overloaded third chakra people tend to be very successful and are good at acquiring all the trappings of success and power. However, they are also prone to losing it all in one fell swoop because they take risks and don't usually consider other points of view. This can be a lonely way to live, so balancing that third chakra is well worth the effort.

Healing an Overloaded Solar Plexus Chakra

Healing an overloaded third chakra means draining out some of that excessive "all-about-me" energy to make room for other kinds of energy, such as grounding energy, compassion, and love. Remember, personal power is great as long as it doesn't take over and exercise its power at the expense of others. Balance is best. Try these strategies:

- Practice deep relaxation techniques, such as meditation or *Savasana* (see Chapter 7).
- Aerobic exercise, such as running or working out at the gym, to drain off aggressive energy.
- Practice deep breathing exercises. Take long, slow, and deep breaths, filling up your lungs completely and then exhaling completely. Try inhaling to the count of five and exhaling to the count of ten, increasing these intervals with practice.

- Engage in noncompetitive activities or activities that force you to work with others.

- Slow down. Practice eating, walking, even working in a slower and more measured way.

- Hone your listening skills. Practice hearing what other people are saying. Try posing the question to yourself: "What if they really are right and I'm wrong?" It's not the end of the world if that turns out to be true. It can be good for you, like eating vegetables … or humble pie!

- Get counseling to learn to increase your sensitivity toward others and for anger management issues.

Yoga Poses to Balance the Solar Plexus Chakra

The best yoga poses for balancing both blocked and overloaded Solar Plexus chakras are those poses that help you to feel powerful but balanced, and those poses that strengthen your core. The Warrior (*Virabhadrasana*) series is ideal for this purpose. So is Boat pose (*Navasana*), which not only builds core strength, but also teaches you balance from the inside out. Yoga breathing exercises, such as Bellows Breath, which you'll learn in Chapter 14, can also help to heal a second or third chakra imbalance of passion and power.

When you first begin practicing yoga's Warrior poses, it is not uncommon to feel fears and anxieties arise in these challenging poses. Warrior II was Betsy's least favorite pose for years. Despite a strong yoga practice, she always experienced an irrational fear that her legs wouldn't be able to support her. As her teacher kept the class in this pose, Betsy would routinely feel panicky, and her mind would begin to race with fears of collapsing. It wasn't until Betsy worked with a Phoenix Rising Sun yoga therapist that she began to connect her personal struggle of stepping into her own potential and power with her difficulty in Warrior II pose. Warrior II suddenly became easier as Betsy worked on increasing the fire in her third chakra; burned through old and limiting fears; began to believe in herself; and took some risks in her life that forced her to be the powerful woman she is. Betsy now joyfully holds Warrior II with steadfastness, inner fortitude, and a calm mind.

Warrior I (*Virabhadrasana I*)

The first Warrior pose (Virabhadrasana I) *aligns your personal power as the life force energizes the third chakra, or Solar Plexus chakra.*

1. Stand in *Tadasana* (as described in Chapter 7) in bare feet and with your feet hip-width apart. Experience stability. Take a deep breath and allow the strength of something greater to support you as you prepare to become a Warrior.

2. Inhale and step or jump your feet about 3 to 4 feet apart. Turn your right foot in a little, and open your left leg 90 degrees to the front of your yoga mat. Square your hips to face the front of your mat. If you feel unsteady, you can walk your right foot more to the edge of your mat to create a wider base from which to work.

3. Firm your muscles and hug your shins toward each other. Keeping your right leg straight, exhale and bend your left leg into a square. Your left knee should track to the little toe side of your left foot.

4. Inhale and stretch your arms toward the ceiling, reaching up through your finger-tips. Your upper arms should be on either side of your ears. Align your head over your torso with a strong gaze forward.

5. Take your internal reproductive organs and move them back, spreading them open. Maintaining the thighs back now, lengthen the tailbone down toward your heels as you lunge deeper into your front leg. Press your feet firmly into the mat, sending energy from the core of your pelvis down into the Earth.

6. Inhale and straighten your front leg. Turn your feet to be parallel, and then step or jump your feet back together. Repeat Warrior I pose on the other side.

Warrior II (*Virabhadrasana II*)

Correct   Arched   Flat

The second Warrior pose (Virabhadrasana II) *gives the third chakra, or Solar Plexus chakra, power as support while the outstretched arms lengthen through the chest and open the fourth chakra, or Heart chakra.*

1. Stand in *Tadasana* (as described in Chapter 7) in bare feet, with your feet hip-width apart. Experience stability. Take a deep breath and allow the strength of something greater to support you as you prepare to become a Warrior.

2. Inhale and step or jump your feet about 3 to 4 feet apart. Turn your left foot in a little, and open your right leg 90 degrees to the front of your mat. Your right foot should be directly in line with the arch of your left foot. You should be able to feel your front foot connect with the floor, neither too arched nor too flat. Open your arms before and behind you, lengthening through your fingertips, your palms facing down. Your ankles should be in line with your wrists.

3. Firm your muscles and hug your shins toward each other. Keeping your left leg straight, exhale and bend your right leg into a square so your knee is directly over your ankle. Your right knee should track to the little toe side of your right foot. Turn your head and gaze out over your right hand.

4. Concentrate on feeling power in your legs. Rely on your breath to support you in this challenging pose. With every inhalation, elongate your spine; with every exhalation, feel grounded down into your legs as you lunge more deeply into your right leg. You are a Warrior!

5. Inhale and straighten your bent leg. Step or jump your feet back together. Repeat on the other side.

Boat Pose *(Navasana)*

Practicing Boat pose (Navasana) *with a partner builds core strength and shares balanced power.*

1. Sit on the floor and stretch your legs straight out in front of you.

2. Keeping your body straight and your core muscles firm, exhale and lean back, raising your legs to 60 degrees and lowering the trunk by 30 degrees. Balance on the front of the buttock bones. Extend energy out through the legs, keeping the feet flexed.

3. Raise the arms to shoulder level, palms facing each other, and stretch your arms long to loosely grasp your partner's hands. Your elbows should align with your knees. Place the flat of your foot against your partner's, touching as lightly as possible. (Don't push the feet into each other.) Breathe evenly and try to balance together, riding on the waves of breath for as long as you can.

4. Come down slowly together. Sit comfortably in a cross-legged position with your hands on your knees. Breathe as you look deeply into your partner's eyes.

Astrology for the Awakened Solar Plexus Chakra

Now, we're going to look more closely at the astrological correspondences for the third, or Solar Plexus chakra. In Chapter 4, you learned:

- The planetary rulers of the Solar Plexus chakra are Mars ♂ and Pluto ♀.
- The signs for the Solar Plexus chakra are Aries ♈ and Scorpio ♏.

Planetary Ruler	Sign(s) Ruled
Mars ♂	Aries ♈, co-ruler of Scorpio ♏
Pluto ♀	Scorpio ♏, co-ruler of Aries ♈

Knowing the energy of astrology's planets and signs that correspond to the Solar Plexus chakra helps you understand how to bring awakened third chakra power to life. Yoga Warrior and Boat poses use concentration, strength, and balance to stimulate third chakra power in your body. Astrology gives that spinning power a meaning and a purpose in your life. To look at how the chakras are interpreted in an astrological birth chart, see Appendix A, where we'll look at Michelle Obama's birth chart. Transiting planetary energy can also affect astrological cycles and the way they are felt and experienced.

How Mars ♂ Awakens the Solar Plexus Chakra

Mars ♂ is one of astrology's *personal* planets. Mars ♂ is the natural ruler of Aries ♈ and the first house of identity, personality, the physical self, and childhood. Mars ♂ is the natural co-ruler of Scorpio ♏ (its energy is weaker than the ruler's) and the eighth house of sex, death and regeneration, rebirth, psychic powers, higher mathematics and atomic energy, and political resources. As a personal and inner planet, Mars ♂ governs personal expression, core identity, and your inner being.

Mars ♂ is the champion of assertiveness and personal courage, and it generates physical energy, emotional desires, and boosts your ego. Bold and decisive with the strength needed to compete, Mars helps you know how to pick your battles, learn to manage anger, and act to achieve your goals. Mars lends power to the Solar Plexus chakra, spinning core strength at the center of your being (and fueled by the passions of the Sacral chakra). In a balanced Solar Plexus chakra, Mars is strong without hurtful aggression. It avoids indecision and indolence by nurturing the courage for you to feel secure in your passions and confident of your path.

How Pluto ♀ Awakens the Solar Plexus Chakra

Pluto ♀ is one of astrology's *transpersonal* planets. Pluto is the natural ruler of Scorpio ♏ and the eighth house of sex, death and rebirth, psychic intuition, and higher mathematics. As a transpersonal or outer planet, Pluto ♀ (with its longer orbit) governs astrological cycles influencing whole generations of people. Astrologers continue to designate Pluto ♀ with planetary status. There are indications that astronomers might reverse Pluto's downgrade to "dwarf planet" and reinstate its full planetary status as well.

Pluto ♀ is the planet of your soul's journey, charting its evolution. The Solar Plexus chakra feels the influence of Mars ♂ because it is the weaker co-ruler (with Pluto ♀) of Aries ♈. This means the transformative disruption of Pluto ♀ receives the support of Mars's ♂ bold and courageous action in awakening Solar Plexus energy. Mars provides the push that gets *Kundalini* energy to spin the Solar Plexus chakra with Pluto's power of creative destruction and personal rebirth.

How Aries ♈ Awakens the Solar Plexus Chakra

Aries ♈ with its yang, Fire element energy, is ruled by the warrior Mars ♂. Aries's rush to take on the world with wholehearted enthusiasm suits Solar Plexus's chakra energy perfectly. Eager, inquisitive, and straightforward to the point of bluntness, Aries loves to meet any challenge. The Solar Plexus chakra welcomes strong-willed Aries's hard-charging passion to get there *first*. With Aries's influence, awakened *Kundalini* serpent power in the Solar Plexus chakra is channeled from the Sacral chakra to spin with the desire to act and to go where no one has gone before.

How Scorpio ♏ Awakens the Solar Plexus Chakra

Scorpio ♏ is ruled by Pluto ♀, with Mars ♂ as its co-ruler. As the weaker planetary ruler of Scorpio ♏, Mars's ♂ influence lends a warrior's courage to the Scorpion's probing intensity. Mars directs the Scorpion's emotional intensity from Pluto into the magnetism of leadership. By awakening the Solar Plexus chakra's power, Scorpio's laser focus on the evolution of the soul (led by Pluto) is given the awesome force of persistence by Aries and its Mars ruler.

Solar Plexus Chakra Rising

The pioneering spirit of Aries ♈/Mars ♂ provides the surge to push *Kundalini* energy from the passionate Sacral chakra to the powerful Solar Plexus chakra. That power surge risks coursing offtrack or petering out without the soulful magnetism of Scorpio ♏/Pluto ♀ to draw the soul upward to its unknown potential. To give the Solar Plexus chakra its proper balance, both zodiac signs must be present.

Once you've hit upon the right cause to liberate your soul's passions, the Solar Plexus chakra will activate. Filled with purpose and the desire to act, a perseverance that never gives up, your Solar Plexus chakra spins with a power whose source resides below in the passions of your Sacral chakra. The life force rises up to meet your compassion in the fourth chakra, or Heart chakra.

Chapter
10

Heart Chakra (*Anahata*): Love Is Everything

Do we have to tell you that your fourth chakra is all about love? Of course it is. This is your Heart chakra, the place where loving energy pours out of you to wash over the world and make life better. Your bonds to other human beings; your sense of caring and compassion; your altruism; your urge to give to others; and, just as importantly, your ability to love, cherish, and take care of yourself all start here.

Plus, the Heart chakra is the center chakra, halfway between the three lower, earthier, and more physical chakras and the three higher, more cerebral, and spiritual chakras. The Heart chakra is the fulcrum where you find balance between Earth and Heaven and between body and mind. Love holds it all together and makes you human. In other words, this chakra is a V.I.C. (Very Important Chakra!).

When your Heart chakra is strong, balanced, and open, you know how to love and give to others freely, but you also know how to love and take care of yourself. However, when the Heart chakra is blocked, you might feel cut off from your connection to others. By contrast, an overloaded Heart chakra is linked to giving *too* much at the expense of your physical and emotional health. Let's explore the Heart chakra in more depth, so you can get your center of balance *back* into balance and celebrate what might just be the very best quality of human beings: the ability to love with true healing compassion.

Heart Chakra 101

The fourth chakra, or Heart chakra, also sometimes called the Love or the Air chakra, is called *Anahata* in the traditional Sanskrit. This word can be translated as "unstruck" or "intact." Some scholars call the Heart chakra the "place of the unstruck sound" because the heart sings without having to be played. (We feel that's such a nice way to think about the Heart chakra.)

The fourth chakra is associated with the Air element, perhaps because you breathe from here. This is the realm not only of the heart but of the lungs—the entire cardiovascular system. Life force energy moves in and out from this center of the body. You could think of your fourth chakra as your very own Grand Central Station. The Heart chakra's symbolic color is green, and the traditional lotus symbol depicting this chakra has 12 petals. The sound associated with this chakra is the seed sound *YANG* (rhymes with "song"). Chanting this sound helps to activate the Heart chakra.

You can guess where the fourth chakra is located—deep in the center of your chest behind your heart, radiating in and around your heart (the mediastinum), lungs, chest, and even out to your shoulders, down your arms, and into your hands. Your thymus gland and your cardiac nerve plexus are associated with the fourth or Heart chakra. For women, the breasts are also a part of the realm of the Heart chakra.

Balance

At the heart of the Heart chakra is the notion of balance. As we mentioned earlier, the Heart chakra sits squarely between the three lower chakras and the three higher chakras. Your first (Root), second (Sacral), and third (Solar Plexus) chakras have everything to do with the physical body, whereas the fifth (Throat), sixth (Third Eye), and seventh (Crown) chakras are more about intuition, the mind, and the spirit. The Heart chakra helps these two halves of you speak to each other and act—not out of pure physical instinct or completely in-your-head braininess—but with active love and compassion.

Finding balance, strength, and openness in your fourth chakra will transform your life into one of balance, strength, and openheartedness.

The fourth chakra, or Heart chakra (Anahata), is compassion in action, providing the balance between the three lower chakras and the three upper chakras.

Love Fest

Love. It makes the world go around. It's what the world needs. It's the answer. Our culture is obsessed with love, and this is obvious by the music we create and play over and over again; by the movies and television shows we watch; by the stories that move us to tears; and even by our entire value system, which champions such notions as marriage, true love, soul mates, love at first sight, and romance.

We have a huge capacity to love—so huge that we extend that love beyond our own species. We love our dogs, our cats, our birds, even our fish. We love our plants. We love the earth and its gardens. We love mountains and starry skies and flowing streams. In other words, *we love*. And it all comes out of the Heart chakra.

When we lose love or when our hearts are broken, we can literally *feel* it in our fourth chakras. That feeling of pain, grief, or a shattered heart is very real, even if a doctor can't pinpoint it with a diagnostic test. If you've ever had your heart broken, you know what we mean.

Betsy sees so many people in treatment with fourth chakra heart issues! She believes this is the chakra we shut down most often, as a means of protecting ourselves. Yet what starts out as self-preservation often turns into isolation and disconnection from those relationships that we are wired to need in our lives.

Children who don't feel loved or who feel their love is rejected by a parent or a sibling often develop blocked Heart chakras. They fear more rejection, so they close down this sensitive chakra and refuse to make themselves vulnerable. Sometimes, children grow up with an opposite reaction: an overloaded Heart chakra so focused on giving to others in an effort to make up for a lack of love and attention in their life that they never learn how to take care of themselves or how to receive love. Consider how your family handled issues of love, compassion, and giving to others, as well as caring for themselves. Are you repeating or reflecting those patterns in your adult life?

Fortunately, the Heart chakra is also an expert healer.

Healing Power

The fourth chakra energy naturally flows not only around your heart and lungs but also down your arms and out the palms of your hands. This means that when this chakra is strong and energized, your hands actually have healing power. This healing might be subtle, but it is very real. Think about how a mother's loving touch on her child's wounded knee seems to make everything better. You can even use this natural healing ability on yourself to cycle your own loving energy back through your body. This is one of the best ways to love yourself and make yourself strong, healthy, vibrant, and able to love others well.

You can use your own healing energy to help speed the healing of your aches, pains, strains, sprains, and even your emotional pain, from a bruised ego to a broken heart. Just try this healing meditation:

- Sit comfortably anywhere. Close your eyes. Visualize your Heart chakra as an emerald-green wheel of light spinning around your heart.

- Breathe deeply and imagine the light growing brighter and more vibrant, illuminating your lungs. Imagine the wheel spinning faster. Imagine the chakra getting larger and more brilliant.

- Visualize that green light now, and picture it flowing out from the sides of the fourth chakra, up through your shoulders, flowing down your arms, and out your palms.

- Bring your palms about 2 inches apart and try to feel the energy between them. Continue to visualize that heart energy flowing, like an eternal spring, from out of your Heart chakra, down your arms and out your hands.

- Touch your palms together and feel the healing energy moving in a two-directional circle, from your heart, down each arm, and back up each opposite arm at the same time.

- Now, put your palms onto any part of your body that hurts. Imagine the green light filled with tiny sparks of healing energy, pouring into the spot and knitting and mending everything back together, healing and connecting tissues and strengthening bones and joints, and freeing internal energy to move where it needs to go.

- ○ Stay like this, with your palms on the hurt area, for as long as you like. Repeat several times each day, for as long as you need to send healing Heart chakra energy to that spot.

Your Compassion Center

The fourth chakra is not only about love, but it's also about other impulses that are born out of love, especially compassion. To live a life of loving kindness and compassion toward others is to live a life with the Heart chakra wide open. Our culture admires people who feel compassion for others and act on that compassion. We act on our compassion in many ways, from formalized expression such as volunteering for a charity, to quieter ways, like being a good listener for a friend, being open to family members who need help, and even feeling compassion for ourselves and our own needs. It's there in the soothing sound of Sufjan Stevens's beautiful song "Love Yourself."

A recent client came to Betsy for treatment because she was dissatisfied with her marriage. She had been married for about three years, and she felt that her husband didn't communicate his feelings to her enough. She also didn't feel like he heard her when she was speaking. She feared their relationship was doomed and had already begun to shut herself off emotionally from her husband. Betsy soon learned that this woman came from a supportive and nurturing home where open and loving communication was the norm. Her parents were still married after 35 years and had a very loving relationship. The woman had never seen her parents fight or even be cross with one another.

While it might seem like such an upbringing would be a recipe for a healthy fourth chakra, the problem was that this woman had very specific expectations for her own marriage. When it didn't look like her parents' marriage, she assumed something was terribly wrong and her marriage was destined to fail. Through their work together focusing on the fourth chakra, Betsy helped this woman to reopen her heart and see that she and her husband were not her parents. They had to forge their own way through love, rather than turning into a mirror image of the woman's past. She also realized that she could not compare her 3-year marriage with her parents' 35-year relationship. The woman expressed great relief. Now she understands that fighting doesn't have to mean divorce and that in letting go of her colossal expectations, she can embrace what love is for *her*.

But compassion has a dark side, too. Some people are so open and overloaded in their Heart chakras that compassion for others takes over their lives. They dedicate all their energies to helping others, while completely neglecting their own needs. A balanced fourth chakra can feel compassion for others while also feeling compassion for the self.

Let's Talk About *You*

You've probably heard the old saying that you can't love others until you love yourself. That's not exactly true. You *can* love others without loving yourself, but it will be a needy, clingy, immature love compared to love that comes from an autonomous and full heart. Your fourth chakra reflects your self-love in the same way it reflects your ability to give love and receive love from others.

You are in a primary relationship with yourself. As you treat others, so you should treat yourself, and vice versa. Do you speak to yourself with the same compassion and care that you use to speak to your loved ones? Most people admit that they are much more cruel, judgmental, and harsher toward themselves. Without self-love, self-care, self-nurturing, and compassion for your own needs and desires, your fourth chakra will never be completely open and vibrantly healthy.

Physically opening your Heart chakra can actually make more room to get Heart chakra energy flowing in a healthier way. It can change the way you stand for love. If you usually slump and hold your shoulders and head forward, you are actually physically sheltering your Heart chakra, as well as constricting your Solar Plexus chakra, the source of your personal power. To get more open, pull your shoulders back, look up, and imagine lifting your heart toward the sky. Yoga back-bending poses like the ones at the end of this chapter are a great way to open the heart, but even a good stretch that expands the chest and pulls your shoulders back can make a difference.

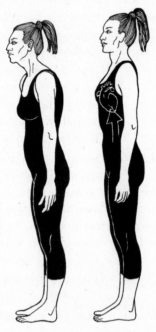

You can open your Heart chakra by improving your posture. Lift your heart!

What Goes Out Must Come In

The fourth chakra gets a lot of attention for being all about loving others, but a healthy fourth chakra can also receive love *from* others. Don't think of the fourth chakra as a waterfall; instead, think of it as the entire water cycle.

There is an old Hindu legend that Shiva and Shakti, the primordial God and Goddess, make love constantly on a mountaintop. Their passion is so intense that it melts the snow, which runs down the mountain and becomes the sacred Ganges River. But the story doesn't stop there. That river water evaporates in the intense heat, forms clouds, floats over the mountain, and snows down again onto the loving couple, and the cycle begins anew. That's how your fourth chakra should work: your love flows outward, but it comes back to you, too.

Girl Talk (Boys Allowed)

Gentlemen, you might think you can feel free to skip this section. However, a man also feels a desire to shelter and protect what rises from his breast, the need to fold someone into the warmth and safety of his arms and hold them there, or to let a babe snuggle for a nap small upon his broad chest. Compassion that rises from the breasts lives in both genders, as it should. Yet men know the fourth chakra holds a special significance for women, who carry within their breasts the power to nurture life. So, we'll indulge in a bit of girl talk. Ladies, let's talk about The Girls. The Twins. The Two Sisters. That's right, we mean your breasts.

Yes, the fourth chakra has everything to do with this most female of female body parts. A woman's breasts literally transmit love to her baby by feeding the most perfect food. But even if you've never breastfed a baby, you still understand to the heart of you that your breasts are all about love. Your sense of womanhood wells up from your breasts and is woven into your fourth chakra throughout your life. From the time a girl's breast buds signal her transition to a young woman, to the time a new mother's breasts ache and swell with milk, and to the time a grandmother or beloved auntie's breasts lower and soften to the perfect comforting pillow, a woman's breasts give constant expression to the compassion she carries within.

We would be remiss if we didn't mention breast cancer, as millions of women (and men) each year are diagnosed with it. Although researchers understand a lot more about how genetics, lifestyle, diet, and hormones may put women at risk, it still is nearly impossible to pinpoint why certain people get it and others do not. From an energetic perspective based upon chakra theory, breast cancer is likely related to an imbalance in the fourth chakra energy. Breasts represent love and nurturing. If disease shows up at the Heart chakra, it could be important to ask yourself how you can better support and nurture your own practice of self-care. Ask yourself what you want and need. When disease comes into our lives, it can help us to understand ourselves more deeply as we seek to restore our balance and to heal.

Your breasts are particularly sensitive to how well you love yourself and how well you receive love. Breasts are, by their very nature, all about giving, so if they don't receive love in return, you feel it. Love yourself, love your female nature, take care of yourself, and honor yourself for the goddess that you really are. If you do these things, you'll be taking care of your breasts, too.

When Betsy gave birth to a beautiful baby boy—her second—life was wonderful. Everything was going well until Betsy developed a nasty case of mastitis, which is an infection of the milk ducts in the breast characterized by pain, fever, and flu-like symptoms. Betsy believes that her mastitis was directly linked to an overflowing amount of love, nourishment, and protection that she was giving away, not only to her new infant but to her three-year-old son and to her fledgling yoga studio (her other baby). Betsy was focused so intensely on the needs of others that she was doing absolutely nothing for herself in terms of rest and self-care. Her fourth chakra was so wide open that her body went into emergency alert mode. Voilà—mastitis. Betsy didn't just get mastitis once; when she didn't get the message the first time, she got mastitis a second time. When she finally realized she needed to drop some of her less-important responsibilities (such as those at the yoga studio) and began to say "no" to requests from other people, and when she sent her three-year-old to visit his grandma and focused on nothing but feeding her baby, resting, and nourishing herself, she finally got … and stayed … better. Lesson learned.

Heart Chakra Correspondences

Your Heart chakra corresponds with so many aspects of your life because humans live with love so central to their consciousness. Consider the associations in the following chart and consider how your Heart chakra fits into who you are.

Fourth Chakra	Correspondence
Sanskrit name	Anahata (unstruck, intact, dwelling place of the unstruck sound)
Element	Air
Color	Green
Seed sound	YANG
Location	Behind the heart
Associated cultural phrases	"Love makes the world go 'round."
	"All you need is love."
	"Love is the answer."
	"My heart is broken."
	"Bleeding heart."
Associated anatomy	Heart, lungs, shoulders, arms and hands, chest, breasts, thymus gland, cardiac nerve plexus

Fourth Chakra	Correspondence
Associated psychological and life issues	Giving and receiving love, balance, healing, charity, compassion, self-love
Physical issues related to fourth chakra blockage	Heart problems related to blockage (angina, heart disease, heart attack); lung and breathing problems (asthma, shortness of breath, pleurisy, emphysema); pain in the chest, shoulders, or arms; immune system suppression; depression
Psychological issues related to fourth chakra blockage	Withdrawal from intimate relationships, coldness, intolerance, irritability and impatience, being overly critical of others, lack of compassion and empathy for others, chronic relationship failure
Physical issues related to fourth chakra overload	Enlarged heart, low blood pressure, depression, exhaustion, breast problems (breast cancer, mastitis, benign lumps)
Psychological issues related to fourth chakra overload	Constantly putting needs of others above yourself, martyr complex, burnout, codependency in relationships, clinginess, self-neglect, jealousy, chronic relationship failures
Fourth chakra therapy	Deep breathing and breathing exercises Eating lots of fruits and vegetables Backbends Volunteering and charity work (for blockages) Spending more time with animals Spending more time with children Counseling or therapy to help with relationship issues, grief/loss issues, and/or self-esteem and self-care issues

Awakening the Heart Chakra

When *Kundalini* energy is free to move through your fourth chakra, you've accomplished something important: connecting your body and mind in a powerful way. When you awaken your Heart chakra, you are likely to experience strong feelings of love and compassion, both for the people you already know you love and for all living things—people, animals, and the natural world. No, you won't become some flaky, disconnected, head-in-the-clouds love guru. We promise. But you will become more loving, and be able to both feel and express your loving energy in a more meaningful way. You will be filled with loving kindness, or a compassion for all living things.

Awakening the Heart chakra also means you'll feel more comfortable being loved, and that's a big step for some people. And finally, you'll be better at loving yourself. You might even begin to understand why that is so important.

Anything that physically or metaphorically opens your heart and chest area will help to awaken your Heart chakra. The other key: breathing. Deep breathing and yogic *pranayama* exercises are essential for Heart chakra activation. Remember, this chakra's symbolic element is Air, and breath is the aspect of the Air element that you can control.

To get more Heart chakra energy into your environment, emphasize the color green. Wear green, paint your family room green, or put green plants around the house. Just seeing the color can help to awaken the Heart chakra. Also, include more Air elements in your home, such as fans to move air and wind chimes and mobiles to produce sound and movement when the air moves. Open the windows whenever you can to get fresh air moving through your home.

You can also try this exercise for awakening the Heart chakra:

1. Sit on the floor, legs crossed, seat on a pillow or a folded blanket. Feel your pelvic bones and imagine roots anchoring those bones to the Earth. Place your hands slightly behind you, and move your shoulders back to widen or open your chest.

2. Take several long, slow, deep breaths, and then draw your attention to the area just behind your heart. Imagine your fourth chakra as a brilliant, emerald-green circle spinning slowly.

3. Imagine your chakra radiating a green circle of brilliant light that encompasses your entire chest. Feel the warmth melting your heart, so that any hardening falls away and you feel open and radiating with love.

4. Take a deep breath in and in a low, resonating tone, say the word: *YANG*, holding the "A" sound (pronounced "ah"; the word rhymes with "song"). Imagine the green light filling your entire body with slow, steady pulses, like a heartbeat.

5. Continue to breathe and let the warm waves of love and compassion continue to radiate from your fourth chakra for as long as you like.

Aligning the Heart Chakra

Set your heart right, and all your other chakras above and below will get pulled into alignment as love moves both up and down from this central fourth chakra. To get your Heart chakra properly aligned, try this exercise:

1. Stand in Mountain pose (*Tadasana*), with your feet about hip-width apart, and arms at your sides.

2. Imagine your fourth chakra just behind your heart, and try to feel it spinning and getting warmer. Imagine your heart softening. Feel your heart beating.

3. Visualize a strong green cord moving straight up out of your Heart chakra, up through the crown of your head into the Air to the Heavens, and filling your entire upper body with healing energy. Now, visualize this strong green cord of healing energy shooting straight down from your heart, down through your third (Solar Plexus), second (Sacral), and first (Root) chakras and down into the Earth. Imagine the entire cord filling your body with healing energy as it beams straight up and straight down.

4. Lift your arms straight up overhead and imagine the green light flowing up and down and radiating to the center of the Earth and all the way to the Heavens. Your Heart chakra should now be aligned.

Blocks in the Heart Chakra

Many people have Heart chakra blocks! We believe many things can cause Heart chakra blockages, from childhood all the way up to what happened to you five minutes ago. However, because this is such an important, central chakra it is essential to keep the heart unblocked. For many people, unblocking the Heart chakra might be a daily priority. When your Heart chakra flows freely after being blocked, your life will change because you will see the entire world—the Universe, and everybody and everything in it—in an entirely new way. You will begin to understand what it means to *love*, even when love is difficult. You will be filled with loving kindness.

To have an open heart is to fulfill your destiny as a sentient being. When the Heart chakra is blocked, you withdraw from people and from real connection. You may judge others and yourself harshly. You get irritated and you run from intimacy. Maybe you have commitment issues, or even rage issues. You might be lonely, but at least you are autonomous, and strong. Or, at least, that's what you tell yourself.

But in reality, you are lonely because a blocked Heart chakra is characterized by deep spiritual longing. Not only does a blocked Heart chakra keep you from connecting with other people, but it also blocks the connection between your body and your mind. It might even block your connection with something larger, with Spirit, with God or a Higher Power, or with the power of the Universe.

Many people fall into the habit of systematically keeping their Heart chakras blocked. They learn this pattern when they get their hearts broken and don't want to feel that pain again. This could have happened as a child or as an adult after profound loss, after a failed relationship, or by getting hurt by anyone for any reason.

But that's not your destiny. Your Heart chakra knows (and that means *you* know) that what is easiest is not always what is best. Your heart knows that love is the life force that endures all things. And in the words of Shakespeare's famous Sonnet 116:

> *Love is not love*
> *Which alters when it alteration finds,*
> *Or bends with the remover to remove.*
> *O no! It is an ever-fixed mark*
> *That looks on tempests and is never shaken.*

That's the power of love!

Blocked Heart Chakra Health Issues

Fourth chakra health issues have everything to do with your heart, lungs, and chest. When your Heart chakra is blocked, your heart can physically become blocked, resulting in heart disease, clogged arteries, angina (chest pain), heart arrhythmias, and even a heart attack. (Of course, not everyone with heart disease has a blocked Heart chakra. This can be caused by many other environmental and genetic factors.) A blocked Heart chakra can also contribute to blocked breathing passages, asthma, and shallow breathing, as well as to lung pain.

Blocked Heart chakra types can also experience depression because of the loneliness and isolation they maintain. You can see a blocked Heart chakra in someone with a sunken chest or a hunched upper back. Instead of leading with the heart, the body is literally protecting and guarding the Heart chakra by coiling forward. Simply being more consciously aware of your sitting and standing posture and prompting yourself to lift your heart and breathe deeply when you catch yourself guarding can begin a cascading flow of beneficial change to your heart and lungs that enhances your whole experience of life and being alive. That's the healing power of the Heart chakra!

Blocked Chakra Psychological Issues

When the Heart chakra is blocked, there are multiple psychological implications. Most obviously, people with blocked Heart chakras have problems relating to other people, commitment issues, and relationship problems. The people who are afraid to make relationship commitments in intimate partnerships have blocked Heart chakras, while the people who are overloaded in their Heart chakras may find themselves in dysfunctional codependent relationships where they are so enmeshed with their partner that they lose all sense of individuality and independence.

Heart chakra blockages also reflect a judgmental attitude. These are the people who are so critical of others (and most of all, of themselves) that every fault small or large in someone else becomes an obstacle to a relationship. No one is ever quite perfect enough—although in reality, what people with blocked Heart chakras are actually feeling is that *they* aren't perfect enough, or deserving enough, to ever experience enduring love.

When someone breaks your heart, it is very important to nurture your fourth chakra back to health again. Your Heart chakra might need to close down for a while, and that's fine. Be patient with yourself, and most of all, take care of yourself. When you nurture and attend to your own needs, the love you give to yourself will help coax your Heart chakra open again. Remember, the Heart chakra is the healing chakra. Only when it opens again can you truly experience self-healing.

Healing a Blocked Fourth Chakra

To heal and strengthen a blocked Heart chakra, Betsy encourages her clients to care for themselves. You can't control how or whether others love you, but you can control how and whether you love yourself. She reminds her clients that the most important relationship one will ever have is the relationship with oneself. This means you better put some effort into this relationship, because it is literally the only relationship you are guaranteed to have up to your dying day. If you are always pulling away from others, look first into your own heart. Are you pulling away from yourself? Heal your fear of self-love first; by doing so, loving others, as well as accepting love from others, will happen automatically. If you don't know how to do this, a licensed mental health therapist can help you explore your heart's needs.

The Heart chakra also heals and opens when you practice loving things that are easier to love than human adults. Animals—especially companion animals like dogs and cats, children, even nature can soften and open your heart when it has closed down. If you don't have pets or children, take some time to volunteer at an animal shelter or a local school. Spend more time outside in direct contact with nature. Walk in the park or hike in a natural area. Tend to a small garden of flowers or vegetables. All these activities can help to fill up your heart so that it opens again.

Also focus on your breath. Anything that gets your breath moving will help to open your heart. Try some of these activities to open a blocked Heart chakra:

- Practice deep breathing and the yoga breathing exercises called *pranayama* (like the one later in this chapter called *Nadi Shodhana*).
- Eat green foods like salads, spinach, kale, collard greens, Swiss chard, green beans, artichokes, and sweet peas.
- Reach out to help others in need, through volunteer work or through simple, kindly gestures to strangers.
- Get up in the air. Climb a tree. Ride a Ferris wheel. Hike up a mountain, or just go up on a roof (safely) and take in the view.
- Hug someone who loves you. You don't have to say a word.

- Spend time with children, preferably outdoors.

- Meditate on your loving feelings for someone. Dedicate your day to someone you love.

- Make a list of all your own good qualities. If you are having trouble, ask someone who loves you to help.

- Exercise, especially anything that increases your breathing, such as brisk walking, running, or dancing.

- Engage in *Anusara* yoga. This form of yoga literally means "flowing with grace, following your heart." *Anusara* is a heart-oriented style of yoga that combines attention to alignment and a life-affirming philosophy. Every *Anusara* class focuses on a heart-opening theme.

- Recite these mantras:
  - *I love and nourish myself.*
  - *I deserve love.*
  - *It's okay to love.*
  - *I will open my heart and allow others to love me.*
  - *The world is a better place because I love.*

An easy way to tune up your Heart chakra is to pay attention to the ways other people express love, not only to you but also to others in their lives. How do other people show love to their partners, to their children, to their friends, and even to their pets? Watch and you might learn something. You can even copy some of their words or gestures to try them on for size. Some people are very good at loving.

Overload in the Heart Chakra

Maybe you don't have any problem loving others. Maybe your problem is that you love *too much*. But wait. Is that really possible? Can there be too much love in the world?

The problem with an overloaded Heart chakra is not that you have too much love; it's that you are out of balance in expressing it. You let your Heart chakra dominate your other chakras, at their expense. A full, open, and loving Heart chakra is a wonderful quality, but if the power of your Solar Plexus chakra (below) and the truth of your Throat chakra (above) atrophy because your Heart chakra is so huge, you can lose a sense of who you are and what is really best for you.

People with overloaded Heart chakras are those people who give and give and give until they burn out or suffer from immune system collapse or heart failure. Can you say *martyr complex?*

A martyr complex is a psychological term referring to someone who suffers on purpose, often in the name of helping or serving someone else, suffering for love, or suffering for a cause, and they do all this suffering at the expense of personal needs or desires. This type of person often becomes resentful because the love they shower on others isn't returned to them in the way they want or feel they need. These people might be trying desperately to gain the love of others—perhaps because they didn't receive enough as children—so much so that they go overboard. They often end up in codependent relationships or are clingy and smothering to their partners and/or children.

Overloaded Heart Chakra Health Issues

Physical signs of an overloaded fourth chakra include low blood pressure, an enlarged heart, exhaustion, depression, and self-neglect. Women with overloaded Heart chakras might develop breast problems, such as benign cysts, breast pain, and sometimes even cancer because they keep pouring out love without saving some of that love for themselves. People with overloaded Heart chakras sometimes stand with their chests forward, though not in the overpowering way that overloaded third chakra people lead with their solar plexus. Instead, this kind of chest-forward stance looks more barrel-chested and vulnerable, with the head pulled back, almost as if they are physically offering their hearts out to anyone.

In many relationships, one person gives much more than they receive, and the other person receives much more than they give. Considering that the fourth chakra is the chakra of balance, this is definitely a Heart chakra problem. Consider whether you give more than you get in your relationship or whether you take more than you give. Either way, you aren't getting everything you could because your relationship is unbalanced. What could you do to shift the power more toward the fulcrum? Ironically, sometimes the best way to get more is actually to give more. Try meditating on that with your Heart chakra open.

Overloaded Heart Chakra Psychological Issues

Overloaded fourth chakras result in big relationship problems because the overloaded Heart chakra person is constantly giving but also constantly clinging, which ultimately pushes a more self-confident person away. Resentment and anger often build in a person with an overloaded fourth chakra because they aren't getting what they want, but they never express this for fear the other person will leave and they cannot imagine a life without the relationship. So, they stuff the resentment deep down inside themselves, which leads to bigger problems down the line, such as depression. Often, these people get into codependent relationships with those who like this unequal balance of power, so that both people feed into each other's weak spots. For instance, an overloaded Solar Plexus chakra person might be happy to use his personal power to take from an overloaded Heart chakra person, but that's not good for either person because it sends both out of balance.

Codependency is a term used in psychology to describe a situation in which someone becomes so preoccupied with giving to and caring for someone else that they neglect themselves. They believe that something or someone outside of themselves will make them fulfilled and happy. To these people, life is only okay if those around them are happy and well, thanks to their actions and care. Codependency is common in families of alcoholics, where the codependent partner believes that if he or she works hard enough to help the alcoholic sober up, the healed family will be free of shame and anger. This only leads to disappointment because alcoholics ultimately sober up only when they decide to sober up, not solely because someone else worked hard to get them there.

Overloaded Heart chakras also tend to be overloaded in one direction only: outward. People in service positions, such as teaching, nursing, counseling, or the clergy, or those attracted to activist causes or charitable organizations, sometimes develop overloaded Heart chakras because they spend so much of their energy focusing outward on the suffering of others. But when it comes to loving themselves, these people often are blocked. When all your heart energy pours out, you leave nothing left to nurture and heal yourself, and that results in a severe internal imbalance that will eventually deplete your energy and even impact the strength of your immune system.

Healing an Overloaded Heart Chakra

One great way to calm and balance an overloaded Heart chakra is to practice *pranayama* breathing techniques. Try this exercise called *Nadi Shodhana* for greater internal balance:

1. Sit comfortably and hold your right hand up. Curl your index and middle fingers in. Put your thumb next to your right nostril and your ring finger and little finger by your left nostril.

2. Gently close your left nostril by pressing your ring and little fingers against it as you inhale deeply through your right nostril.

3. After inhaling, pause as you release your left nostril and press your right nostril closed with your thumb. Exhale deeply through your left nostril.

4. Inhale deeply through your left nostril, and then switch nostrils again, closing your left nostril and opening your right. Exhale deeply through your right nostril.

5. Repeat for two to five minutes.

Following are some other good strategies for healing an overloaded Heart chakra:

- Engage in self-care activities. Self-care is anything you do solely for yourself that brings you joy, happiness, and balance. Treat yourself to a massage, get a pedicure, take a walk outside in nature, or sign up for that class you've been wanting to take. Do something *you* (not anyone else) want to do.

- Yoga poses that rein in your heart and relax and balance you can help. Try Child's pose (described later in this chapter) and Tree pose (see Chapter 7).

- Meditate for at least 5 minutes every day, working up to 15 or 20 minutes. Sit comfortably, relax, and watch your thoughts and emotions, rather than letting them carry you away. With practice, you will begin to see that you are not your thoughts; you are not your emotions. Your thoughts and emotions are only a small part of who you are. Let your mind relax and expand as you discover and explore your true beautiful nature.

- Use *mudras* during meditation. These powerful specific hand positions are designed to take the energy coming down your arm into your hand and reroute it back up so it stays inside your body and becomes more concentrated. *Mudras* affect the internal energy of the body in specific ways. They are used in several ancient Eastern traditions, including yoga and Buddhism. To reroute *prana* back into the body for greater healing, try *prana mudra*—a *mudra* that joins the index and little fingertips with the thumb. Stretch out all your fingers, and then bend your thumb and your ring and little fingers so that the tips all touch. Leave your index and middle finger extended. Do this with both hands, and rest your hands, palms facing up, on your knees while sitting on the ground or while lying down. Breathe deeply.

Yoga Poses to Balance the Heart Chakra

The best yoga poses for healing both blocked and overloaded Heart chakras are those poses that help encourage building a bridge that creates balance. For blocked Heart chakras, work on backbends that open the chest. For overloaded Heart chakras, work on poses that draw heart energy within. In all these poses, use your breath to fill your lungs and draw life force *prana* to activate the Heart chakra and draw balance between the three lower and three upper chakras. Remember the Heart chakra's element is Air.

Bridge Pose (*Setu Bandha*)

Bridge pose (Setu Bandha) builds a healing bridge to an open, balanced Heart chakra.

This pose opens the heart and lungs while maintaining safe, solid contact grounded upon the Earth.

1. Lie on your back on the floor with your arms at your sides, your knees bent, and your feet on the floor. Move your heels as close to your body as you can while keeping your feet pointing straight out.

2. Inhale and soften your body as you expand your heart center, literally relaxing your chest and letting it release to widen and soften. Exhale and lift your hips up. Walk your shoulders side to side so that your shoulder blades lengthen and move more into connection with your back body, as your chest and heart begin to lift.

3. Clasp your hands underneath your hips, and lift your hips a little higher as you focus on opening your chest. Try to keep your chin relaxed and slightly away from your chest. Keep your gaze looking up. Avoid turning your head side to side. Breathe deeply.

4. Hold the position for about 30 seconds, then slowly unclasp your hands and exhale as you come down.

Cobra Pose (*Bhujangasana*)

Cobra pose (Bhujangasana) *opens your heart and lungs from a position of strength.*

You first learned yoga's Cobra pose when learning about *Kundalini* serpent power (see Chapter 5). You learned that Cobra pose is summoned to begin activation of coiled *Kundalini* energy by gathering strength in the first chakra, or Root chakra. Using Cobra to activate the fourth chakra, or Heart chakra is to invite *Kundalini* energy to rise up from the Root chakra through the Sacral and Solar Plexus chakras to shine in an energized Heart chakra. This heart opener is designed to mimic the shape of the cobra. As you do this pose, think about how an open heart doesn't have to mean a vulnerable heart. Opening your heart takes the strength and courage of the Cobra. Imagine the movement of the uncoiled *Kundalini* as an energy bridge of *prana* activation linking the lower chakras to the Heart chakra.

1. Lie on your stomach with your palms on either side of your upper chest. Keep your legs together and press the tops of your thighs, shins, and feet into the floor.

2. Inhale, relax and soften your body and mind. Exhale and push yourself up with your arms to raise your shoulders, head, and chest up off the floor. Curl into a baby backbend. Flex the muscles in your arms as if you were going to drag your hands back toward your hips. At the same time, push your chest forward. Imagine your Heart chakra's healing power flowing from your Root chakra through your Sacral chakra, to your Solar Plexus chakra, and out through your Heart chakra. Hold the open pose for about 30 seconds.

3. Exhale and come down slowly, resting for about 30 seconds with your forehead on the floor. Feel Heart chakra energy entering the Earth through the palms of your hands.

Child's Pose (*Balasana*)

For a relaxing heart stretch, extend your arms in this variation of Child's pose (Balasana).

This easy, nurturing pose is perfect for calming an overanxious heart and for restoring yourself when you are depleted from too much giving. Child's pose is a beneficial *asana* for shielding the Heart chakra in a healthful way, avoiding the destructive posture of guarding. Think of this pose as a great way to nurture your own inner child. Let Child's pose care for you in the same way you would comfort any young one in need of healing support.

1. Sit on your heels with your big toes touching, and widen your knees to the outside edge of your mat.

2. Exhale and bend forward to the floor. Extend your arms straight out and reach your hands, walking them out on the floor in front of you until you achieve a comfortable lengthening. Rest your forehead on the floor.

3. Relax in this position until you feel better.

Astrology for the Awakened Heart Chakra

Now, we're going to look more closely at the astrological correspondences for the fourth chakra, or Heart chakra. In Chapter 4, you learned:

○ The planetary ruler of the Heart chakra is Venus ♀.

○ The signs for the Heart chakra are Taurus ♉ and Libra ♎.

Planetary Ruler	Sign(s) Ruled
Venus ♀	Taurus ♉, Libra ♎

Knowing the energy of astrology's planets and signs that correspond to the Heart chakra helps you understand how to bring awakened fourth chakra compassion to life. Yoga uses Boat pose (*Setu Bandha*), Cobra pose (*Bhujangasana*), and Child's pose (*Balasana*) to open the torso, improve breathing, and relax anxiety held in your body during stressful times, allowing you the opportunity to recognize and nurture a heart full of compassion. Astrology gives that spinning compassion a meaning and a purpose in your life. To understand how chakra energy is at work in your astrological birth chart, see Appendix A, where we'll look at the chakras in Michelle Obama's chart. Transiting planetary energy in the Heavens also affects astrological cycles and the way we feel and experience them here on Earth.

How Venus ♀ Awakens the Heart Chakra

Venus ♀ is one of astrology's *personal* planets. Venus ♀ is the natural ruler of Taurus ♉ and the second house of possessions, values, resources, self-esteem, self-worth, and earning potential. Venus ♀ also is the natural ruler of Libra ♎ and the seventh house of personal partnerships, friendships, marriage, sharing and cooperation. As a personal (also an inner) planet, Venus ♀ governs personal expression and core identity, your inner being.

Venus ♀ is the planet of love, art and creativity, and the appreciation of beautiful things. Venus also governs the social graces, balance and harmony. As the planet of value, Venus represents your possessions, your gifts, and even your money. Venus nurtures compassion in the Heart chakra, spinning toward a harmonic balance of yin and yang energy at the center of your being (and supported by the power of the Solar Plexus chakra below). In a balanced Heart chakra, Venus understands the value of give and take in intimate relationships, and the need for it. A strong Venus looks past the superficial to redeem the pure essence of the beloved, and is willing to invest precious time and resources to find or create beauty.

How Taurus ♉ Awakens the Heart Chakra

Taurus ♉ with its yin, Earth element energy is ruled by the sensuous, physical Venus ♀. Taurus's quiet, industrious effort to make things grow suits Heart chakra's energy harmoniously. Whether creating a home or family, a garden, a friendship, or an investment portfolio, Taurus devotes all the senses in full-bodied service of building value. The Heart chakra welcomes down-to-earth Taurus's settled homebody, happy to shelter in place with a good book or a knitting project, hide away in the studio to paint or sculpt, plant a savory kitchen garden, or increase home value with a DIY project. With Taurus's influence, awakened *Kundalini* energy is channeled from the Solar Plexus chakra to spin with dependable warmth, grounded by inner serenity.

How Libra ♎ Awakens the Heart Chakra

Libra ♎ with its yang, Air element energy is ruled by harmonious, balanced Venus ♀. Libra's diplomatic charm and active mind suits Heart chakra balance energetically. Always weighing the strength of opposites, Libra looks for the most durable partnerships and embraces them wholeheartedly. The Heart chakra seeks idealistic Libra's appreciation of art and beauty, along with its judicious eye for harmonious equilibrium. With Libra's influence, awakened *Kundalini* energy is channeled from the Solar Plexus chakra to spin by encouraging a union of body and mind that creates stability, unity, and inner peace.

Heart Chakra Rising

Down-to-earth dependable Taurus ♉/Venus ♀ balances the reconciler of opposites Libra ♎/ Venus ♀ to draw *Kundalini* energy from the powerful Solar Plexus chakra in search of the compassionate Heart chakra. As the natural ruler of both Taurus ♉ and Libra ♎, Venus's ♀ dual nature of Earth and Air, yin and yang, seeks at its best a pure alliance that allows true compassion to fill the Heart chakra. Without the partnership of both zodiac signs, the Heart chakra risks becoming either too openhearted or too closed hearted.

Once you've reached the perfect union of physical earthbound Taurus and fair-minded thoughtful Libra, the Heart chakra will activate. Filled with the clear light of love, the Heart chakra spins with a compassion whose source resides below in the power of the Solar Plexus chakra. Of the seven healing chakras, the fourth, or Heart chakra, spins balanced between the three lower chakras of the body's passions and the three upper chakras of the blissful mind. The Heart chakra itself is the balance of peace. The life force rises up from the Heart chakra's compassion to meet your voice in the fifth chakra, or Throat chakra.

Chapter 11

Throat Chakra (*Vishuddha*): Express Yourself

Tell us *all about it*. Or can you? If you have an open and healthy fifth chakra, you can. The Throat chakra is the center for communication, sound, vibration, and ultimately, truth. This is where you express yourself in every way, and it's also how you receive the self-expression of others. People with strong Throat chakras have clear voices that people love to hear. This may also be expressed in a clear ability to write, draw, or express themselves with just the right words because people with strong Throat chakras tend to have good writing abilities and musical abilities. Many also have a good sense of rhythm and timing, not just musically speaking, but saying the right things at the right time. Our inner vibrations are expressed from this chakra and so is our ability to be good listeners.

We all talk, listen, and understand others from this chakra. Through the Throat chakra, you understand what people say, as well as what they actually *mean*. You understand metaphorical and figurative language here. You also begin to understand Spirit.

The Throat chakra is the first of the Spirit chakras. Some people believe you can't open this chakra on your own, but instead need the guidance of a teacher. Others believe you can open your own Throat chakra with the right focus. This chakra is certainly different than the Earth-centered ones below it. Associations aren't as straightforward. This chakra, along with the two above it, enters the realm of Mind: vibration, visualization, intuition, and thought. What you say, what you see, what you imagine, and what you think are all reflected in the upper three chakras. It all starts here with the fifth chakra, where your internal vibration is expressed through words, symbols, music, hand gestures, and expressions—all the ways you communicate with the outside world. In this chapter, we look deeply into that place from which you speak to help you figure out what you know, what you understand, and what you *really* have to say.

Throat Chakra 101

The fifth chakra, the Throat chakra, is also sometimes called the Communication or the Truth chakra. The Throat chakra is called *Vishuddha* in the traditional Sanskrit; this word can be translated as "purity" or "purification." The traditional element associated with the fifth chakra is Ether. Think of Ether as space or the void—the place where nothing exists. Part of the understanding of the void in traditional yogic thought is that the void came out of pure sound vibration. The original sound that created the Universe is the sound of *om*. Some contemporary writers, such as chakra expert Anodea Judith, prefer to say that the element associated with the fifth chakra, or Throat chakra, is simply Sound.

Om, sometimes spelled *aum,* is a sacred symbol in Hinduism, representing the impersonal, omnipotent, absolute source of all creation. According to Hindu thought, the sound of *om* encompasses the past, present, and future and was the original vibration that created the Universe. It is often used as a mantra in meditation or prayer, and speaking this intonation is thought to penetrate the soul (see Chapter 15).

The fifth chakra's symbolic color is blue, and the traditional lotus symbol depicting this chakra has 16 petals. The sound associated with this chakra is the seed sound *HANG* (rhymes with "song"). Chanting this sound helps to activate the fifth chakra.

The Throat chakra is located in the throat and encompasses the entire neck and upper chest, radiating around your jaw, mouth, ears, and down through your collarbones. Other physical structures associated with the fifth chakra are your thyroid, trachea, esophagus, parathyroid, neck vertebrae, and pharyngeal nerve plexus.

The fifth chakra, or Throat chakra (Vishuddha), resonates in tune with the Celestial harmonies of the Universe. It informs our communication, imbuing speech with sound and movement.

Let's Talk

What is talking? It's a strange ability we humans have. We make vibrations in our throats that come out of our mouths to make sounds that we all understand to symbolize other things. When you talk about a flower, the flower doesn't have to be anywhere near you. It doesn't even have to exist. But others who hear you (and speak your language) understand exactly what you mean. Language is all about symbols—including both speaking and writing. In the Throat chakra, we begin to grasp the concept that one thing represents something else.

We understand this kind of symbolism in no simpler way than through what we say. Can you imagine how difficult it would be to function in the world today without being able to speak? If you've ever had laryngitis (a classic fifth chakra issue), you know how frustrating it can be. Even the shiest among us need to speak out. How else will anyone know what we need, what we want, or *who we are?*

Your voice comes from your Throat chakra, and the quality of your voice says a lot about the *state* of your fifth chakra. A weak, timid, shaky, or cracking voice indicates a blocked chakra, while a loud, booming, or overpowering voice indicates an overloaded chakra. The condition of your voice isn't your fault, but it is a reflection of what is going on in your fifth chakra, which is, in turn, a reflection of what's going on within *you.*

When your fifth chakra is strong and healthy, your voice will be clear, pure, resonant, and pleasing to hear. People will enjoy listening to you speak, and they will be likely to understand what you say (unless they have their own fifth chakra issues with listening). The fifth chakra reflects your ability to communicate your thoughts and intentions clearly, and just as importantly, it reflects your ability to listen to and understand the expressed thoughts and intentions of others.

When you were younger, were you allowed to speak your mind, or were you told to be quiet all the time? Were children supposed to be "seen and not heard" in your home? Or was your home filled with too much talking, noise, yelling, and voices used to express negative emotions like disappointment or anger? How you were raised to use or not use your voice is significant for the health of your fifth chakra today. Children who are discouraged not just from talking but from telling the truth, or who are told lies, often have Throat chakra issues as adults. To get a better feel for the state of your own Throat chakra, think about how talking, listening, and telling the truth were handled in your childhood home.

Listen Up

Do you really know how to listen, or do you usually just wait to talk? When asked to consider the question, many people admit that they usually wait to talk. It's not surprising, really. In such a loud, raucous world, it's hard to get a word in edgewise, and it can be easier to focus on getting your own words out than to focus on letting others get theirs out.

However, knowing how to listen is a very important trait. If you balance the words you send out with the words you take in, you will feel calmer, more centered, and have a better understanding of your environment. Plus, listening is an important part of being a good friend, family member, and partner. It's also an excellent way to hone your intuition, which supports the health of your sixth chakra, or Third Eye chakra, the chakra governing intuition (see Chapter 12). Listening is powerful, and all you have to do to listen is stop talking and pay attention. It's worth a try.

Truth or Consequences?

You could call the Throat chakra the Truth chakra because this is also the place from where you speak your own truth and discern the truth in what others say and do. This is a most powerful skill, and one everybody possesses. Many of us don't use it like we could, though. When people constantly suppress their own truths—for example, they don't say what they really mean or refuse to acknowledge something true about themselves—they often develop a block in their Throat chakras. To keep this chakra open and strong, spend the time to discover what really *is* true for you. Then spend the time to listen to what others say, including the meaning behind the words and the meaning between the words. Soon, you'll be hearing their truths, too.

One way to hear the truth behind people's words is to pay attention not only to what they say but also to how they say it. People who study nonverbal communication say that nonverbal cues tell us more than the actual words people say. One study estimated that up to 93 percent of communication is nonverbal. To begin your study of nonverbal communication, start observing facial expressions, posture, what people do with their hands and feet when they talk, how they stand or sit, which way they lean, and where their gaze falls. For example, people tend to lean toward things that interest them and lean away from things they fear or don't like. They tend to blink a lot and don't look people directly in the eyes when they are fudging the truth. Also, they tend to move more when they are nervous and less when they are engaged. See what you notice as you watch what people do and whether it does or doesn't match what they say. Also, pay attention to what your eyes, hands, feet, and body do when *you* talk.

Your Inner Music

The fifth chakra is about vibration and rhythm as much as it is about words. People with healthy Throat chakras often have nice singing voices (although not all of them do) and can carry a tune and keep a beat. Although their singing voices might not make them the next American Idol, people with open fifth chakras tend to enjoy singing, even if they only sing in the confines of their own cars! People with strong fifth chakras might have strong, unusual, sonorous, or memorable voices, though their voices aren't necessarily society's version of *good* voice. Instead, they might have more of a distinctive or interesting voice. People who are tone deaf, or who can't seem to hear rhythm, or keep a beat very well may have blocked Throat chakras.

The entire Universe is made out of vibration (see Chapter 15), and music is one of the most beautiful and poignant ways that we shape and celebrate vibration. Music is an excellent fifth chakra therapy, for both blocked and overloaded chakras, so listen to or play some music every day. It's good medicine for your fifth chakra, or Throat chakra.

Betsy was working with a client who was a singer. She mentioned in therapy that she was having a difficult time with her voice. Sometimes, her voice lost its strength or became too nasal and shrill, and she couldn't seem to control when this happened. The woman also said that she found it very difficult to express the right emotion for the song she was singing, an essential part of being a good singer. Through therapy, Betsy discovered that this woman grew up in an abusive family where she was either ignored or told to "shut up and be quiet."

Betsy's client was literally prevented from having a voice as a child, and when she did try to express her feelings or emotions, she was punished for it. Thus, she learned to swallow her feelings because she had learned that expressing herself was bad. Yet, how interesting it is that this client chose a career path that forced her to use and develop her voice! Betsy says we often unconsciously choose the experiences we need most. As Betsy began to focus on the client's fifth chakra and free the energy here, the woman noticed almost immediate changes in her singing voice. Her tone became more even, and the strength of her voice became more powerful. Finally, she began to feel more comfortable exploring the emotions behind the songs she sang because her Throat chakra had opened.

The Write Stuff

Although the second chakra, or Sacral chakra, is an important source of creativity, so is the fifth chakra, or Throat chakra. Music comes from here, as does writing. Writers often have healthy, open fifth chakras because they constantly use them. A blocked Throat chakra can sometimes reveal itself through writer's block. In the same way speaking uses spoken-word symbols to represent other things, writing uses written-word symbols. We all know how vivid and powerful a book can be, or even just a really descriptive paragraph. Words are our staircase to the mind, and writing helps you climb up there to look around. Writing, like music, is excellent therapy for both blocked and overloaded fifth chakras.

If your Throat chakra needs work, or even if you just want to keep it healthy, try writing a little bit every day. Some people like to keep a journal of what they do and how they feel, while others would rather write stories, poetry, or an autobiography. What you write doesn't matter as much as just putting pen to paper or fingers to keyboard.

Throat Chakra Correspondences

Your voice, your words, and your music—they all tie together with the other Throat chakra correspondences. See them all at a glance in the following chart.

Fifth Chakra	Correspondence
Sanskrit name	Vishuddha (purity)
Element	Space/the void, sound
Color	Blue
Seed sound	HANG
Location	In the throat
Associated cultural phrases	"Tell it like it is." "Speak of the devil and he will appear." "Speak up!" "Talk is cheap." "The sound of silence." "Silence is golden." "Truth or dare."

Fifth Chakra	Correspondence
Associated anatomy	Throat, trachea, esophagus, neck, thyroid gland, pharyngeal nerve plexus, cervical spine, mouth, jaw, and teeth
Associated psychological and life issues	Communication, ability to express feelings, ability to listen, speaking and hearing the truth, understanding meaning behind or beyond words, and musical and writing ability
Physical issues related to fifth chakra blockage	Lump in the throat, laryngitis, sore throat, jaw pain and tightness, neck pain, stiff neck, neck arthritis, vocal nodes, recurrent strep, hypothyroidism, hearing loss, tinnitus, tone deafness (can't hear the difference between musical notes), and no sense of rhythm
Psychological issues related to fifth chakra blockage	Problems with self-expression, weak voice, fear of speaking, lying, inability to discern the truth, inability to say what you mean, taking things too literally, and writer's block
Physical issues related to fifth chakra overload	Hyperthyroidism, neck pain from hyperflexibility, vocal nodes from talking, yelling, or singing too much, tooth decay, tooth loss, cold sores, and canker sores
Psychological issues related to fifth chakra overload	Talking too much, talking too loudly, interrupting, speaking without thinking, inability to listen to others, and automatically speaking the truth without sensitivity to others
Fifth chakra therapy	Mantra meditation, chanting, singing, drumming
	Speaking in front of others (for blocks)
	Going without speaking (for overloads)
	Quiet time of vocal rest
	Keeping a journal/freewriting
	Purposeful listening without commenting
	Practicing taking turns talking
	Lowering your voice (for overloads)
	Raising your voice (for blocks)
	Therapy for improving communication skills

Awakening the Throat Chakra

When your Throat chakra awakens, your voice becomes clearer, you say what you really mean, you listen to others and really hear them, and you discern the truth. Fire up your creative expression by literally opening your throat. Carefully tilt your head back and breathe. Feel your Throat chakra opening.

Another great, powerful way to awaken and energize the Throat chakra is through sound. Singing, chanting, humming, and saying mantras are all fifth chakra enhancers. Sing in the shower, hum while you make breakfast, and belt out your favorite tune in the car. Your Throat chakra will feel great.

To get more Throat chakra energy into your environment, emphasize the color blue. Wear bright sapphire blue on your body, or paint your office shades of blue, or put blue flowers around the house. Just seeing the color blue can help to awaken your Throat chakra. Also, include more of the Sound element in your home: wind chimes, noise machines that produce sounds such as waves or birds in a forest, and of course, music. Play music often to keep your Throat chakra energized.

You can also try this exercise for awakening the Throat chakra:

1. Sit on a pillow or folded blanket on the floor with your legs crossed. Feel your pelvic bones, and imagine roots anchoring those bones to the Earth. Place your hands slightly behind you, and move your shoulders back to open your chest.

2. Take several long, slow, and deep breaths in and out, and then draw your attention to the area inside your throat. Imagine your fifth chakra as a brilliant, sapphire, blue circle spinning slowly.

3. Imagine your chakra radiating a blue circle of brilliant light that encompasses your entire throat, jaw, and upper chest. Feel the cool electric blue in your throat, opening all your channels of communication.

4. Take a deep breath in, and in a low resonating tone, say the word: *HANG*, holding the "A" sound (pronounced "ah," the word rhymes with "song"). Repeat the word slowly 16 times. Every time you speak the word, extend the sound as long as you can and feel the vibrations in your entire body, radiating from your Throat chakra.

Aligning the Throat Chakra

When your Throat chakra is properly aligned, you can use communication to help those you love, to improve your love relationships, and also to fully utilize your natural intuition. To get your Throat chakra properly aligned, try this exercise:

1. Stand in yoga's Mountain pose (see Chapter 7) with your feet about hip-width apart and your arms at your sides.

2. Imagine your Throat chakra just behind your voice box, and feel it spinning and getting cooler. Imagine a cool blue breeze blowing through your entire body.

3. Visualize a blue ray of light moving straight up out of your Throat chakra, up through the crown of your head, and filling your head with blue light. Now, visualize this blue beam of light shooting straight down from your throat and down through your fourth (Heart) chakra, third (Solar Plexus) chakra, second (Sacral) chakra, and first (Root) chakra and down into the Earth. Imagine the entire ray of light filling your body with cool sapphire-blue energy.

4. Lift your arms straight up overhead and imagine the blue light flowing up and down, radiating to the center of the Earth and all the way to the Heavens. Your Throat chakra should now be aligned.

Blocks in the Throat Chakra

A blocked Throat chakra can be a major impairment in our culture. It's the Information Age, and those who can communicate effectively are usually well rewarded. People with blocked Throat chakras tend to be afraid to speak and have weak or quiet voices. They may come across as very shy. In our loud society, this can annoy people who might always be snapping, "Speak up!"

People with blocked Throat chakras also tend to have problems expressing their thoughts and feelings. People often misunderstand their texts and social media posts, and this can frustrate the blocked Throat chakra person so much that they are even more likely to clam up. Or they consistently say what they don't really mean. This is because they aren't willing to see and speak their own personal truths, or they fear a backlash or loss of love by speaking their truths, so instead, they say exactly what they think others want to hear.

Healing a blocked Throat chakra is incredibly important, both so you can communicate in society and so you can express your true self. This is essential for psychological as well as physical health. Pent-up feelings and lack of acknowledgement of what is really going on can become major obstacles to contentment and well-being. However, some people fear what can happen if they *really* begin to speak. This fear can come from childhood experiences, or it can come from a fear of consequences. And yet, the real consequences come from long-term stifling of truth and words. These clog up the body and can manifest as physical illness if you don't get them out. So, let your Throat chakra open and set your voice, your words, and the truth free.

Blocked Throat Chakra Health Issues

Fifth chakra health issues usually settle into the throat and neck. They can include such minor or temporary complaints as a lump in the throat, laryngitis, a sore throat, strep throat, or a stiff neck, and they can include more chronic problems like jaw pain and tightness, neck pain, arthritis in the neck vertebrae, a stiff neck, neck muscle spasms, throat problems like vocal nodes or recurrent strep, and hypothyroidism. Your ears can also suffer from a blocked Throat chakra, which can manifest as tinnitus (ringing in the ears) or hearing loss, being tone deaf (which means you can't hear the difference between musical notes), or having no sense of rhythm.

Blocked Throat Chakra Psychological Issues

When the Throat chakra is blocked, the psychological implications usually have to do with self-expression. This can include speaking quietly or not using one's voice with conviction, fear of speaking in front of people, fear of speaking one's own truth, compulsive lying, inability to discern the truth in what others say, inability to say what one means, taking things too literally, and writer's block.

Sometimes, you can spot someone with a blocked fifth chakra not only by the sound of their voice but by the way they tuck the chin in or bow their head to protect the Throat chakra. You might even watch this type of person literally "swallow" their words. It's as if the voice wants to speak up, but the words get stuck and nothing comes out.

When you lose your voice, consider that there might be something more going on than the common cold virus. People with blocked fifth chakras tend to be more vulnerable to colds, and their cold symptoms tend to settle in their throats. If you've lost your voice or have a sore throat, consider whether there is something you are not saying or some truth you are refusing to see. Perhaps the problem is that you haven't been listening to someone, and your fifth chakra has intervened to make you stop talking so you can hear. Consider it a sign from your fifth chakra that something is awry in your communication system. Start by reviewing your texts and your social media posts and comments for clues to what might be amiss. (Of course, that doesn't mean you shouldn't drink a warm cup of tea and spend the whole day in bed!)

Healing a Blocked Throat Chakra

To learn how to heal and strengthen a blocked Throat chakra, we turned to one of Betsy's colleagues, Joseph Mizelle, a licensed massage therapist, certified yoga teacher, and Reiki master and teacher who practices sound energy healing. Joseph has a beautiful voice and can make all kinds of amazing sounds, but his advice for people who need to unblock their fifth chakras is simple: sing (see Chapter 15). "Singing, humming, any kind of toning is activating and empowering for the fifth chakra," Joseph says. "This chakra is about creative expression, and just making sound gives people the opportunity to get in touch with what they need to say in their lives."

Don't worry if you think you can't carry a tune or you don't like your voice. Learning how to use it is key to unblocking your Throat chakra and freeing up your communication energy.

Joseph also suggests meditating on the fifth chakra and asking the body: "What am I not saying that I need to be saying?"

Then, start singing and see what comes out. You might be surprised at how relevant it is.

You can also try some of these activities to open a blocked Throat chakra:

- Call a trusted friend to get together in person or on video chat and just talk. Be sure to listen, too.
- Eat blue foods like blueberries, blue corn chips, blue popcorn, and blue potatoes (naturally blue foods, not dyed foods!).
- Handwrite someone an old-fashioned letter. You don't even have to send it. Just the physical act of writing it by hand will help open your Throat chakra.
- Play music. Stream your favorites, regardless of the musical genre. Close your eyes and soak up the sound.
- Play a drum, or just drum on a tabletop.
- Listen to a new podcast. Ask your friends and colleagues for their favorite podcasts, and give them a listen as well.
- Get a shoulder and neck massage.
- Recite these mantras:
  - *I say what I mean.*
  - *I speak the truth.*
  - *Everyone hears me.*
  - *I hear others; I listen when they speak.*
  - *I express myself openly and freely.*

Joseph Mizelle, sound energy healer, says that when you randomly start singing a song, the song that comes to mind is indicative of your psyche. In other words, the songs you choose to sing for no apparent reason often hold messages for you. Whenever you get a song stuck in your head, stop for a minute and think about the words. What might they mean for you right now? Are they telling you what you aren't saying by yourself? Are they expressing your current mood? Are they solving a problem you have? In many cases, the answer to one of these questions will be "yes." That's the power of sound and your fifth chakra at work.

Overload in the Throat Chakra

If your problem is that you talk too much, too loudly, or you say things that aren't very considerate, you might have a Throat chakra overload. People with an overloaded Throat chakra have an entirely different kind of communication problem. They just can't stop talking.

These people talk over others, interrupt, dominate conversations, and are definitely more likely to be waiting to talk rather than listening. These people also use their voices in ways that hurt others. They might say too much, be unable to keep secrets, gossip, or sometimes, even lie.

We've all had times when we say more than we should have, but people with overloaded chakras do this chronically and have a very hard time controlling the problem.

Overloaded Throat Chakra Health Issues

An overloaded fifth chakra means there is too much energy in the throat. Physical signs of this can include hyperthyroidism (an overproduction of thyroid hormone); neck pain from being too flexible and wearing away cartilage between the vertebrae; and vocal nodes caused by talking, yelling, or singing too much. People who have to talk a lot in their professions can be prone to these problems, including professional singers, coaches, public speakers, and teachers.

Overloaded fifth chakras can also cause problems in the mouth, including tooth decay, tooth loss, cold sores, and canker sores.

Overloaded Throat Chakra Psychological Issues

When you have too much energy in your fifth chakra, you will tend to talk too much, talk too loudly, and interrupt. People with overloaded fifth chakras speak without thinking first. Because of this, their words often hurt others. Just because something is true doesn't mean you have to *say* it. These people also tend to talk over others and aren't able to stop talking long enough to listen.

The problem with an overloaded fifth chakra is the way in which it compromises relationships, personal power, emotions, and even safety. In other words, an overloaded fifth chakra puts the health of all the lower Earth-centered chakras at risk. When you talk without thinking or say everything you are thinking out loud, people begin to withdraw from you. It's great to be able to express yourself, but you don't have to express every single detail of yourself. What about everyone else? Would you want to hear them talk about what is coming out of your mouth? Would you really be interested? Sometimes, silence is golden.

As for the upper chakras, how can you focus on your inner voice if your outer voice never stops talking? In the same way that overloaded fifth chakra people need to back off a little bit and learn how to listen to others, they also need to learn how to listen to their own inner voices, which are quieter, but might have much more important things to say.

Eve has always been a talker, so it's no surprise she grew up to be a writer. She's had her fair share of chakra blocks, but her fifth chakra always seems to be wide open—maybe too open. When Eve was a child and her family went on car trips, they used to play the game "Who can stay quiet the longest?" While Eve thought this was a fun and exceptionally challenging game, she had no idea that her parents were just trying to get a few blessed moments of silence! Eve now has her own kids, and her youngest son is the same way. He loves to sit and talk, and talk, and talk … and that's great! He's very good at self-expression. However, Eve now finds herself proposing that same game on car trips ….

Healing an Overloaded Throat Chakra

Healing an overloaded Throat chakra means burning off some of that excess vibrational energy, but unlike the lower, more physical chakras, the solution isn't exercise (except that if you are breathing hard enough, you probably can't talk!). Instead, the solution is simple: silence.

Take a vow of silence, even for just one hour. Or why not try a whole day of silence? Of course, some people can't be silent all day if they need to speak for their jobs or they have children. However, on a day when it could work, try it. Singers and performers call this "vocal rest." Refusing to speak can be a transformative experience. You'll begin to hear things you never knew existed. You can keep a pad of paper and a pen handy for emergencies, but try not to use them. Unplug the phone. No text messaging, social media posts, or even email—that's cheating. Stop the words and see what else lives out there in the world.

Some other good strategies for healing an overloaded Throat chakra:

- Meditate on the sound of your breath, or just sit quietly and listen to the sounds of the room without making any noise yourself. See if you can go for five minutes. Try to do this every day.

- Practice waiting three seconds to respond to any question or comment someone makes. This three-second wait time can allow you a space to breathe and consider what is appropriate and kind to say, rather than whatever random thing comes into your head first.

- Do people sometimes tell you to lower your voice? Try telling yourself first. Start to become aware of the volume of your speaking voice relative to others. Can you dial it back?

- Practice listening like it's a sport. Spend some time every day consciously listening to someone who is talking to you. Make sure you understand what they are really saying before you respond. Try repeating back what they said, like this: "So, what I understand you to be saying is …." Rather than focusing your mental efforts on what *you* think of what they said, focus instead on what you think *they* think. (Got that?)

Yoga Poses to Balance the Throat Chakra

The best yoga poses for balancing both blocked and overloaded Throat chakras are those poses that physically open the neck, shoulders, and throat. Even an overloaded Throat chakra can get into better balance through throat-opening poses because these poses tone and strengthen the Throat chakra so it can better keep its normal shape. Think of it like a muscle that is either too tight or overstretched. Both can benefit from strength training.

Camel Pose (*Ustrasana*)

Moving into Camel pose opens the Throat chakra.

This pose opens both the chest and the throat, so it is perfect for fourth chakra, or Heart chakra and fifth chakra, or Throat chakra balancing.

1. Kneel on the floor with your knees about hip-width apart. If this hurts your knees, kneel on a folded blanket. Focus on keeping your tailbone pointing straight down. Rest your hands on your hips.

2. Inhale and relax, softening your body and mind. Exhale and release any fear or tension. On your next inhale, feel your side body, or the space between your waist and armpit, open and lengthen as your shoulder blades engage and come more onto your back body. (The anterior edges of your scapulae press in toward your backbone.) Your heart lifts in an expression of openness and gratitude. Move your upper inner thighs back; you will feel your buttocks begin to stick out slightly. From here, scoop your tailbone down toward the mat, and feel your belly tone.

3. Keeping your hips in line with your knees, exhale, and start to curve back. Your heart and chest begin to shine up toward the sky. Release your hands, stretch your arms down, and hold your heels. If you cannot reach your heels, rest your hands on your calves, or keep your hands on your hips, keeping the action of bending back and lifting the chest up.

4. Take your head back, if that's comfortable, and breathe evenly. Stay here for 10 seconds to 1 minute, depending on what feels best to your body.

To come out, lead with your heart. Place your hands back on your hips; inhale and lift your torso from the heart, your head coming up last. After you are done, rest in Child's pose (see Chapter 10) for up to one minute.

Jhalandara Bandha

Tone the Throat chakra with this yoga *bandha*. *Bandhas* are interior body locks used in yoga practice to help lock in and control the flow of *prana* life force energy in the body. *Jhalandara bandha*, in particular, is perfect for toning the Throat chakra. Here's how to do it:

1. Sit in a cross-legged position on the floor. Relax.

2. Inhale so your lungs are about three-quarters full. Hold your breath and then drop your chin down and draw it back toward your throat. This locks the breath in.

3. Hold this position (and your breath) for a few seconds or as long as feels comfortable.

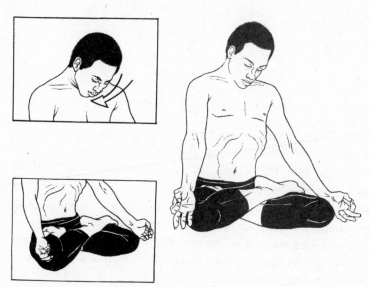

When you practice a yoga **bandha**, *you learn how to hold* **prana** *lifeforce within your body.*

4. Raise your chin back to a normal position and exhale. Repeat a few times, working up to 16 repetitions.

Astrology for the Awakened Throat Chakra

Now, we're going to look more closely at the astrological correspondences for the fifth, or Throat chakra. In Chapter 4, you learned:

- The planetary ruler for the Throat chakra is Mercury ☿.
- The signs for the Throat chakra are Gemini ♊ and Virgo ♍.

Planetary Ruler	Sign(s) Ruled
Mercury ☿	Gemini ♊, Virgo ♍

Knowing the energy of the planet and signs that correspond to the Throat chakra helps you understand how to bring awakened fifth chakra truth through communication to life. Yoga uses throat-opening poses and poses that incorporate focus on the breath to nurture and tone the body's instrument of speech. Astrology gives that spinning expression of truth a meaning and a purpose in your life. To see how chakra energy is expressed in your astrological birth chart, see Appendix A, where we'll study the expression of the chakras in Michelle Obama's birth chart. Transiting planetary energy in the Heavens also affects the way we feel and experience astrological cycles as we live through their influence here on Earth.

How Mercury ☿ Awakens the Throat Chakra

Mercury ☿ is one of astrology's *personal* planets. Mercury ☿ is the natural ruler of Gemini ♊ and the third house of knowledge, logic, information collection and sharing, brothers and sisters, early education, and your immediate environment. Mercury ☿ is also the natural ruler of Virgo ♍ and the sixth house of service, personal responsibility, health maintenance, and a desire to be skilled and efficient. As a personal (also an inner) planet, Mercury ☿ governs personal expression and core identity, your inner being.

Mercury ☿ is the planet of mental acuity, speed of thought, communication, and intelligence. As the planet in charge of information, Mercury loves language in all its forms—from data, to mathematics, to the words we speak, to genetics. Mercury is all about transmitting information as well as listening to, processing, and understanding it. Mercury imbues the Throat chakra with an innate quickness of communication, spinning at the speed of truth to the quickening life force energy at the center of your being (and steadied by the compassionate balance of the Heart chakra below). A strong Mercury searches all the knowledge available to it, evaluating with a logical mind able to prioritize and balance at speed without spinning out of control.

How Gemini ♊ Awakens the Throat Chakra

Gemini ♊ with its yang, Air element energy is ruled by the quicksilver speed of messenger Mercury ☿. Gemini's twinned talent of seeing both sides of every idea suits Throat chakra's questioning energy. Gemini knows when to speak the truth and when to listen hard to perceive it amidst all the noise of our Digital Age. The Throat chakra searches out intelligent Gemini's strength of voice—whether through writing, singing, painting, or calculating. With Gemini's influence awakened, *Kundalini* energy is channeled from the Heart chakra to spin with a mind that considers all its options and dares you to keep up, resting its truth on a balanced, centered heart.

How Virgo ♍ Awakens the Throat Chakra

Virgo ♍ with its yin, Earth element is ruled by the shrewd, considered thought merchant Mercury ☿. Virgo's relentless pursuit of sacred perfection suits the Throat chakra's quest for knowledge. Virgo wants nothing more than to put what it learns to use in service—to family, community, and to the world. The Throat chakra seeks responsible Virgo's appreciation of sacred patterns, its ability to see cycles and model outcomes. With Virgo's influence awakened, *Kundalini* energy is channeled from the Heart chakra to spin a devotion to order, duty, efficiency, beauty, and sacred patterns of perfection.

Throat Chakra Rising

Quick-witted seeker Gemini ♊/Mercury ☿ speaks out the truth that calls *Kundalini* energy to rise from the compassion of the Heart chakra to the sacred voice of the Throat chakra. That voice risks going unheeded without the orderly persistence of Virgo ♍/Mercury ☿ to practice perfection in the performance of service to humankind. To give the Throat chakra its full and highest expression, the energy of both zodiac signs must be present. Once the swiftness of thought is coupled with a devotion to living its most sacred truth, the Throat chakra will activate.

Filled with the quest to learn and teach, to listen and speak, the Throat chakra spins as the Heart chakra provides the compassion that grounds knowledge with empathy. The life force rises to meet your wisdom in the sixth chakra, or Third Eye chakra.

Chapter
12

Third Eye Chakra (*Ajna*): In Sight

You know that *feeling* you get when the phone rings and you just know who it is? Have you ever been singing a song, and when you choose a random playlist, that song is playing? Do you sometimes know what someone is thinking or have a feeling something is about to happen and then it does? Have you ever dreamed about someone and then they contact you?

Life is full of these so-called coincidences, and according to yogic tradition, this "second sight" comes from the Third Eye chakra. Our two physical eyes see the past and the present. Our Third Eye sees the future. It's no coincidence that our "sixth sense" lives inside our sixth chakra.

The Third Eye chakra is the center, not just of our sense of what's coming, but of our intuition: what we *know* without seeing directly. As with the fifth chakra, or Throat chakra, we are now in the realm of the mind, rather than the body. The sixth chakra is the chakra of perception, imagination, and visualization, as well as of dreams, visions, and inspiration, the sixth chakra is that inner voice we recognize as our conscience, which tells us what is right and what is wrong. In India, people often mark the sixth chakra, or Third Eye chakra with a bright scarlet or yellow dot to help activate it, but you can activate yours just by reading this chapter.

Third Eye Chakra 101

The sixth chakra, the Third Eye chakra, is also sometimes called the Intuition chakra or Psychic chakra, and is called *Ajna* in the traditional Sanskrit. This Sanskrit word can be translated as "command," although some people also translate the word to mean "perceive." The notion of commanding relates to the notion that the Third Eye contains our intuitive perception and our conscience. Our perception is not necessarily neutral, but it has a sense of right and wrong and a moral compass that can guide us in how to act.

The traditional element associated with the sixth chakra, or Third Eye chakra, is called *mahat,* which means "supreme or great" element. This is where all the elements combine into one. However, chakra expert Anodea Judith writes that the Third Eye chakra is associated with the Light element. This makes intuitive sense because we cannot see without light, and we cannot "see" with our Third Eye chakra (in other words, we can't tap into our own inner vision, intuition, and imagination) without an inner light to illuminate those perceptions. If the Third Eye chakra is closed, the light—our life force energy—cannot penetrate through, and we are in inner darkness.

The Third Eye chakra's symbolic color is sometimes described as a deep indigo and sometimes described as purple. Throughout this chapter, as you tune in to your own sixth chakra, use your intuition to discover what color rings more true to you. The traditional lotus symbol depicting this chakra has just two petals, on either side of a central circle, like two eyes on either side of the Third Eye. The sound associated with this chakra is the seed sound *AUM* (or *OM,* both rhyme with "home"), the original, primordial sound of the Universe's vibration. Chanting this sound helps to activate the sixth chakra, as well as to bring unity to all the chakras.

The Third Eye chakra is located just between or slightly above the eyebrows and encompasses the entire face and head. Other physical structures associated with the sixth chakra are your pituitary gland, pineal gland, carotid nerve plexus, brain, eyes, nose, and sinuses.

The sixth chakra, or Third Eye chakra (Ajna), brings your intuition to light.

I See …

What do you see? Just the objects around you, or do you see more? Although you could list things you see in front of you, you might have trouble putting into words everything you "see" as you move through your life. You see a sunrise, but you also "see" that your friend is worried about something. You see a math problem, but then you suddenly "see" how to solve it. You see someone you love in front of you who is trying to explain how they feel, then you "see" what they mean.

The Third Eye chakra is all about what you see in every sense of the word. It influences your physical eyes and your imagination, your ability to perceive information both literally and metaphorically, and your inner wisdom that sees what has to be done. It's all going on right there in the middle of your forehead.

Psychic Moments: Your Intuition

What is being psychic? Many believe those who are psychic simply have a more finely honed intuition. Intuition is the part of you that picks up on cues in the environment that are so subtle, your conscious mind doesn't even notice them. You "get a feeling" you should cross the street, avoid that lane of traffic, get out of the elevator when someone else gets in, or call your mom.

Some of what you might be picking up are mental pictures that come through your sixth chakra. When the sixth chakra is open and healthy, your intuition can speak up and encourage you to take notice. Don't ignore it. Studies show that people who follow their intuition are more likely to avoid dangerous situations. Those who ignore the sixth sense because they think they are just being silly, paranoid, or overly sensitive often find out too late that their intuition was spot on.

Children have amazing imaginations, but they also have amazing perceptions. They see things adults don't always perceive with their busy, stressed, crowded brains. Sometimes, children might misinterpret the things they see, but if they are constantly told that what they see doesn't exist, they quickly learn to stifle their perceptions and ignore their intuitions. When a child thinks she sees a ghost, believes her dream really happened, tells you that grandma was in her room when grandma lives in another state, or is quite sure she knows exactly what her goldfish is trying to tell her, imagine what happens when a trusted parent says, "You are wrong." If you were told that your childhood visions weren't real, you might have learned not to listen to your inner voice or heed your inner vision. Children whose visions are acknowledged, considered, discussed, and honored—even if the adult ends up explaining what might really be going on—learn that their own Third Eye might really know something after all. That's an empowering gift to give a child.

Imagination Station

Remember all the things you used to imagine as a child? Imagination is fun, but adults often push it to the side or forget about it entirely. Yet our imaginations—even if they lie dormant—stay with us for our entire lives, and people with healthy, open sixth chakras have an all-access pass.

Adults can use their imaginations in many productive and wonderful ways, from daydreaming and pass-the-time fantasies to actually charting a course for the future; your imagination can be used for career development, relationship improvement, retirement planning, or learning how to finally live your dream (whatever that dream may be). People in creative professions use their imaginations regularly, but they don't have to be limited to the realms of their jobs. If you let your imagination work for you, it will. This is the place inside yourself where you can do and be anything. Using your imagination can be just plain fun without the aim of manifesting the things you imagine. However, begin here if you want to live your dreams or if you want to make what happens in your head happen in your life. If you imagine it, then you might just be able to make it so.

Picture This

If you've ever taken a yoga or meditation class, you have probably experienced *visualization*. Visualization is the act of forming mental images of something for various purposes. Some people use visualization to help with centering, relaxation, or focus during meditation (see Chapters 17 and 19). They might visualize a calming environment such as a beach, a meadow full of flowers, or a mountaintop with a beautiful view. Some people use visualization to help something actually happen in their lives, such as visualizing money coming to them or visualizing being at their ideal weight. Elite athletes have been known to visualize consistently making the free throw or making the perfect putt. Some people use visualization to enhance creativity, or they do it just because it's fun.

Your mind's ability to see what isn't actually there is reflected in the state of your sixth chakra. From here, you can form mental pictures of anything from the relationships you want the most to heal you to understanding and dealing with the things that most frighten you.

Some people find visualization easy, particularly those with healthy sixth chakras. For others, picturing something that isn't there is challenging, but energizing the sixth chakra can help. Practice helps, too. The more you use your imagination to visualize the things you want to see, the more skilled at visualization you will become. It's enjoyable to picture things in your mind, from memories of happy times in the past to visions of places you would like to go and things you hope to achieve someday. Visualization can even help you find solutions to your problems and ways to overcome obstacles in your life. It's a powerful tool, and all you need to do to start learning is to close your eyes.

Many of the exercises in this book require visualization. Every time we ask you to visualize, to see one of your chakras as a certain color or see it spinning, radiating, or anything else, that's visualization.

Try this powerful exercise if this insight has been difficult for you (or even if it hasn't). It's excellent for honing your visualization skills, and it can also help you use your intuition to discover some new things about yourself:

1. Sit comfortably and close your eyes. Take a few deep breaths.

2. With your mind's eye, picture yourself descending a long staircase. At the bottom you come to a hallway with three doors on each side of the hallway and a door at the end. All the doors are closed.

3. Imagine walking down the hallway and looking at each door. Every door looks a little different. Try to imagine the details of each door.

4. Now, choose a door and open it. Let yourself imagine what you see behind that door. Walk inside the space you imagine and take as long as you like to visualize every detail. Is it an ornate living room? Is it a meadow full of flowers? Is it an office of glass and steel? Is it a balcony overlooking the mountains? Or is it something completely abstract? Whatever it is, let yourself examine your surroundings for as long as you like, adding details as you go.

5. Use all five of your senses to help your visualization take form. What smells are behind the door? Are there certain sounds unique to this place? What colors do you see? Do you have a taste in your mouth connected to this place? What does

your body feel like, physically, when you are here? Your inner vision may not be complete at first, but that's okay. When you've spent as much time as you want to spend in the room of your imagination, go back out the door into the hallway, and open another door. Step in and visualize this new place.

6. Continue with this visualization until you have opened every door in that hallway. Visualize the space behind each door as well as you can. After you are finished, sit for a few minutes thinking about what you saw behind each door in your mind and what it might mean in your life right now.

Wise Up

As much as the Third Eye chakra is about seeing in all its many manifestations, it is also about knowing. This is where wisdom lives, as well as conscience. Through your sixth chakra, you not only see what is going on, but you know what it means. You understand if it is right or wrong, and you also simply understand it. You are wise in your Third Eye chakra. Close yourself off here, and you will lose your moral compass and your ability to make a decision based on more than just surface-level knowledge. An open sixth chakra allows you to tune in to your aha moments of recognition, discovery, and understanding. Here, you can tap into a deep inner and eternal knowing. Close it off and you lose this center of wisdom.

Dream On

Sometimes, what we see in our dreams can seem just as vivid as what we see when we are awake. Dream energy lives in the sixth chakra, and tuning into your dreams is an excellent way to energize the Third Eye. Each morning, try to remember your dreams and think about what they might tell you to get a new perspective on what is going on in your life. Dreams speak in symbols and pictures, and what they tell you is wise. (For even more help on interpreting your dreams, check out *The Complete Idiot's Guide Dream Dictionary,* which Eve coauthored with Gayle Williamson.)

Anyone can develop better dream recall. Keep a journal and pen next to your bed, so that you can write down visual impressions from your dreams the moment you wake up in the morning. Before you go to sleep, tell yourself you will remember your dreams.

Third Eye Chakra Correspondences

Tap into your inner wisdom by becoming aware of the many areas of your life that correspond to your sixth chakra, or Third Eye chakra.

Sixth Chakra	Correspondence
Sanskrit name	Ajna (purity)
Element	All elements combined, Light
Color	Indigo or purple
Seed sound	AUM (OM)
Location	Between and just above the eyebrows
Associated cultural phrases	"Sixth sense." "What you see is what you get." "Picture this." "I see what you mean." "Seeing is believing." "She has second sight." "Use your head." "Get out of your head." "Don't lose your head." "You are living in a dream world." "His head is in the clouds." "Get your head screwed on straight."
Associated anatomy	Brain, nerves, forehead, eyes, nose, pituitary and pineal glands, and carotid nerve plexus
Associated psychological and life issues	Intuition, perception, wisdom, imagination, ability to visualize, and dreams
Physical issues related to sixth chakra blockage	Headaches (including migraines); nasal congestion; sinus infections; near-sightedness and other problems seeing clearly; night blindness; stroke because of blockage, brain tumor, and head injury (can cause a blockage)
Psychological issues related to sixth chakra blockage	Lack of imagination, can't remember dreams, no intuition, chronic bad decision-making, denial of reality/self-deception, and sociopathic behavior
Physical issues related to sixth chakra overload	Headaches (particularly from dilated blood vessels), hallucinations and other visual disturbances involving seeing things that aren't there, hyperventilation, brain hemorrhage; brain tumor, and head injury (can cause an overload)

(continues)

Sixth Chakra	Correspondence
Psychological issues related to sixth chakra overload	Psychic visions that interfere with normal life, can't tell dreams from real life, disconnection from reality, psychosis, and being "too much in your head"
Sixth chakra therapy	Visualization Meditation Drawing and painting Practicing tuning in to your intuition Keeping track of your dreams Therapy to help clarify your inner vision Hypnosis—a state of altered consciousness during which there is increased focus and a greater openness to suggestion

Awakening the Third Eye Chakra

When your Third Eye chakra awakens, you become more perceptive and intuitive. You notice more of those little signs that urge you in the right direction, and your inner voice becomes clearer. People with awakened Third Eye chakras also tend to have exceptionally creative imaginations, good vision, and can remember and understand their dreams.

Awakening your Third Eye chakra can be as simple as touching your forehead to the ground, but meditating, drawing or painting, keeping track of your dreams, or practicing visualization are all great ways to get the Third Eye chakra activated.

To get more Third Eye chakra energy into your environment, highlight the color indigo or deep purple. Wear indigo on your body, paint the room where you meditate indigo, or put deep purple flowers around the house. Also include more Light elements in your home: interesting light fixtures; candles; or crystals and prisms that hang in the window, catch the light, and throw rainbows on the wall.

You can also try this exercise for awakening the Third Eye chakra:

1. Kneel on the floor; bring your big toes together and your knees wide apart. Put a folded blanket in front of you.

2. Bend forward and rest your forehead on the blanket. Close your eyes. Take several long, slow, and deep breaths, and then draw your attention to the area inside your Third Eye. Imagine your sixth chakra as a brilliant, deep indigo purple color that is spinning slowly. See if you can feel a vibration on your forehead where it touches the blanket.

3. Take a deep breath in and in a low resonating tone, say the word *AUM* slowly two times. (Pronounce this in three parts, holding each part for a few seconds: *ah-oh-oomm*.) Feel the word vibrating into your Third Eye chakra.

4. Rest quietly with your head down for a few minutes and imagine the deep indigo color spinning in your forehead.

Aligning the Third Eye Chakra

When your Third Eye chakra is properly aligned, your intuition will become fine-tuned. You'll be able to hear your inner voice and heed its wisdom. To get your Third Eye chakra properly aligned, try this exercise:

1. Stand in yoga's Mountain pose (see Chapter 7) with your feet about hip-width apart and your arms at your sides.

2. Imagine your Third Eye chakra in your forehead, between and just above your eyebrows. Visualize a deep indigo curtain opening to reveal your radiating sixth chakra.

3. Visualize a deep indigo ray of light moving straight up out of your Third Eye chakra, up through the crown of your head, and filling your head with indigo light. Now, visualize this indigo beam of light shooting straight down from your sixth (Third Eye) chakra and down through your fifth (Throat), fourth (Heart), third (Solar Plexus), second (Sacral), and first (Root) chakras and into the Earth. Imagine the entire ray of light filling your body with indigo energy.

4. Lift your arms straight up overhead, and imagine the light flowing up and down, radiating to the center of the Earth and all the way to the Heavens. Your chakra should now be aligned.

Blocks in the Third Eye Chakra

When your Third Eye chakra is blocked, you just don't *notice things*. Not only is your intuition blocked, your direct perception is blocked, too. Have you ever looked for something like your car keys, and then suddenly you see them right in front of you on the table, even though you swear you had already looked there? Has someone ever tried to send you subtle hints and had to resort to kicking you in the shins because you just didn't pick up on what they were trying to tell you nonverbally? Do people say you can't take a hint? Have you ever been startled because somebody snuck up on you, even though in reality, you just didn't see or hear them approaching? These are all signs of sixth chakra blockages. It's that feeling that you are "checked out" or just don't have your head screwed on straight.

Blocked Third Eye Chakra Health Issues

Sixth chakra health issues usually settle into the head. Anything that physically blocks up the processes in your head can be related to sixth chakra blocks, including headaches (including migraines), nasal congestion, and sinus infections. Other issues related to sixth chakra blocks include visual problems, such as a sudden onset of nearsightedness, night blindness, blurred vision, and other problems seeing clearly. Brain abnormalities can be reflected in a blocked sixth chakra. A head injury can also precipitate a blocked Third Eye chakra.

Blocked Third Eye Chakra Psychological Issues

When the Third Eye chakra is blocked, the psychological implications usually have to do with a lack of perception and imagination. People with blocked Third Eye chakras seem to have no "vision" of their own futures, the world, or even for what they want to accomplish at any given time. Or they might seem practical but not creative because their imaginations are stifled. Visualization is difficult for people with sixth chakra blocks, and they rarely recall their dreams.

These people are often in denial. They don't want to see what is going on in their lives, perhaps because they believe it is too painful, so they close themselves off to their inner vision and their inner voices. They might ignore their conscience or continue on in a bad situation because it is easier or more comfortable than seeing the truth. They don't seem to realize that listening to and following their own intuition, which resides in the sixth chakra, will lead them to their best possible lives.

To help unblock your Third Eye chakra, keep a drawing journal. Use a journal with unlined pages or a sketchpad and a pencil. Take 10 or 15 minutes to draw anything that comes into your mind. The point is to focus on the visual and translate what you see to paper. Even if you think you can't draw, give it a try.

People with a blocked sixth chakra also tend to proceed through life as if they have blinders on. They seem to be narrow-minded because they only see things one way or perceive things to be black and white with no shades of gray. They have trouble perceiving subtle differences in things or accepting that there are exceptions to every rule. They miss out on much of the complexity and diversity of life because seeing it is too difficult or painful, or they never really learned how to see the world through that Third Eye lens.

Healing a Blocked Third Eye Chakra

To heal and strengthen a blocked Third Eye chakra, focus on honing your vision, both outer and inner. Really look at things. Tune in to the colors and shapes in your environment. Close your eyes and visualize places, people, and situations. Try to visualize things that could never actually happen or places you've never actually seen. Fantasize. (How often is someone going to tell you to do *that* for your health?)

You can also try some of these activities to open a blocked Third Eye chakra:

- Paint. Watercolors and acrylics are easy to use. Experiment with color. Don't worry about skill; just have fun seeing.

- Keep a dream journal, and write down dream impressions each morning. The more regularly you try to remember your dreams and write down the images you recall, the more you are likely to remember.

- Eat dark blue and purple foods like purple and black grapes, eggplant, plums, red cabbage, and blackberries.

- With a partner watching to ensure your safety, try wearing a blindfold for a while. See how your perceptions change without your outer vision.

- Have someone give you a head rub or get a facial massage.

- Spend time in a steam room breathing deeply.

- Recite these mantras:
  - *I can see clearly.*
  - *I have an inner vision.*
  - *I trust my inner voice.*
  - *I listen to the deep and eternal wisdom that resides within me.*

Beauty might be in the eye of the beholder, but that shouldn't stop you from celebrating whatever *you* think is beautiful. Looking at beautiful things is incredibly therapeutic and excellent for unblocking the Third Eye chakra because it makes seeing highly rewarding. We're not talking about being obsessed with superficial beauty. We're talking about things that radiate inner beauty. Gaze at a beautiful view, take a walk in a beautiful setting, or stare at a beautiful sky, whether it's bright blue or dark and speckled with stars. Look at and appreciate beautiful objects, beautiful animals, and people you think are beautiful or who are doing something beautiful, like dancing, walking, reading, or just sitting and thinking.

Overload in the Third Eye Chakra

For some people, the Third Eye chakra takes over and visions are all they have. A sixth chakra overload can be a real problem for someone who has to function in the mundane world. Overloaded Third Eye chakras can reflect hallucinations, delusions, and obsession with memories of the past. If you live in a fantasy world, spend too much time daydreaming, or have a lot of trouble focusing on your current situation and environment, you might be overloaded in your sixth chakra.

People with overloaded Third Eye chakras sometimes have psychic abilities or think they do. However, these inner visions impair normal life because the person experiencing them can't distinguish them from outer visions. These people might also have such vivid dreams that they mistake them for reality, or they might have terrifying nightmares that stay with them and which they can't stop replaying in their minds. These are the people who are so convinced their visions are true that they skew their own intuition, taking every leap of imagination as "a sign" and every visual image as a dire warning or prediction. People grappling with PTSD might also have overloaded Third Eye chakras. If thoughts and visions become too overwhelming, seek the assistance of your primary care doctor or a licensed therapist to help you understand what you are seeing and what might be happening.

Overloaded Third Eye Chakra Health Issues

People with overloaded sixth chakras tend to have headaches caused by dilated blood vessels, such as tension headaches. They might suffer from hallucinations and other visual disturbances (such as migraine auras) that involve seeing things that aren't there, including extremely vivid dreams. In extreme cases, they might experience a brain hemorrhage or other brain abnormalities. As with sixth chakra blocks, a head injury can also cause a sixth chakra overload.

Overloaded Third Eye Chakra Psychological Issues

When you have too much energy in your sixth chakra, you tend to be so focused on your inner vision that you can lose touch with the real world. In extreme cases, a sixth chakra overload can indicate *psychosis*, a state of altered consciousness during which there is increased focus and a greater openness to suggestion, signaled by a total break from reality. More commonly, however, the overloaded Third Eye chakra person tends to be overly tuned in to intuition and the inner voice to the point that this focus interferes with normal life. Sixth chakra overloaded people also tend to think too much and at the expense of acting. If this is you, people might sometimes tell you to "get out of your head" or "stop thinking so much."

If you have an overloaded sixth chakra, you might also have extremely vivid dreams and remember many of them in the morning. Keeping a dream journal can be helpful for you, too; doing so won't help you remember more, but it will help you process all those images. Write down what you remember, and think about what it might mean for your waking life.

Healing an Overloaded Third Eye Chakra

First chakra, or Root chakra, grounding can be helpful for an overloaded sixth chakra. Get into your body more, and you'll have an easier time balancing your tendency to live inside your head. Exercise, preferably outside where you can focus on beautiful surroundings. Take a walk through the woods or a park. Tune in to what is really there, rather than spending the entire time thinking or fantasizing about other things.

Consciously working to be present is excellent for an overloaded Third Eye chakra. Pay attention to where you are, what you are doing, and what is going on around you periodically throughout the day. When you focus on your physical environment and the task at hand (instead of always living in your head and thinking about the past or the future), you will help heal your Third Eye chakra and you will also notice that you can concentrate better and get things done more efficiently. An overloaded Third Eye chakra can definitely predispose some people to chronic multitasking. Your mantra: *one thing at a time.*

Some other good strategies for healing an overloaded Third Eye chakra:

o Practice *mindfulness meditation,* a form of meditation in which you sit and observe your present state from moment to moment, without letting your thoughts carry you away to some other mental place.

o Practice noticing what physically exists around you. Remind yourself periodically throughout the day to *be here now.* Take a vision break every two hours and spend just two minutes observing actual objects in your immediate environment.

o Go back and review Chapter 7, which is all about the first chakra, or Root chakra. The stronger your first chakra, the better you will be able to remain grounded and to feel your connection to the Earth element. Having a stronger first chakra also means you won't be stuck in your head as often or feel blinded by the Light element of the sixth chakra. The Root and Third Eye chakras balance each other in many ways.

Yoga Poses to Balance the Third Eye Chakra

The best yoga poses for blocked Third Eye chakras are those poses that encourage *pratyahara,* the yoga principle of withdrawing the senses and turning inward. It's one of the Eight Limbs of Yoga, as described by Patanjali in the *Yoga Sutras.* Regular sensory withdrawal results in greater control over the senses, so they are not mistaken for more than they are. The yoga poses that help to balance an overloaded Third Eye chakra are those that encourage grounding in one's physical surroundings. Following, we've included a few of each.

Sensory Withdrawal Yoga Poses

We've already introduced you to two great poses that are perfect for withdrawing the senses to focus on the Third Eye chakra.

o Child's pose (as described in Chapter 10). Rest your forehead on the floor or on a folded blanket during this pose, and focus your attention on the Third Eye.

○ Corpse pose (as described in Chapter 7). In this yoga pose, as you lie perfectly still and relax every part of your body, bring your mind to the Third Eye chakra and try to see and feel it. Let the sixth chakra become your point of focus so that all your senses converge here, energizing and awakening the inner vision of your Third Eye.

Grounding Yoga Poses

The poses best for balancing an overloaded sixth chakra and bringing the mind back to the body are those that require maintaining concentration and balance.

○ Mountain pose and Tree pose (both described in Chapter 7). These yoga poses work to help balance the sixth chakra's insights into your inner and outer reality.

○ Partner Mountain pose (see Chapter 18). When two partners' Third Eye chakras synchronize, the healthier, more open chakra tends to "fix" the overloaded chakra, bringing it back into balance. Overloaded chakras can't negatively affect healthy, open chakras.

○ *Prana* Arch pose (as described in Chapter 19). This yoga pose opens and aligns the upper chakras to balance your perception, while remaining grounded in the Earth-centered chakras below.

Astrology for the Awakened Third Eye Chakra

Now we're going to look more closely at the astrological correspondences for the sixth chakra, or Third Eye chakra. In Chapter 4, you learned:

○ The planetary rulers of the Third Eye Chakra are the Sun ☉ and the Moon ☽.

○ The signs for the Third Eye Chakra are Leo ♌ and Cancer ♋.

Planetary Ruler	Sign(s) Ruled
Sun ☉	Leo ♌
Moon ☽	Cancer ♋

Knowing the energy of the planets and signs that correspond to the Third Eye chakra helps you understand how to bring sixth chakra wisdom through intuition to life. Yoga uses poses that encourage sensory withdrawal and physical grounding so that your body is calm and centered to receive psychic perceptions. Astrology gives that spinning wisdom of inspiration a meaning and purpose in your life. To understand how chakra energy is revealed in your astrological birth chart, see Appendix A, where we take a peek at Michelle Obama's birth chart chakras. Transiting planetary energy in the Heavens also affects astrological cycles and the way we feel and experience them here on Earth.

The Sun ☉ and Moon ☽ Open the Third Eye

The Sun ☉ and the Moon ☽ are astrology's *luminaries*. The Sun ☉ is the natural planetary ruler of Leo ♌ and the fifth house of creative potential, self-expression, romance, children, fun-loving joy, and risk-taking. The Moon ☽ is the natural planetary ruler of Cancer ♋ and the fourth house of home and family, your roots, emotional security, and the foundation of your life. As luminaries (considered planets in astrology), the Sun ☉ and the Moon ☽ govern your self (your willpower, life spirit, and essential waking nature, as well as your intuitive, emotional, instinctive dreaming self).

Together, the Sun ☉ and the Moon ☽ imbue the Third Eye chakra with the wholeness of being, the perfect yin/yang balance of light and dark, outgoing and reserved, leader and lone seeker, waking visions, and lucid dreams. The luminaries spin the Third Eye chakra, opening a mind's eye portal to the wise life force energy at the center of your being (and supported by the truth of the Throat chakra below). Strong luminaries give your body-mind-spirit access to the best of your whole, integrated self—a self that balances leadership in action with visionary perception and emotional intelligence. Without the luminaries in balance, the Third Eye chakra can spin toward too much doing or too much dreaming … and not many results in real life.

How Leo ♌ Awakens the Third Eye Chakra

Leo ♌ with its yang, Fire element energy is ruled by the warmth of the Sun ☉. Leo's exuberant, creative, can-do stamina suits Third Eye chakra's energy wisely. Leo can be the life of the party but also knows how to take the lead to get projects going and how to bask in the spotlight of social media, regaling all its many accomplishments. The Third Eye chakra reaches for Leo's big-hearted enthusiasm for living—the wisdom of experience. With Leo's influence awakened, *Kundalini* energy is channeled from the Throat chakra upward, to spin with a joy of living while grounded in a strong voice and sense of purpose.

How Cancer ♋ Awakens the Third Eye Chakra

Cancer ♋, with its yin, Water element energy is lit by the Moon's ☽ light, which is the reflected light of the Sun ☉. Cancer's nurturing sensitivity suits the Third Eye chakra's desire to bathe in illuminating emotion. Cancer loves the security of traditions and proves dependable, adaptable, and self-sacrificing. The Third Eye chakra seeks sensitive Cancer's desire to lead with the heart and to feel with the mind. With Cancer's influence, *Kundalini* energy is channeled from the Throat chakra upward, to spin with a joy of loving while grounded in the truth true love holds.

Third Eye Chakra Rising

The imaginative leader Leo ♌/Sun ☉ joins with the sensitive caregiver Cancer ♋/Moon ☽ to urge *Kundalini* energy from the raw data of the Throat chakra to the deciphered wisdom of the Third Eye chakra. Without the Third Eye chakra's balance of bright tenacity with deep intuitive knowing, the Throat chakra's message risks being lost in translation. To give the Third Eye chakra the fully developed personhood capable of creating wisdom, the energy of both zodiac signs must be present. Once the received wisdom can be explored through the portal of the mind's eye, the Third Eye chakra will activate.

Filled with the potential of the Universe waiting to be seen and known, the Third Eye chakra spins as the Throat chakra sounds the celestial music resonating with perfect harmony into the mind's eye. The life force rises to meet Spirit's understanding in the seventh chakra, or Crown chakra.

Chapter
13

Crown Chakra (*Sahasrara*): Thousand-Petaled Lotus

To be a whole person with complete body-mind-spirit integration, one must involve the seventh chakra—the part that reflects the human spirit. Spirit means a lot of different things to different people, and in the context of the Crown chakra, it also has a range of meanings.

This is the realm of higher brain function, so not only does the seventh chakra reflect our connection (in a traditional sense) with the Higher Power or energy of the Universe that some people call God, but it also reflects our "big picture" sensibility. The impulse to understand who we are and where we fit into the broad scheme of things comes out of the seventh chakra. This is the place where we question the meaning of life, as well as the place where we learn and where we integrate what we learn into who we are. This is also where we receive inspiration, sudden aha moments of understanding, and a deep sense of connectedness to all of life and the energy that connects all life. We might not feel it all the time, but when we get those flashes of unified feeling, they come from the Crown chakra.

Betsy rarely sees people with closed Crown chakras, and she believes this is because we are all deeply connected to each other and to universal energy, even if we don't realize it consciously.

Crown Chakra 101

The seventh chakra, the Crown chakra, also is sometimes called the Spiritual chakra, or Thousand-Petaled Lotus chakra, and is called *Sahasrara* in the traditional Sanskrit. This Sanskrit word is usually translated as "thousand-petaled" or "thousand-spoked," which refers to the thousand petals of the lotus flower that symbolically represents this chakra.

Traditionally, the Thousand-Petaled Lotus chakra is pictured as inverted on the crown of the head with the thousand petals extending downward (instead of being pictured as sitting upright atop the head). The lotus is an ancient symbol for spiritual flowering because it floats in ponds and its roots extend deep down into the mud at the bottom of the pond. In the same way the lotus is rooted in murky mud but produces a beautiful white flower above the surface of the water, so must we be rooted in the sometimes dark and murky physical world, but we have the potential to blossom spiritually.

However, the fact that the lotus flower is inverted on the body in its traditional representation also suggests that the Crown chakra is rooted in the Heavens and extends down to each of us, as if the Divine Presence, Spirit, or Goddess/God has reached down to touch you reassuringly on the crown of your head. This is your connection to something greater than yourself, and your sacred proof that you are an integral part of that greater something.

There is no traditional element associated with the seventh chakra, which extends beyond the physical notion of Earthly elements, although chakra expert Anodea Judith says the element of this chakra is Thought itself. Just as we touch Spirit here, we also expand the mind, which is the tool that enables us to understand and communicate with Goddess/God or the energy of the Universe.

The seventh chakra's symbolic color is sometimes described as purple and sometimes described as pure white. As you work with your own seventh chakra, use whatever color makes sense to you. The traditional lotus symbol for the seventh chakra is typically depicted sitting inverted on the crown of the head. There is no element associated with the Crown chakra; there is also no literal sound. Instead, the seed sound of this chakra is the sound of Goddess/God or the Universe speaking *AUM*, rather than a human voice saying anything at all. Some people also interpret the seed sound of the Crown chakra to be the sound of breath. It is typical in chakra meditations *not* to speak when reaching this chakra. Instead, feel the Universe vibrate.

*The Crown chakra (**Sahasrara**) is the realm of Thought and the highest expression of human understanding of the Universe.*

The Crown chakra is located slightly above the crown of the head. It encompasses the brain and especially the cerebral cortex, the external layer of gray matter that covers the cerebrum and cerebellum. The cerebral cortex is the most highly developed part of the brain and is responsible for the most advanced human brain functions, such as thinking, understanding, and integrating information.

Will the Real You Please Stand Up?

Who are you? This is probably a question you have thought about periodically throughout the course of reading this book, but the question is never more relevant than when you are working with your Crown chakra; this is where all the parts of you come together. In some systems of belief, spirituality is something separate from the physical, and physical reality is considered unreal or inferior or, even worse, something to deny. However, the concept of the chakras defies this ideology. From the first through the seventh, each chakra represents an integral part of who you are, and each part develops out of the one below it so that by the time *Kundalini* energy reaches the Crown chakra, you can experience complete integration of all your parts: your instincts, your physical urges, your feelings, your relationships, your compassion, your communication with others, your intuition, and your place in the Universe.

Within your seventh, or Crown chakra, you have the capacity to see all these parts together and integrate them into one exciting, fascinating, and endlessly revealing *you*. Even as you connect to something greater, that doesn't obliterate who you are. Rather, it enhances and clarifies you.

The Spirit Link

The nature of Spirit is complex and takes our highest brain function to understand. Even then, we can probably only hope to scratch the surface of what it means. Different cultures define Spirit in different ways, too—as something within us, something outside of us, or both.

The Crown chakra encompasses our connection both to our own spirituality and to a universal spirit that exists within and beyond us. The seventh chakra is like a door that opens to welcome God or universal life force energy. Call it what you want to call it and envision it in whatever way works for you, but the sense is the same. We are a part of something bigger, and we join with this greater energy through our seventh chakras. We send *who* we are out this door, and the Universe sends *what* we are back in, so that we recognize we are part of something grand. We are never alone because of this sacred link.

For those who don't spend much energy on spiritual pursuits or who were never raised in a religious tradition, this can be a difficult concept to swallow. Don't worry about that. If the seventh chakra doesn't speak to you—if you don't feel like you need it right now—that's fine. It is still open, giving, and receiving like a great cosmic modem, linking you to everything else that has ever lived, breathed, or existed. Trust in that if you want to. Or don't worry about it until you need to. For some, understanding the Crown chakra may come through the lens of their religion, but the Crown chakra does not have to be related to religion. Whatever way you look at it, it is about connection.

Spirituality is easy for kids. Spiritual visions and perceptions seem unsurprising to them. However, a child's spirituality is a delicate and sacred thing. Children who grow up in restrictive religious environments often have later difficulty with spirituality, especially if they reject their childhood religious experiences and retain negative memories from it. Conversely, children with absolutely no spiritual experiences might have a hard time opening up to spirituality later in life because it is foreign territory that never had a chance to develop. While every parent has different priorities, the most important way to help a child's seventh, or Crown chakra develop in a healthy way is to never deny them the reality of their own spiritual perceptions.

The Religion Connection

Betsy has worked with many clients on issues relating to religion. She believes that religion can be an incredibly positive force, and although it isn't for everyone, for some people, it is healing and supportive. Sometimes, however, people can develop anxiety and other issues connected with negative religious experiences. In these cases, the Crown chakra can provide a lifeline.

Betsy had a client named Sarah who was having panic attacks. Saddled with frequent anxiety, the college student came to see Betsy because her anxiety was interfering with her life. Through therapy, Betsy learned that Sarah was raised in an extremely religious household that emphasized sin and an angry, punishing God. Sarah always had huge fears of letting down God and being subject to Divine wrath. She had vivid memories as a child of being told that if her behavior didn't change, she would go to Hell. She regularly experienced fear, guilt, and shame related to the way religion was practiced in her childhood home.

As she matured, Sarah began to feel so oppressed by the moral expectations placed upon her by her church and her parents that she began to separate from her childhood church and from her family. Eventually, Sarah abandoned anything to do with religion and spirituality and decided the only way she could progress was to become an atheist (someone who does not believe in God).

As Betsy began to help Sarah explore her belief systems, it became obvious that Sarah was in mourning. She was grieving the loss of the idea that there was some Higher Power in the Universe and that she was connected to this powerful force. Sarah was missing the positive aspects of religion because she had rejected the entire concept, rather than just those parts that had hurt her in the past. Instead of fearing sin, Sarah's anxiety stemmed from her fear of isolation from God.

Sarah had decided that the God of her childhood no longer fit into her worldview, so she thought that meant there could be no God. However, Betsy discovered that from the very first session, Sarah's seventh chakra was open and strong. Sarah found this difficult to believe. How could her Spiritual chakra be open when she was an atheist who had purposefully cut herself off from anything spiritual?

As they worked, Sarah began to reevaluate the meaning of her open and balanced seventh chakra. Week after week, as her chakra remained open, Betsy began to feel a sense of relief that maybe Sarah was still connected to a Higher Power after all.

During therapy, Betsy helped Sarah to clarify what she was really feeling and to discover that it was not necessary for her to carry the same strict religious beliefs her parents held to have a spiritual life. As an adult, she could figure out what spirituality and God meant to her.

Sarah began to practice meditation to connect with a larger life force. With regular meditation practice, Sarah rediscovered her spiritual self and was able to free it from the chains of negativity based in her past. Sarah's anxiety eased and she felt calmer, balanced, and integrated.

Higher Education

The seventh chakra also governs your ability to learn. All knowledge you take into yourself comes in through the Crown chakra, which also reflects the state of the cerebral cortex. You know what they say: never stop learning. To energize the seventh chakra, keep learning. When learning stops, the seventh chakra falters. Fortunately, for most people who are living an active and interactive life, learning never stops because knowledge isn't just about taking a workshop to build a webpage, learning to play the ukulele, or going back to finish your degree. Knowledge is about engaging with the greater world—stepping out of your comfort zone to discover what that means for who you are and what you are becoming at any given moment.

The Big Picture

When you are conscious, your seventh chakra is at work. In this way, the seventh chakra encompasses a wide range of thinking, from philosophical musing to simply being awake. When you are unconscious, such as while you are sleeping, if you faint, or if you are in a coma, your seventh chakra closes. But you don't necessarily have to be asleep to be walking through this world in an unconscious state. If you wake up to your life and live with intention and engagement, your seventh chakra will open again.

Seat of the Soul

Not everyone buys into the idea that each of us has a soul, something apart from our physical bodies that survives after our bodies die. However, for those with open seventh, or Crown chakras, the presence of the soul is self-evident. You can just feel it. For those who have been around someone who has died, you might even have seen or sensed the soul leaving the body as that person took the last breath. (This isn't always at the exact moment of physical death; sometimes, it happens just before or just after death.)

While nobody has ever proven the existence of the soul, many people believe that the soul is the part of you that lives within your body but is not part of your body. You can't see it on an X-ray or even measure it with a pendulum. It is the presence of life force energy within you that is imprinted with your individual signature and with the signature of the Universe, like a jointly signed contract.

In other words, the seventh chakra reflects both the body's consciousness and the Spirit's consciousness. The Crown chakra is the soul's home. The state of the soul and what it says about spiritual health is reflected in the energy of the Crown chakra. This doesn't mean whether the soul is "saved" or "damned." These concepts are foreign to yogic philosophy.

Crown Chakra Correspondences

Your spiritual life is reflected all over your physical life, and the Crown chakra has many correspondences that can help you tap into its power. These correspondences are summarized in the following chart.

Seventh Chakra	Correspondence
Sanskrit name	Sahasrara (Thousand-Petaled Lotus)
Element	No element; or, Thought
Color	Purple or white
Seed sound	The Divine speaks the sound; or, the sound of breath
Location	At the crown of the head
Associated cultural phrases	"That's the spirit!" "Believe in me." "You've got to have faith." "God willing." "Look at the big picture." "I think, therefore I am."
Associated anatomy	Skull, brain, and cerebral cortex
Associated psychological and life issues	The true self, unity in all things, knowledge and understanding; spirituality; connecting to a Higher Power or the Universe; seeing the big picture; or the soul
Physical issues related to seventh chakra blockage	Learning disabilities, nervous system failure, headaches (at the crown of the skull), autism, brain tumor, coma, amnesia, and senility/Alzheimer's disease
Psychological issues related to seventh chakra blockage	Feelings of isolation, depression, lack of inspiration, and spiritual crisis/"dark night of the soul"
Physical issues related to seventh chakra overload	Headaches (at the crown of the skull), Savant Syndrome, brain seizures, and health problems related to poor hygiene or physical neglect
Psychological issues related to seventh chakra overload	Obsession with or addiction to spiritual or intellectual practices, religious or spiritual delusions/hallucinations, nervous breakdown, uncontrolled out-of-body experiences, dissociation with the body, over-intellectualizing, and feeling ungrounded
Seventh chakra therapy	For blocks: meditation, prayer, spiritual study, self-study, learning something new and challenging like a musical instrument or a language, therapy to deal with spiritual crisis For excess: grounding, balancing all seven chakras, physical exercise, therapy to reintegrate the mind with the body, therapy to put spiritual beliefs and practices into perspective

Awakening the Crown Chakra

When your Crown chakra awakens, you see beyond the limits of your own ego. The Universe gets bigger and begs the question: "why?" The lifelong quest to answer that "why" is the province of the seventh chakra; your Crown chakra is the tool for uncovering the answer. Learning, experiencing new things, seeing things in a new way, and generally expanding the mind more and more to encompass each new facet of life as it is encountered are all activities that awaken the Crown chakra. Ultimately, when the inner gaze turns even more fully outward and beyond human experience to seek meaning in a broader, universal perspective, the question becomes something like

- "Who is running this show?"
- "What drives it all?"
- "What is the nature of the fuel for this energy?"
- "What is Goddess/God?"

You nudge your Crown chakra open every time you gain new knowledge or experience. Whenever you reach out into the Universe with a question, your seventh chakra activates—it comes to life.

To get even more Crown chakra energy into your environment, highlight the colors purple or white. Wear these colors, use them in your home, and fill your home with the tools for gaining knowledge, such as books and digital media. Also, consider reserving a space in your home for meditation or prayer where you can be quiet and reflect on things. A meditation room is nice but not necessary. Any space that is clean, uncluttered, and quiet will work. Use it every day, and your Crown chakra will remain open and strong as a conduit for the *prana* life force energy of the Universe.

You can also try this exercise for awakening the Crown chakra:

1. Kneel on the floor and put your palms together in front of your chest in prayer position.
2. Bow your head in supplication to Spirit energy greater than yourself. Close your eyes. Take several long, slow, and deep breaths, and then draw your attention to the area at the crown of your head.
3. Raise your head up so your neck is aligned perfectly over your spine. Imagine your Crown chakra. Try to see what color it is, deep purple or bright white. Imagine it glowing brilliantly and spinning slowly. Try to feel it at the top of your head or just above it, as vibrating, swirling energy.

4. Breathe evenly and listen to the sound of your breath. Now, imagine Goddess/God or the vibration of the Universe uttering the sound: *AUM*. Don't make any sound yourself other than breathing. Just listen and hear the sound coming from outside yourself and vibrating inside you.

5. Once again, bow to Divine energy, and then rest your hands on your knees, lift your head, and open your eyes. Breathe. Your Crown chakra is awakened.

Aligning the Crown Chakra

When your Crown chakra is properly aligned, you feel grounded, connected to others, and connected to the Universe. You perceive the unity in all things, and yet you appreciate your own individuality and ability to gain knowledge and interpret information as part of your personal growth. Aligning your Crown chakra is the final act of alignment; when all your chakras are straight, open, and permitting the free flow of *prana* life force energy, you will gain ultimate balance. You can live in the world while still knowing Goddess/God energy, the Source, and the All.

To get your Crown chakra properly aligned, try this exercise:

1. Stand in yoga's Mountain pose (see Chapter 7) with your feet about hip-width apart and your arms at your sides. Feel your feet firmly planted on the floor. Connect with the energy of the Earth and imagine your body-mind-spirit becoming grounded.

2. Imagine your seventh chakra at the crown of your head. Visualize a deep purple or pure white light shining out of the top of your head and extending in a brilliant beam up toward the sky. Imagine energy flowing up and out of your seventh chakra, and then imagine a matching beam of light coming down from the Heavens and from far beyond the place where you could see its Source, and imagine that light beaming directly into the crown of your head so that Divine energy flows up and down.

3. Now, visualize this beam of light shooting straight from the Source down from the Heavens to your Crown chakra, and then down through your Third Eye chakra, your Throat chakra, your Heart chakra, your Solar Plexus chakra, your Sacral chakra, your Root chakra, and out from the base of your spine straight down into the Earth, reaching all the way to the Earth's core. Imagine the entire ray of light filling your body-mind-spirit with glittering, radiating energy.

4. Lift your arms straight up overhead and imagine the light flowing up and down, into the Heavens and down from the Heavens, into the core of the Earth, and back up again to Earth's surface. Your Crown chakra—all seven of your chakras—should now be aligned. You are both in and of the world. Invite *Kundalini* serpent energy to activate and rise within you, urging you to engage in the Divine life of the world.

Blocks in the Crown Chakra

When your seventh chakra, or Crown chakra is blocked, you feel cut off. It's as if someone cut the power to your house and your source of energy and heat is gone. With a blocked Crown chakra, you can still function in the world. You can (and will) talk to other people—even love them. You can feel, do, and speak. However, you cannot spark a connection to the Goddess/God, you cannot feel engaged with energy of the *prana* life force, and you will have trouble seeing the big picture. You'll struggle to learn, and you won't have any context for your knowledge. Spirit is stifled and you feel lost, even when you know exactly where you are in space and time.

Fortunately, Crown chakra blocks aren't common. The Universe has a way of whispering to us even if we aren't listening. Even if we give up on the Goddess/God or a Divine life force, the Universe does not give up on us. It takes powerful negative experiences to close down a Crown chakra, but when it does close, you might experience a spiritual crisis. The question, "What does it all mean?" suddenly seems like it has no answer, and the consequences of that non-answer might suddenly seem more dire to you than you ever imagined possible.

People with blocked Crown chakras also tend to have problems learning. They have trouble grasping new concepts and settle into such a comfortable sameness that the idea of experiencing anything new becomes terrifying. Healing a blocked Crown chakra is incredibly important so you can live fully and be spiritually whole. Your whole brain functions properly with an open Crown chakra. Don't despair! Growing through a spiritual crisis, a "dark night of the soul," can strengthen your sense of purpose and give you a renewed understanding of life. What was clouded can shine anew with Divine light.

Blocked Crown Chakra Health Issues

Seventh chakra, or Crown chakra, health issues, like sixth chakra, or Third Eye chakra, health issues, settle in the head, but seventh chakra issues have more to do with the top of the head and higher brain function. A blocked Crown chakra can result in headaches, especially those on the top of the head. The sudden onset of learning disabilities, memory loss (like amnesia), or other brain dysfunction is common with seventh chakra blocks. Temporary loss of consciousness, including coma, also are common with seventh chakra blocks.

Blocked Crown Chakra Psychological Issues

When the Crown chakra is blocked, the psychological implications relate to both learning and spiritual matters. Blocked seventh chakra people have trouble comprehending new information and sometimes isolate themselves to avoid dealing with the repercussions of a learning disability or cognitive malfunction. They might refuse to see beyond a narrow set of beliefs or to experience anything new. Even some religious people have closed seventh chakras because they actually worship their own narrow idea of the Goddess/God rather than being open to the experience of actual divinity. This can happen out of fear, force of habit, or simply a lack of courage and curiosity. The result is often narrow-mindedness, prejudice, hate, depression, and a life that grows smaller and smaller.

Blocked seventh chakras are also related to spiritual crises, which are common when someone rejects a spiritual tradition and has nothing to take its place or becomes filled with doubt in which all previous faith is called into question. When someone gives up on learning, rejects new knowledge, or turns away from Spirit, the Crown chakra can shut down.

Mother Teresa's much-publicized spiritual crisis is a perfect example. Her words to the Reverend Michael Van Der Peet in September 1979 express this block: "Jesus has a very special love for you. As for me, the silence and the emptiness is so great that I look and do not see, listen and do not hear." Even though she was famous all over the world for her selfless work and spiritual devotion, she had doubts, fear, and a feeling of isolation from the Divine.

You don't have to be religious to have an open seventh chakra. You don't even have to believe in a particular Goddess/God or even the concept of a Higher Power. Many people are spiritually connected to life force energy despite their rejection of organized religion or what they think of as spiritual pursuits. Some are so devoted to *not* believing in Goddess/God, logic, science, or secular humanism, that this devotion becomes, in itself, a sort of religion of the mind and generates its own brand of spirituality. Being passionate about living, learning, and *being* is a reflection of an open Crown chakra. In other words, the seventh chakra does not demand any particular adherence other than the one devoted to the quest for knowledge of the meaning of life. When the quest for knowledge is active, so is the seventh chakra.

Healing a Blocked Crown Chakra

To heal and strengthen a blocked Crown chakra, work your mind by gaining knowledge. Purposefully have new experiences, even if you don't necessarily find doing so comfortable. Think, consider, philosophize, theorize, and never stop learning. Let your quest for knowledge encompass both the physical world and the world beyond. Question what you learn and don't just believe everything you hear. Be open to not only facts but also those realities that might not be provable. Have both doubt and faith and have a willingness to see beyond the obvious. If it's good for your brain, it's good for your seventh chakra.

You can also try some of these activities to open a blocked Crown chakra:

- Meditate, especially on the nature of the Universe, the Goddess/God, or any other spiritual matters you find interesting. Try listening for the answers to your deepest questions.

- Pray or reach out to a Higher Power in whatever manner fits in with your belief system. Ask for what you need and want. The Universe will hear you.

- Learn something new. Studies show that choral singing or learning a language or a new musical instrument are some of the best ways to maintain cognitive brain function.

- Eat purple or (naturally) white foods like purple grapes, plums, purple or white eggplant, white radishes, potatoes, or onions.

- Catch snowflakes or raindrops on your tongue, or take off your hat and feel them landing on your head.

- Do word or number puzzles.

- Have someone give you a head rub.

- Recite these mantras:

  - *I can learn anything.*

  - *I honor my body, my mind, and my spirit equally.*

  - *I am filled with life force energy.*

  - *Goddess/God lives within me.*

  - *I am a Divine being.*

  - *I never stop learning.*

Overload in the Crown Chakra

When the Crown chakra is too open and overloaded with energy, spiritual matters not only prevail, they push other matters off the radar. These are the people who get addicted to religious practices or are so overzealous in their spiritual pursuits that they forget to live in the world. This is fine for monks and nuns in monasteries and hermits in caves who have devoted their lives to the singular pursuit of spirituality, but for the rest of us who have to live in the world, a sense of balance with the more mundane aspects of life is essential. (For that matter, even monks and nuns need to make the food, do the dishes, and weed the garden.) An overloaded seventh chakra tips the scale away from the real world, the body, and even other people in favor of a vision that always and only looks upward.

But an overloaded Crown chakra can also be about an obsessive devotion to learning and gaining knowledge at the expense of actual practical application of knowledge. People with unusual intellectual abilities sometimes have overloaded seventh chakras when these abilities control their lives. Maybe you are so devoted to spiritual pursuits that you don't remember to eat, sleep, or brush your teeth. Or maybe you are a scholar, an intellectual, or so fascinated with learning that you spend your days in endless reading, become overly interested in political policy debates, or plumb the depths of digitized sacred texts online to find answers to your most philosophical questions, but you ignore the people around you. Whatever the case, an overloaded seventh chakra can result in being completely out of touch with the real world, your actual body, your job, your daily duties, and your relationships.

Overloaded Crown Chakra Health Issues

People with overloaded seventh chakras tend to have headaches at the crown of the heads, rather than in other areas like the forehead or sinuses. An overloaded seventh chakra sometimes can be reflected in a brain abnormality, especially one that grows quickly. Savant Syndrome, a condition characterized by having unusual skill at something such as art, music, math, or remembering dates, can be a sign of an overloaded seventh chakra if that person is (as is often the case) impaired in other ways. Howard Hughes, billionaire businessman of the Great War generation, comes to mind. Hughes was a brilliant thinker, doer, and genius, but he was saddled with obsessive-compulsive disorder and other problems that made it extremely difficult for him to live a normal life.

People with overloaded seventh chakras can also have overactive nervous systems and can suffer from seizures or nervous breakdowns. Because they often lose touch with their bodies, people with overloaded seventh chakras might also have poor hygiene or health problems related to physical neglect.

Overloaded Crown Chakra Psychological Issues

When you have too much energy in your seventh chakra, you tend to be so focused on your mind that you lose touch with your body, which can cause not just health problems but problems with relationships and daily functioning. If you forget to shower or change your clothes, you are probably going to start having problems out there in the world.

Overloaded seventh chakra people also tend to be addicted to spiritual or intellectual practices like prayer, meditation, or constant study. They might suffer from religious or spiritual delusions or hallucinations, and might even have out-of-body experiences because they are so much in their heads and so little in their bodies. Also, they might feel separate from their bodies, as if their bodies don't belong to them. Overintellectualizing is a common problem for overloaded seventh chakras, as is a feeling of not being grounded.

If you have an overloaded seventh chakra, or Crown chakra, chances are you have a closed first chakra, or Root chakra, because these two chakras often reflect each other's imbalances. Likewise, an overloaded first chakra sometimes coincides with a blocked seventh chakra. To balance your Crown chakra, look back at the exercises for energizing and opening your Root chakra.

Although we are all spiritual beings who are having human experiences here on Earth, it is important to remember that we are also living on the physical plane within Earthly bodies, and we need to pay attention to the body and the world around us, rather than constantly focusing exclusively on the spiritual world beyond.

Healing an Overloaded Crown Chakra

First chakra grounding can be very helpful for overloaded sixth and seventh chakras. Get into your body more and you'll have an easier time balancing your tendency to live inside your head or in front of a screen. Move your body, feel your feet on the ground, jump up and down, dance, and exercise. Pay attention to the world. List physical details you see in front of you. Touch things. Smell, taste, and feel. Remember, you are here in your body right now for a reason. You aren't up in Heaven yet or even in an ivory tower. Live while you are alive. It isn't all about thinking or the unending intellectual search.

Following are some other good strategies for healing an overloaded Crown chakra:

- Practice balancing all seven chakras each day to remind you that you are more than just your brain.

- Tune in to your five senses. Sit quietly and focus on everything you can see in the room around you. Then notice everything you can hear, from the sound of traffic or birds outside to the creaking floors and ticking ceiling fan. Next, tune in to everything you can feel: the air on your face, your clothing, and your jewelry. Can you smell anything? Breathe in deeply and find out. What taste do you have in your mouth right now?

- Eat something. Eating is very grounding. Foods that come from the earth, especially those that grow deep in the soil like potatoes, onions, and carrots, are especially grounding. Eat slowly and notice the taste and texture of the food.

- Exercise outside. Get your heart rate up and your muscles moving.

- Spend less time in front of a screen. Focus on the time you spend engaging with digital media. How much of your life has moved online? Try to manage the amount of time you spend online, as well as how and where you use it. Balance time online with time doing real-world activities.

- Therapy can help you reintegrate your mind and body, or it can help you put your spiritual or intellectual practices into perspective so you can also function in the real world.

- Practice noticing what physically exists around you. Remind yourself periodically throughout the day to "be here now." Take a "vision break" every two hours, and spend just two minutes observing actual objects in your immediate environment.

○ Leave the house, the library, or the office. Do errands. Take a walk. Visit a parent or friend. Force yourself to engage with the world outside your enclave of work and/or study.

Yoga Poses to Balance the Crown Chakra

Two good yoga poses for balancing the Crown chakra are Corpse pose (*Savasana*), which you first learned in Chapter 7, and Headstand pose, also called *Sirsasana*.

When doing Corpse pose to balance the Crown chakra, focus on the feel and weight of your body sinking into the ground, but also envision your crown opening and energy flowing through all your chakras.

Headstand is an advanced yoga pose, and we don't encourage you to try it for the first time on your own. Go to a yoga class where an experienced teacher can lead you safely into this pose. However, go ahead and try our easier variation, explained in the following section.

Modified Headstand (*Sirsasana*)

A full Headstand pose draws blood to the head and nourishes the Crown chakra. Work on achieving this pose with the instruction of a qualified yoga teacher.

A Headstand against a wall is a great place for people to start who are ready for this pose. If you've been practicing yoga for a while and a skilled teacher can demonstrate for you in person how to do headstand, then go for it. Eventually, you might even be able to do a Headstand in the middle of the room. This is an excellent pose for both opening a blocked Crown chakra and for calming an overloaded Crown chakra because it puts your portal to the mind directly in contact with the Earth.

However, not everybody can do Headstand pose or can do it yet. Why not get all the benefits without all the pressure? Try this modified version:

1. Kneel on all fours in front of a folded blanket. Place your hands on the blanket, and come down onto your forearms. Clasp your hands together making a space about the size of your head with your hands. Keep your elbows wide apart, and make sure your wrists remain pushing down into the blanket.

2. Raise your hips and come onto your feet so that your hips are in the air, your feet are on the ground, and your upper body is supported by your forearms and hands.

3. Put your head down into the space between your forearms so your crown rests on the blanket and your clasped hands cup your head. Walk your feet in a little closer. If this is too difficult, come out of the pose and move to a wall so your back can lean against the wall as you walk your feet in closer to your arms. Or don't come up onto your feet. Stay on your knees as you rest your head on the floor.

4. Take a few deep breaths, and feel the crown of your head against the blanket. Stay in this position as long as you like.

5. To come out of the pose, come back down onto your knees with your forehead resting on the floor. Stay here for at least 30 seconds. Sit up slowly.

Astrology for the Awakened Crown Chakra

For each of the chakras, we have charted the rise of *Kundalini* energy up from the activated first chakra, or Root chakra, through the energies of the astrological planets and signs corresponding to each. An understanding of astrological influences has shown how one chakra blossoms into another—aligning and giving full expression to the life force energy within us. When these energies reach a fully activated and waiting Crown chakra, the understanding of enlightenment awakens within you. Because the realm of Spirit, the nirvana of enlightenment, exists beyond the physical Universe in all its expansiveness, the Crown chakra itself spins beyond expression through astrology's planets and signs. This kind of knowing transcends articulation.

To awaken the Crown chakra, the life force energy must first move through astrology's planets and signs, healing each chakra we have charted, with the help of the Heavens. Let's review the astrological chakra correspondences as they unfold in the body.

ASTROLOGICAL CHAKRA CORRESPONDENCES FOR EACH OF THE CHAKRAS WE HAVE CHARTED

Chakra	Planetary Ruler	Sign(s) Ruled
Seventh, or Crown	Union with the Divine	
Sixth, or Third Eye	Sun ☉ Moon ☽	Leo ♌ Cancer ♋
Fifth, or Throat	Mercury ☿	Gemini ♊, Virgo ♍
Fourth, or Heart	Venus ♀	Taurus ♉, Libra ♎
Third, or Solar Plexus	Mars ♂ Pluto ♇	Aries ♈ Scorpio ♏
Second, or Sacral	Jupiter ♃ Neptune ♆	Sagittarius ♐ Pisces ♓
First, or Root	Saturn ♄ Uranus ♅	Capricorn ♑ Aquarius ♒

Kundalini rises. How wonderful it will be to reach the fullness of this awakened healing! Upon arrival, the seventh chakra opens its Thousand-Petaled Lotus as a union with the Divine unfolds a crown above our heads. Here on Earth, you embody our Divine humanity.

Part 4

High Octane Healing Bliss ... No Caffeine Necessary!

Once you really know your own chakras and what's going on inside, you can begin enjoying the benefits of healing chakra work. You'll learn about how to increase your energy through stimulating chakra energy. Plus, you'll find out how to use mantra, chanting, and other sound techniques to resonate through and further awaken your chakras, and you'll even explore how your chakras relate to your sex life with some enlightening Tantric techniques. This part ends with a chapter on meditation, one of the best ways to get in daily touch with your own chakras to integrate their healing energy force into your life.

Energize: How Chakras Help You Feel Better

You can understand what chakras are, what they do, how they work, and what aspects of you are reflected in each one, but we know that what you really want to do is to be able to use their awakened energy for self-healing to make your life better. That's what this chapter is all about.

Energy on Tap

If you have read these chapters in order, you've already learned how energy moves through the meridians in your body, pooling and circulating in your seven primary chakras. This energy comes into your body with the breath, and the chakras transform that breath into life force energy known as *prana* that your mind and body can use.

As you read in Part 3, the way each chakra translates *prana* is unique.

- The first chakra, or Root chakra, turns energy into instinct, the will to survive, courage, a sense of security, and the ability to make yourself safe.

- The second chakra, or Sacral chakra, transforms energy into passion, creativity, and connection.

- The third chakra, or Solar Plexus chakra, turns energy into personal power and action.

- The fourth chakra, or Heart chakra, transforms energy into love, compassion, and the balance that brings harmony and peace to your relationships.

- The fifth chakra, or Throat chakra, makes energy into messages and channels creativity through your voice to the outside world.

- The sixth chakra, or Third Eye chakra, turns energy inward to access inner wisdom and intuition.

- Finally, the seventh chakra, or Crown chakra, sends energy out into the Universe, so you can find your place in the scheme of things and experience bliss.

When you have to deal with real-life challenges each day, the different ways your chakras transform *prana* can be immensely helpful because you have access to that life force energy. You can use this energy even more effectively when you customize chakra healing you need for the task at hand. You wouldn't put jet fuel into your car, eat gasoline for lunch, or heat your home with a sandwich. You also wouldn't plumb the depths of your first chakra to hone your intuition or tap into your seventh chakra for better digestion.

But using chakra energy isn't exclusive to a single chakra either. Many issues can best be served by tapping into the energy from more than one chakra, boosting the healing awakened in each in a way that makes the energy flow from several chakras that are greater than the sum of their parts.

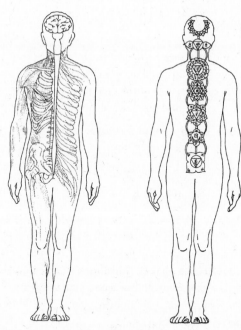

Your chakras are energy centers of concentrated life force energy (prana) that correspond to nerve centers in your body.

Feel-Good Power

Working with your chakras makes you feel good for a variety of reasons. First and most obvious, chakra work helps to open blocked chakras and ease the pressure on overloaded chakras, so awakened healing life force energy flows unimpeded through your body. When every part of you gets its fair share of *prana*, you feel better than you do when part of you and part of your life get too much or too little energy.

Chakra work also feels good because it requires you to pay attention to *you*. It's easy to put yourself at the bottom of your priority list, especially when you have to take care of other people and multiple responsibilities in your life. The more you increase your internal energy supplies, the more effectively you can provide care for the people who depend on you.

Chakra work literally feels good, too. When you have a physical problem, such as insomnia, chronic pain, anxiety, or fear, accessing energy from the right chakras can resolve the problem. Also, this energy can support and facilitate your other healing efforts to work on your issues. Here are some ways to awaken chakra energy to make your life work better.

Getting Your Zzzs

Americans, along with people all over our modern world, are chronically sleep-deprived. The World Health Organization and the National Sleep Foundation in Washington, D.C., both stipulate an average of eight hours of sleep a night for adults. Yet, according to sleep expert Matthew Walker, PhD, in his groundbreaking bestseller, *Why We Sleep: Unlocking the Power of Sleep and Dreams:* "Two-thirds of adults throughout all developed nations fail to obtain the recommended eight hours of nightly sleep." Because this is an average, it means that a lot of people all over the world get even less sleep. Plus, it is now known that sleep lost is gone forever; the harmful effects of missing sleep cannot be "made up" or "balanced out" by oversleeping. There is no catching up on missed sleep.

Too little sleep isn't always just a matter of having too much to do or binging your favorite show too late at night. People with *insomnia,* a sleep disorder, can't fall asleep or stay asleep, even when they try. Not only is this inability to fall asleep a miserable experience, but it also has been linked to physical illness, chronic pain, depression, and anxiety, among other issues. Insomnia is almost always caused by stress and tension in a person's life that prevents them from falling asleep. However, insomnia can also be caused by a sleep disorder such as sleep apnea. Thus, discussing your sleep problems with a physician is important, so you can determine the cause of the difficulty getting those ZZZs.

Because insomnia can cause so many problems, from daytime sleepiness and lack of focus to anxiety, depression, and irritability, solving a sleeplessness problem can make a big difference in your life.

Sleep is a survival act. Our bodies require sleep for physical healing, emotional balance, and mental decluttering. That means the energy for sleeping comes primarily out of the first chakra, or Root chakra, the place that reflects your survival instinct. Fear and a deeply rooted sense of insecurity can also be reflected in the first chakra, and if these issues contribute to sleeplessness, then the healthy life force energy of the first chakra can help to resolve this barrier to a good night's sleep.

Other chakras also are related to insomnia because insomnia occurs when the mind can't stop chattering. Thinking is the realm of the sixth chakra, or Third Eye chakra, and anxiety happens here. The Third Eye chakra also energizes and influences our dreams, helping us process mental activity. With insomnia, there is typically too much energy in the Third Eye chakra and a lack of energy, or grounding, in the Root chakra.

To receive the best, most regenerative sleep possible, get your energy moving down from your Third eye chakra into your Root chakra to decrease some of the anxious energy in your mind.

Try this whenever you are having trouble getting to sleep. As with other exercises, you can record your own voice or someone else's reading these cues, or you can just read them over a few times, so you can guide yourself silently.

1. Lie down on your bed or any other place where you would like to fall asleep. Lie on your back and move your shoulder blades underneath you as if they are cradling your heart. Let your arms rest at your sides, palms facing up, leaving about a foot of space between your hands and the sides of your body. Stretch your legs out, then relax them and let them fall open.

2. Breathe softly, feeling your breath flow in and out, letting it flow naturally without any conscious effort to manipulate it..

3. Bring your awareness to your feet. Notice everything about your feet. Are they warm or cold? Can you feel socks on your feet, or are you barefoot and experiencing the weight of your sheet and blankets on your feet? Begin to experience your feet becoming heavy and warm, so heavy that your feet feel as if they are sinking into the surface upon which you rest.

4. Now visualize a warm red glow at the base of your spine. The light is comforting and makes you feel at home. It turns slowly, anchoring your body to the ground, and you experience its red glow descending down each leg into both of your feet, warming them. Imagine this light is protecting you, keeping you safe, and shielding you from any danger or insecurity.

5. When you feel secure in this red glow, move your attention to your forehead. Imagine a deep indigo glow like an evening sky filled with sparkling stars, slowly rotating like a galaxy over your forehead. Visualize all your scattered thoughts running around inside your head. Imagine the indigo light gently surrounding the scattered thoughts. All the chattering energy in your mind is quieted by this indigo light, and the excess energy here is transported down to your feet. Now imagine the indigo light forming a shield that extends beyond your body and beyond the red shield so that your entire body is encased in a two-layered cradle of red warmth and dark starry sky.

6. Now, imagine you are being gently rocked to the rhythm of the planet's spinning. Your Root chakra still anchors you to Earth and provides safety, while your Third Eye chakra keeps thoughts far away from you, launching you safely into a sweet, quiet sleep filled with regenerating energy and gentle, nurturing dreams.

7. Stay relaxed. Let yourself rest in this quiet place for as long as you need to be there. If you feel compelled to turn onto your side or stomach, that's okay, but if the new position starts to make you restless, return to your back. If you fall asleep, then congratulations! Your chakra energy provided your body with what it needed. If you didn't fall asleep, that's okay, too. This kind of deep relaxation is almost as regenerative as actual sleep.

Easing the Pain

Pain is also a first chakra, or Root chakra issue because our bodies launch into survival mode when we feel pain. However, the fourth chakra, or Heart chakra, is the compassionate chakra. Combining survival energy with compassionate energy can banish (or at least help ease) pain, no matter what the cause.

If you suffer from chronic pain, carefully read the chapters on chakras one and four, and work on the exercises provided in those chapters to energize, align, and balance those chakras. Accessing your inner resources for survival and compassion can make a big difference if you work regularly on healing these chakras.

Sometimes, though, you might be suffering from a flare-up or temporary, acute pain from an injury. Or maybe you have an emotional wound. Both physical and emotional pain can benefit from this quick healing exercise, so try it whenever pain is distracting you from what you are doing. It will only take two minutes and could make a difference in how you feel.

You might find this exercise even more effective than you could have hoped.

1. Sit, stand, or lie down in a comfortable position that does not aggravate your pain. Relax as much as you can. Close your eyes.

2. Take a slow, deep breath through your nose, taking about 10 seconds to fill up your lungs. Pause for five seconds and imagine the energy from your held breath lighting your Root chakra like a struck match flaring into flame.

3. Exhale slowly through your mouth, taking about 10 seconds to empty your lungs. As you exhale, imagine the spark spreading into a warm, red glow all around your Root chakra that is getting warmer and brighter, as if fueled by a bellows filled up with the air of your exhaling breath.

4. Keep that idea of warmth at the base of your spine, and then inhale again for 10 seconds. Pause for five seconds and imagine that held breath igniting your Heart chakra like a struck match.

5. Exhale slowly, taking about 10 seconds to empty your lungs. As you exhale, imagine the spark in your Heart chakra spreading into a bright green flame that surrounds your heart.

6. Slowly inhale one more time for a count of 10 seconds and imagine the warm, red glow rising up and the warm green glow descending down until they meet in the light of the yellow jewel set right in the middle of your Solar Plexus chakra. Hold your breath for five seconds and imagine the energy from your Root and Heart chakras combining and strengthening in the power of the Solar Plexus chakra.

7. Slowly exhale one more time for a 10-second count, and imagine that healing power you've generated pouring into the part of your body that hurts. Allow each exhale to be a release of pain and discomfort. Feel the warmth as your body begins to heal itself and the pain floats far, far away. Visualize that energy knitting the broken pieces back together and putting everything back in alignment. Move your body in any way that it feels like it wants to move, such as shifting positions, sitting up straighter, or standing up. Your own healing energy might be making beneficial adjustments to your physical body.

8. Breathe normally for a few more breaths and continue to feel healing energy processing and eliminating your pain. When you are ready, open your eyes. You will feel more relaxed and alert. Experience the awakened healing strength of your *prana* life force energy moving through your chakras and surrounding you with safety and compassion.

If you have a medical problem or suffer from severe or persistent unresolved pain but aren't sure why, please consult your doctor for a referral to a pain medicine clinic, in addition to practicing chakra healing exercises. Clinicians trained in pain management techniques can work with you to awaken healing and restore comfort and health. Any use of pain medications must always be managed under the supervision of your doctor.

Calming Down

Sometimes, stress gets the best of all of us and we find ourselves freaking out. Whether you are having a full-blown anxiety attack or you are just pacing back and forth and incapacitated by worry or excessive negative energy, your chakras can help process and eliminate some of that overload so you can feel calmer faster.

Anxiety often comes from your first chakra, or Root chakra, if you feel scared or unsafe. However, it can also come from your second chakra, or Sacral chakra, which reflects your emotional state. Lastly, anxiety can come from your third chakra, or Solar Plexus chakra, when you take on too much and suddenly feel overwhelmed, like you just don't have the inner resources or personal power to deal with everything.

In other words, anxiety is a chakra "one-two-three" problem. Even if you aren't sure why you are feeling anxious or can't calm down, try this healing exercise, for a security, emotional, or power boost that will help you let go of the anxiety and relax.

Don't panic! Use this exercise whenever you feel super stressed, overwhelmed, anxious, or panicky. Be sure to do the exercise in a quiet place where you won't be disturbed for at least five minutes by family members, friends, pets, your computer, or the sound of a ringtone from your phone telling you that you have a new text.

1. Sit on the floor on the edge of a folded blanket. Sit straight, as if you were rising from the crown of your head. Pull your entire torso up, as if making space between each vertebra in your spine. Feel a lift in your chest and at the crown of your head, but keep your tailbone tucked in and down.

2. Visualize your first three chakras: the red Root chakra at the base of your spine, the orange Sacral chakra at your navel, and the yellow jewel Solar Plexus chakra just below your breastbone. Imagine each of them, glowing in their separate bright, clear colors.

3. Now, imagine each chakra getting bigger and radiating so that its circle merges with the others. Red becomes orange, orange becomes yellow, yellow becomes orange, and orange becomes red. This continues until each individual chakra dissolves into one bright glowing super chakra that encompasses your entire lower body.

4. Visualize this super chakra turning faster until it begins to generate suction like a funnel. See each individual worry, anxious thought, and panicky feeling getting sucked into this funnel and taken out beyond the perimeter of your physical body. As it continues to spin and suck out anxious feelings like a vacuum, imagine this super chakra getting larger and stronger and radiating and forming a secure shield around your body that keeps those extracted feelings out.

5. Now, imagine this super chakra expanding and encompassing all your other chakras—Heart, Throat, Third Eye, and Crown—reaching beyond the boundaries of your physical body until it encloses you in a safe, secure, warm, and private space. The super chakra expands by pushing individual thoughts even farther back so you can still see them, but they do not activate your mind into a worried state. You stand in the middle of this super chakra, calm, clear, and quiet, with an objective view of your external situation. Let ideas come to you, but not worries or scenarios about the future, which aren't allowed into this sacred space.

6. Continue to exist grounded in this expanded space created by your three lower chakras—Root, Sacral, and Solar Plexus—until you feel steady and calm. During this time, you might suddenly know what to do to improve your situation. Or you will feel clear enough to move ahead without worry because your lower chakras have helped you bring things back down to Earth.

7. Repeat whenever anxiety builds up again.

Courage comes from your Root and Solar Plexus chakras, where you project your feelings of security and personal power. Your chakra power can ground you and light the way, so you can accomplish almost anything without fear stopping you.

When you feel fearful or nervous or are trying to get yourself to do something brave (such as getting up in front of an audience to speak, playing your guitar at a party, or confronting someone with a difficult truth), try this easy exercise. You can do this wherever you are and whatever you are doing:

1. Visualize your deep, red, and strong Root chakra anchoring you to the rich soil like a massive network of thick heavy unassailable tree roots reaching straight down into the Earth.

2. At the same time, picture your third chakra, the Solar Plexus chakra, radiating like a brilliant jewel casting rays of sunlight from just below your breastbone, blinding everyone with power, strength, and the light of truth.

Master of Concentration

Everybody has trouble concentrating once in a while, but concentration is crucial sometimes. When that happens, tap into the energy in your Throat and Third Eye chakras, which are the centers for communication, creativity, thought, and understanding.

The combined power of the fifth and sixth chakras can bring clarity and focus to anything you do, not to mention a creative spark that can carry your work, play, or interaction with others to new levels of brilliance.

To amp up your focus, you just need a warm-up, like stretching before a workout at the gym. *Dharana* is one of the Eight Limbs of Yoga, and it means concentration. Try this mini *dharana* exercise, and then turn your newfound focus to the task at hand. You'll be amazed at how well this works.

1. Sit quietly anywhere. A seat at your desk is just as good as a seat on a yoga mat. Sit up straight so you are not leaning back against anything. Relax your shoulders.

2. Look around and find some small thing to look at. This can be anything small, like the eraser on a pencil, a flower petal, a font chosen for a word typeset in a book, or an earbud for your phone. Center your attention on this visual point of focus.

3. Imagine a deep indigo beam radiating from your Third Eye chakra and hitting this object. At the same time, imagine a bright blue beam radiating from your Throat chakra and hitting this object. Let indigo blue light surround the object and imagine sending energy through these beams to the object. Imagine the energy circulating back, as if the object is beaming the energy or reflecting it back to you.

4. Stay focused on this object for just one or two minutes. Now, get to work!

Weight Loss Made Easy

Okay, disclaimer: weight loss isn't easy. However, chakra power can make it easier than it would be without it. That's because *agni*, the digestive fire, resides inside your third chakra, or Solar Plexus chakra. This is the seat of digestion and metabolism. When *agni* is stoked, you burn your food and fuel rather than storing it as fat.

However, becoming overweight also tends to be a function of the second chakra, or Sacral chakra. Many people overeat because of emotional reasons rather than pure physical hunger. Using food to pacify or smother strong feelings is pretty common, especially among people who are overweight. Process emotions in a healthy way by opening the second chakra, and you won't need to try to smother them.

If you need to lose weight, spend time reading the chapters on the second and third chakras, and do all the exercises for activating, aligning, and balancing these chakras. Losing weight takes a while and works only if you change the habits and ways of thinking that caused you to gain weight in the first place. Temporary diets usually result in regaining the weight and then gaining more after the diet ends.

We could write a whole book on using the chakras for weight loss (and maybe we will someday), but for now, we'll tell you that if you make it a habit to do a once-daily chakra balance of the passionate Sacral chakra and the powerful Solar Plexus chakra, you will stoke your digestive fire, feel more personally empowered, and find yourself better able to manage strong feelings, so you don't keep turning to food when you aren't really hungry. When you do eat, this exercise will also help you burn that fuel faster. You might feel warmer after doing this exercise, but that's a good thing. Your metabolism and your motivation are stoked.

This exercise is based on a yoga *pranayama* practice called *bhastrika*, often called Bellows Breath, a yoga *pranayama* exercise involving quick exhalations to stoke the body's inner fire. Practice Bellows Breath once a day before your first meal or before your largest meal. Don't go too fast before you get used to doing this kind of breath work, or you could hyperventilate. Don't do this exercise before bed, or you might have trouble sleeping. With regular practice, you will increase your metabolism and build your abdominal strength.

1. Sit comfortably on the floor on the edge of a folded blanket. Cross your legs. Rest your hands on your knees.

2. Envision your second chakra, or Sacral chakra, as a bright clear orange light behind your navel, and your third chakra, or Solar Plexus chakra, as a bright clear yellow jewel shining just under your rib cage. Imagine both lights growing brighter.

3. Now, imagine a tiny flame right between your second and third chakras. This flame is small but bright and active, with tongues of orange and yellow.

4. Pretend you are going to blow on this flame to make it brighter and stronger. At the count of one second per inhalation and one second per exhalation, begin breathing in rhythm through your nose—in and out, in and out.

5. Slowly increase the force and sound of your exhalation so that you inhale silently but exhale sharply with a *HHM* or *HA* sound while tightening your abdominal muscles to help force out the air. (You might need a tissue!) Keep your jaw relaxed and your mouth softly closed.

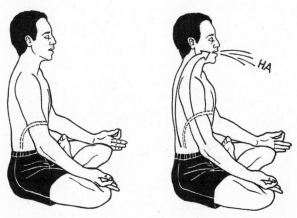

Exhale sharply from the abdomen when practicing Bellows Breath.

6. Repeat this inhale-exhale 10 to 20 times. Every time you exhale, imagine the inner flame getting brighter, larger, and hotter.

7. Repeat once each day, adding a few more breaths each day until you work up to 100. Don't go too quickly, though. It should take you at least one month to reach 100 of these breaths.

8. Enjoy increased metabolism, more inner fire, more confidence and strength, and slow, gradual, and healthy weight loss.

Increase your inner fire even more effectively by spicing your foods with warming spices like ginger, cinnamon, cumin, turmeric, red pepper, and black pepper. Before bed, relax with a cup of warm milk (soy milk or almond milk works, too) with a dash each of ginger, cinnamon, and turmeric, or enjoy ginger or cinnamon tea.

Over time, as you gain strength, Bellows Breath can warm to activate the elements through the lower chakras to the Heart chakra. Coiled *Kundalini* energy is summoned from the Earth-grounded seat of the Root chakra. The serpent energy rises to stir the desires of the Watery Sacral chakra. The powerful bellows of the Solar Plexus chakra stokes the Fire of the breath.

The lungs fill and release *prana* in the balanced exchange of Air that activates *Kundalini* compassion in the Heart chakra. The physical being is now primed and ready to nourish itself through awakening the spiritual bliss of the upper chakras—the healing food of the soul.

Chapter
15

Toning: Singing the Body Chakra

You are energy. You vibrate with *prana*, and it flows through you. Without it, you would not be alive. *Prana* life force energy is the spark that illuminates and animates you, and one of the main ways we feel that energy is by feeling its vibration.

Our chakras spin as *prana* energy moves through and around them, transforming the energy in different ways according to which chakra pulls in that energy and then moves it back out through the body. Chakras change with each passing moment and each new experience, but sometimes they get stuck. They close down to protect themselves, or they get so flooded with energy that they suck all the *prana* from the chakras above and below, throwing the body's functioning out of whack. When this happens, the body's vibrations get out of tune, but you can use your chakras to correct that imbalance. That's what this chapter is all about.

Good Vibrations

Sound is an incredibly powerful tool for tuning up the chakras. This is called *toning* (rather than tuning). This sound can come from a tuning fork or instrument, but it can also come from your own voice. Toning is a technique for balancing, energizing, and strengthening the chakras that uses sound, particularly the sound of your own voice. Toning techniques may employ vowel sounds, sacred syllables associated with each chakra, or improvisational vocalizations.

If you've ever sung in a chorus or even with just one other person, you might know what it is like to be unsure of a note until you hear it. When someone else sings it, your voice slides right into tune alongside the other voice. The vibration of that other voice has coaxed your vibration along with it until the two voices merge. Numerous studies show that singing in a chorus enhances well-being and can contribute to spiritual health and transcendent experiences for the singers. It is known that as their voices harmonize the heartbeats of choral singers synchronize as one heartbeat, and their pulse rates rise and fall together as they sing in unison. Joining a community chorus is a great way to begin voice work with the chakras, encouraging the vibration of *prana* in the body.

Creating the vibration of a chakra with your voice can nudge an out-of-tune chakra back into its natural vibration. This sympathetic vibration is an excellent way to bring the chakras back into tune and help life force energy to flow more freely through them. This, in turn, leads to healing, as each chakra vibrates according to its own nature.

You can start chakra toning right now if you want to, but first, let's talk about making sound and what that means to you. We've read a lot of things about toning and chanting, and we've tried a lot of those things for ourselves to see what works and what doesn't. Each chakra has a sacred syllable, a vowel sound that activates it, and certain sounds that resonate within it. However, what those syllables, vowels, and sounds are varies depending on who you ask.

As far as *you* are concerned, we strongly suggest that you find the sounds that resonate with you. When you make any sound with your voice, you can direct that sound to any part of your body, and it can resonate there, so choose the sounds that feel most natural and right.

For example, is the vowel associated with the Root chakra the sound of *uh*, as in "cup," or *oh*, as in "soap"? Different sources tell you different things, so try them both and see which one resonates most within your first chakra. If you can't tell, then choose the one you like best. It doesn't matter why you like it; just pick the sound that makes you feel good. Your intention and how you decide to use the sounds are arguably more important than what sounds you use.

Much of this chapter involves making sounds that are intuitive. What if you just started making sounds? What if you decided to join a local choral group and tone through singing? Would you be wrong? No. What comes out of your body is what your body produces, and that is what is right for your body.

However, you can learn to tone in a way that increases vibration more efficiently, so before we get into the different sounds associated with each chakra, let's practice a little.

You remember learning the vowels in school, right? A, E, I, O, U, and sometimes Y? Let's start there. Don't worry about what these sounds do right now. Just practice making sounds.

Some people vocalize with ease, while for others, vocalizing doesn't come easily at all. In the latter case, the problem is likely in the fifth chakra, or Throat chakra. The fifth chakra is the center of communication, speaking, listening, music, and sound. This is where you make noise. You groan, giggle, sigh, and sing from your fifth chakra. If this chakra is blocked, you may feel very uncomfortable vocalizing, especially randomly without specific directions. If this sounds like you, skip back to Chapter 11 on the Throat chakra and try the exercises for energizing, aligning, and balancing this important source of sound in your body. Then come back to this chapter and try again. You might need to spend some time finding your own voice, but almost everybody can learn to vocalize, so give yourself a chance to develop your innate vocal talents.

If you have some kind of vocal impairment that makes using your voice difficult, seek the help of a licensed speech pathologist and/or vocal therapist. The act of vocalization is important to developing the vibration of *prana* throughout your body's chakras. Vocal quality does not matter, so shed your vocal inhibitions and engage in the process. Whatever sound issues forth is a joyful noise unto the Heavens.

Make Noise

Are you ready to make some noise?

If you feel self-conscious, you might want to try this when you are home alone or in a room where nobody can hear you. Don't feel silly. Making sound is one of your own body's most joyful acts and powerful healing tools.

1. First, sit on the floor or on a chair with your spine straight. You need plenty of space inside your torso for the sound to resonate, so don't slump against a backrest. If it's more comfortable, you can also stand. If you do find yourself slumping (or even if you don't), this exercise can help.

2. Exhale as you tuck your chin and curl your chest forward. On the inhalation, roll up slowly stacking each vertebra one upon the other as your back straightens. Feel your lungs fill with air. Lift up your heart and bring your head to float balanced upon your aligned neck and spine. Now your breathing apparatus—your voice box and vocal cords, your lungs and diaphragm muscles—is in the proper orientation to maximize your voice. Use this exercise anytime you need to center yourself before speaking or singing. Okay, you are ready to vocalize.

3. Now, say the letter A, as in "say." Just say it once. Hear your voice. Notice the pitch. Say it again and hold it longer. Try to feel it vibrating inside your body. You will feel it in your throat, but where else do you feel it? Does the vibration want to settle somewhere?

4. Try saying the letter at a lower pitch, or a higher pitch. Move it around. Don't worry if it doesn't sound diva-worthy. You aren't trying out for the Metropolitan Opera. Just make the sound. Get used to the feel of your own voice making that sound: *AAAAAAAYYYYYY*. Notice what the vibration of that sound does inside your body.

5. As you practice, notice how you can make the sound in a pinched, tight way that doesn't vibrate very much or in a deep, resonant way that vibrates more. The more resonant the sound is, the better. The more you practice, the more you will get the hang of making a deep, vibrating sound. Don't be intimidated or shy. Try to just let it loose. Open up and relax your throat. Put more breath behind the sound. Try it louder or softer. Be silly. Make wavy sounds or zig-zag sounds. Just make sounds. Most importantly, feel which sounds seem most right, true, and resonant within *you*.

Fun with Vowels

After you've moved your AY sound around and tried it in lots of different ways, go to the next vowel: E. Try that sound: *EEEEEE*. Experiment with different pitches, volume, and vibrations. Notice where you feel this sound in your body. Is it different than when you said *AAAYYY*?

After you've played around with EE for a while, move on to the rest of the vowels: I (*EYE*), O (*OH*), and U (*YOU*).

Keep practicing, and if you feel compelled to make other noises—whether vowels or consonants or suddenly breaking into that song you hear everywhere on social media—go ahead! The point is to set your voice free.

The other point is to determine what sounds make sense to your body and your chakras. Because your chakras are unique to you and your voice and vibrations are unique to you, too, different sounds will work better for you than others.

However, you have to tune in to your voice and the way your body feels to determine this, so if you still feel unsure about the sounds that resonate with you, don't let it hold you back. Keep practicing and using your intuition and your feelings, and your toning skills will quickly improve.

Speaking Chakra

Traditionally, each of the seven primary chakras has a seed sound associated with it. Sometimes, you will see this sound written as (to use the first chakra as an example) *LAM*. In other places, you will see it written as *LANG*, which is the Tibetan version. Because your chakras, voice, and vibrations are unique to you, you might prefer one or the other. It's up to you.

Now that you have warmed up, you can start experimenting with these seed sounds for each chakra. We've listed all the seed sounds in the following chart for easy reference. All sounds rhyme with "mom" or "song," except *OM*, which rhymes more closely with "home," and the seventh chakra, or Crown chakra, which has no rhyme.

Chakra	Seed Sound	Rhymes with
First chakra, or Root chakra	LAM LANG	Mom or Song
Second chakra, or Sacral chakra	VAM VANG	Mom or Song
Third chakra, or Solar Plexus chakra	RAM RANG	Mom or Song
Fourth chakra, or Heart chakra	YAM YANG	Mom or Song
Fifth chakra, or Throat chakra	HAM HANG	Mom or Song
Sixth chakra, or Third Eye chakra	OM (AUM) or ANG	Home or Song
Seventh chakra, or Crown chakra	NNG or no sound (listen)	Home or Song

To practice using these sounds, try this exercise. We use the first seed sound listed in the previous chart (such as *LAM* or *VAM*) instead of the second (such as *LANG* or *VANG*), but you can use either one:

1. Sit on the floor on the edge of a folded blanket. Sit up straight to make room inside your chest.

2. Bring your attention to your Root chakra. Visualize a red wheel turning slowly at the base of your spine. Take a deep breath, then say *LAM,* holding the vowel for as long as you can; leave enough breath to let the final consonant vibrate.

3. Inhale as you bring your attention to your Sacral chakra. Visualize an orange wheel turning slowly in your abdomen just behind your navel. Say *VAM,* holding the vowel for as long as you can; leave enough breath to let the final consonant vibrate.

4. Inhale as you bring your attention to your Solar Plexus chakra. Visualize a yellow wheel turning slowly just beneath your rib cage at your solar plexus. Say *RAM*, holding the vowel for as long as you can; leave enough breath to let the final consonant vibrate.

5. Inhale as you bring your attention to your Heart chakra. Visualize a green wheel turning slowly around your heart. Say *YAM*, holding the vowel for as long as you can; leave enough breath to let the final consonant vibrate.

6. Inhale as you bring your attention to your Throat chakra. Visualize a blue wheel turning slowly just above your collarbone in your throat. Say *HAM*, holding the vowel for as long as you can; leave enough breath to let the final consonant vibrate.

7. Inhale as you bring your attention to your Third Eye chakra. Visualize an indigo or purple wheel turning slowly in the middle of your forehead. Say *OM*, holding the vowel for as long as you can; leave enough breath to let the final consonant vibrate.

8. Inhale as you bring your attention to your Crown chakra. Visualize a purple or white wheel turning slowly just above the crown of your head. Say *NNG* (like the final two consonants in the word *sing*), holding the sound for as long as you can; leave enough breath to let the final consonant vibrate. Or you can just listen during this breath. The seed sound of this chakra is traditionally the Universe vibrating with the sound of *OM* with no sound coming from you at all.

The Sanskrit symbol for OM, the seed sound of the sixth chakra, or Third Eye chakra.

When vocalizing sounds or vowels for each chakra, the usual technique is to start with a low voice when focusing on the first chakra and gradually raise the pitch so that the vocalization for the seventh chakra is the highest pitch of all. This might not work well for you, but try it to see if it makes sense and resonates with your chakras.

The Power of the Vowel

Although any sound can resonate inside the body, vowels seem to have a particular vibration that easily energizes the chakras. In his book *Healing Sounds,* author Jonathan Goldman says one of the reasons he likes to use vowels for chakra healing is that they are not words in other languages that people might find unfamiliar or that might make people uncomfortable, especially if they practice a particular religion and don't want to chant words they feel are associated with a different religion. Motivation aside, vowels do resonate particularly well within the body and are an excellent way to tone the chakras.

However, as we mentioned in the beginning of this chapter, there are different systems that apply different vowel sounds to each chakra. In this book, we show you one of the more common systems, but if other vowels work better for activating your own chakras, you can certainly use those.

To tone your chakras with vowel sounds, practice the same way you practiced speaking the seed sounds in the previous section, but use these vowels as you focus on each chakra, one at a time.

As in the previous exercise, start by doing one vowel sound per breath for each chakra. Or concentrate on a single chakra that you think needs some work, and repeat that vowel sound over and over as you keep your attention focused on the appropriate chakra. When you do this, your vowel sound becomes a sort of mantra. Mantra is the Sanskrit word for a sacred syllable or phrase that is spoken repeatedly during meditation to aid in concentration and focus.

The following chart contains some of the sounds you can use. These are common vowel sounds associated with each chakra, and they're also the ones that resonate best with us.

Chakra	Vowel Sound	The Same Vowel Sound As
First chakra, or Root chakra	UH	Sun
Second chakra, or Sacral chakra	OO	Shoe
Third chakra, or Solar Plexus chakra	OH	Slow
Fourth chakra, or Heart chakra	AH	Saw
Fifth chakra, or Throat chakra	EYE	Sigh
Sixth chakra, or Third Eye chakra	AY	Say
Seventh chakra, or Crown chakra	EE	See

Chakra Singing (and Playing)

With regular practice, you will soon become familiar with speaking seed sounds and toning vowels to tone your chakras and get your *prana* energy flowing, but you can go even further. Try vocalizing according to your intuition. Make sounds—any sounds—that don't necessarily involve the formation of words.

Let your feelings flow from your voice and communicate themselves through vibration rather than a logical linguistic sense. Having a strong, balanced, and open Throat chakra helps, but even if you are having problems with your own personal communication skills, you can still try this. It might be enough to open that Throat chakra right up. Have fun with this. It doesn't have to be serious. Make sounds that fill you with joy.

Random vocalization can be difficult. You might be wondering what the heck you are supposed to be saying. Don't worry about that. We've heard beautiful solos by vocalists who just made sounds according to their intuition at the moment. That's what jazz scat singing is. But you don't have to sound like Ella Fitzgerald or Aretha Franklin. Just make sound. Start with an *AHH* or an *OHH* or an *OOH* or an *EEE*. See where it goes.

Vocalizing according to your intuition can free up your inner voice. Pay attention to what noise you want to make and honor it. Let yourself sing, and your chakras will respond. Nobody has to hear it but you.

Remember, too, that each chakra is also associated with a musical note. Eve loves to vocalize, and when she isn't writing books, she is sometimes singing with her father's jazz band. Occasionally, they play at a nearby casino, and Eve's dad likes to joke that all the slot machines are ringing in the key of C. Actually, musical notes are associated with each chakra, and it's ironic that the slot machines would play C because C is associated with the Root chakra, which is the chakra associated with financial security. Maybe that constant C sound influences people to believe that playing those slots will ensure wealth. If only it were so! Here's a reminder of the notes for each chakra.

- First chakra, or Root chakra   C
- Second chakra, or Sacral chakra   D
- Third chakra, or Solar Plexus chakra   E
- Fourth chakra, or Heart chakra   F
- Fifth chakra, or Throat chakra   G
- Sixth chakra, or Third Eye chakra   A
- Seventh chakra, or Crown chakra   B

Whether you join the harmony of a community chorus, belt out the sacred music at worship, or just sing in the shower, the creation of sound through the human body is a wonderful way to activate the resonant healing power of the chakras. You can also get a similar benefit if you play a musical instrument. Do you ever notice how the great musicians always seem to be at one with their instruments? How you can seem to read the musicians' emotions in their faces, hands, and bodies? Sound vibrates in instruments, and that vibration is transferred to the human body when the instrument is played. Musicians feel (literally) the music they make and experience this resonance through their chakras.

By extension, when audience members hear great singers or musicians, they are moved collectively—causing a shared experience of chakra activation that creates a shared benefit, a fellow feeling among them. There is a great body of scientific study into the effects of music upon listeners (whether listening to live or recorded music) and how those beneficial effects can help calm and restore, as well as boost productivity. Researchers have identified "power songs"—songs that are paced at 121 bpm that generate energy and jump-start metabolism through tempo. (You can search it online and find songs to try.)

Chanting and Mantra Meditation

One of the most common ways to use sound and vocalization as it relates to the chakras is through chanting and mantra meditation. We left this section for the end because we wanted to focus on more basic techniques first. Even if you don't like toning, you might enjoy meditating using mantras.

Mantra meditation is a form of meditation that involves chanting a mantra repeatedly as an anchor or focus for meditation. This keeps the mind centered on one point, and the vibration from the chanting can also alter the course of the meditation in interesting ways. To practice mantra meditation, you can use any of the seed sounds or vowel sounds in this chapter. Sit quietly and repeat the sounds either out loud for maximum vibration power or just in your mind; let these sounds anchor your awareness.

You can also chant when you aren't meditating. Many yoga classes begin with particular chants, like prayers, to set the right intention and mood. When people get together to chant, it is called *kirtan* in India. Musicians typically play and sing chants, and the people participating in the *kirtan* repeat the chants in a call-and-response format. Some people chant at home as part of a daily ritual.

So, make some sound, whether you are meditating, chanting, working with a particular chakra, or you are just celebrating a beautiful day. Make some sound, whether you are a natural born singer with perfect pitch or someone who can't really carry a note. Let your body vibrate with sound from its very core. You have a sacred instrument within you that has the power to tune up your chakras and get your *prana* life force energy flowing again. Discover how to use that instrument that is uniquely your own to have healthier chakras and a more joyful life. Bring your chakras to life through your one true voice.

Chapter
16

Tantra: Chakras and Love

Now for the fun part. Not that the rest of it hasn't been fun, but now we're talking *fun*. In other words, we're talking sex.

Sex is about pleasure, fulfillment, and most importantly, about connection. Because these are all aspects directly reflected in the chakras, working with the chakras can enhance and intensify your sexual health and experience of sex. Chakras are the ultimate relationship aid!

When you look to the chakras to improve your sexual experience, you will quickly understand that this approach takes sex beyond the physical. The idea that sex is a spiritual act is nothing new. Sex as a metaphor for union with the Divine Universal Spirit is ancient and a part of many different traditions. Hinduism explores this metaphor, as do Taoism in China, many of the ancient pagan religions from Europe, and even Christianity, where nuns marry God. In all these traditions, however, sexual energy is transformed into spiritual energy, rather than being "wasted" on plain old physical kicks.

But maybe you didn't sign up for some esoteric spiritual experience. You just want to get healthy, feel good, and have better sex. No problem. We can help you with that. However, to do so, you need a brief lesson in Tantra.

The Truth About Tantra

Tantra is a branch of the yoga tradition often associated with sexual practices, but this is a misunderstanding of this esoteric form of yoga. According to Tantra, our sensory experience and the physical Universe itself is a manifestation of Divine energy, and so it should be celebrated, rather than transcended. Talking about sex in a book about chakras pretty much demands discussing Tantra, even though understanding Tantric philosophy can be the work of an entire lifetime. But we promise to keep things simple.

Tantra is a school of yogic thought that arose as a backlash against the traditional philosophy that the material world, including the human body, is illusory and distracting, a source of suffering, and that it must be transcended to experience enlightenment. Tantra says no! According to Tantric thought, the world is beautiful, the body is beautiful, and physical pleasure is beautiful, too. The physical Universe, including the body, is a manifestation of Divine perfection, so enjoying and celebrating these things is just like worship. Isn't that nice?

Tantra is nice, but it also has a naughty reputation. People automatically associate Tantra with sex and esoteric sexual rituals. Sexual rituals are a part of Tantra—it's true. However, they are just one part—a very advanced part—and definitely not the *point* of Tantra.

Despite what you might have heard, the *Kama Sutra* has nothing to do with Tantra and never mentions the chakras. The *Kama Sutra* is a practical treatise on sexual techniques and the art of love, penned by a Hindu scholar named Vatsyayana in about the fourth century and translated for English audiences in the 1800s by an Englishman named Sir Richard Burton. It is meant to guide, instruct, and counsel a sexual society on everything from handling multiple wives to kissing to the best ways to stimulate the clitoris. You can certainly use some of the techniques in the *Kama Sutra* as you seek to have a deeper sexual relationship, but don't mistake the *Kama Sutra* for a Tantric text.

Tantra is Yin/Yang Union

Tantra means "weaving together," and the Tantric philosophy says fulfillment comes through the weaving together of the yin and yang of opposites: Earth and Heaven; night and day; Moon ☽ and Sun ☉; and of course, female and male.

The Tantric philosophy of the Universe is that (to simplify) there are two Divine parents, not just one male god or female goddess. There is the Divine Feminine and the Divine Masculine. The Divine Feminine is of the Earth, and she is unruly, dark, wild, full of movement, yielding, and even a little dangerous. The Divine Masculine is steady and quick, bright, solid, serene, and infused with Spirit. Each is amazing, fantastic, and fascinating, but neither is whole without the other. Wild shifting ground and Earth nature in motion is steadied by bright serene Spirit, and bright serene Spirit is enlivened and animated by wild Earth nature in motion. Doesn't that sound sexy?

Tantric philosophy also involves *Kundalini*. We go into more detail about *Kundalini* in Chapter 5, and if you've read that chapter already, you probably remember that *Kundalini* is latent, powerful, wild, unruly, and feminine energy that waits inside the first chakra to be awakened. When *Kundalini* awakens, she seeks her mate, the serene spiritual male energy. She moves up through the seven chakras as each is ready to receive her and pierces them as she rises from the Root chakra to the Crown chakra. Once there, she can finally unite in Divine union with her male counterpart who is frequently represented in Hindu literature as the god Shiva.

We think that's pretty sexy, too, and in Tantra, that's just what sex is—a sort of acting out of this Divine partnership where male and female join in ecstatic union that is both intensely pleasurable and significantly spiritual—the best of both worlds.

If you have a same-sex partner, of course you can still experience Tantric sex. Each human being has a mixture of feminine and masculine qualities that seek each other. When you and your partner become immersed in the passionate energy of sexual union, all those energies will find each other, and the merging will be just as sacred and profound in Divine union. The sexual orientation or gender identity of the intimate partners doesn't matter one bit.

The consensual intimate unions of adult sexual partners are sacred—no matter the race, ethnicity, gender orientation, or gender identity of the partners. The striving for balance and harmony through sexual intimacy with a beloved is a hallmark of what it means to be human. We search for that perfect expression of wholeness and Divine union in the body of our loved ones.

What Tantra Isn't

Knowing what you now know about Tantra, it is probably pretty clear that some of the ideas people have about Tantra aren't true. Tantra is not about new complicated sexual positions, role playing, or having multiple sex partners.

Tantra is not just sex, sex, sex either. Most Tantric rituals don't even involve sex. They are about connection, weaving together opposites, and union in all its many forms. Yes, Tantra can increase your physical and sexual energy, but it also channels that energy in a way that increases pleasure, joy, balance, and bonding.

Tantra isn't actually a religion, either. It is a philosophy. If you sign up for a Tantra yoga class, we can guarantee you that you won't be rolling around having sex with the person on the mat next to yours. Tantra is about opening up your mind and body to experience the Divine energy of the Universe to comprehend the truth that we are all part of one great harmonic energy body. There are many ways to do that. Sex is just one of them.

Tantra for One

Is Tantra restricted to sexual unions between partners? Or, can Tantric Divine union be achieved solo? The self-knowledge and acceptance that comes with true self-love can only deepen the bond of union when experiencing love with an intimate partner. Sending loving messages to your body while exploring solo Tantra is a wonderful way to learn how to love your body.

Touch your body to help you get to know how you respond and how emotion and sensation arise within you. Focus, too, on your breath; be aware of breath entering and leaving your body. Breathe into your Sacral chakra to feel the intensity of passion gathering there. Breathe into your Heart chakra to feel the sensation of balance and wholeness rise there. Vocalize the seed sounds into each chakra as you touch its place within your body. Use long steady even breaths and continue to breathe through climax. Solo Tantra can give you a newfound sense of personal wholeness and wellbeing that will make you feel better and that will only be welcomed by an intimate sex partner should you choose one.

The Heart Chakra: Your Sexual Command Center

You might recall from Chapter 8 that the passionate second chakra, or Sacral chakra, is the chakra that reflects our sexual desires, pleasures, and longings. That's true, and we'll get to the second chakra in the next section. However, when it comes to sex and the chakras (doesn't that sound like some new HBO series?), the fourth chakra, or Heart chakra, *really* is your sexual command center.

Remember how the Tantra of *Kundalini* serpent energy works? As Divine Feminine wild, earthy, and unruly *Kundalini* rises from the Root chakra toward the steady, bright, and Divine Masculine waiting for it at the Crown chakra, that steady, bright Divine Masculine can't help being drawn downward toward earthy grounding pleasure, and guess where they meet? All that energy collides and explodes right in the chakra resting exactly between the three Earthly (lower) chakras and the three Heavenly (upper) chakras. Remember, Tantra means weaving together and the union of opposites, and where else to merge those opposites than on neutral ground? The Heart chakra, with its Venus ♀ natural planetary ruler of both Taurus ♉ yin and Libra ♎ yang, celestial balance is that neutral ground (see Chapter 10).

When we talked about *Kundalini* before, you might remember that we talked in Part 3 about how it rises through all seven chakras to find fulfillment at the Crown chakra. That's true, but there's also a lot more going on energetically. *Kundalini* does seek to rise all the way up through each chakra, but Divine Heavenly energy is always seeking the Earth, too, so the person with seven open and balanced chakras experiences all kinds of back and forth and up and down energy.

Although not all sources agree on this, we subscribe to the notion that *Kundalini* can rise, then fall, and then rise again, just as Divine energy can radiate all the way down from the Crown to the Root chakra, and then flow back up. Our bodies—and indeed our chakras—are vessels for our own constantly fluctuating and circulating energies that are both masculine and feminine, Earth and Spirit. However, the real combustion happens in the Heart chakra during sexual union.

That means if you have a blocked Heart chakra, you might experience isolation during sexual intercourse, rather than union. You might also experience personal pleasure but feel nothing for the person helping to provide this pleasure.

During sex, your body does everything it can to orgasm so that chemicals can be released that promote bonding. However, a blocked Heart chakra can reroute those pleasurable feelings so you begin to associate them not with the other person but only with yourself. When sexual pleasure becomes purely self-centered, sexual addiction through casual hookups can be the result—a constant search for the pleasure, rush, and "high" of sex without any feelings linked to the sexual partner and even a profound sense of emptiness in the self after. Sex becomes like a drug of choice, and the Divine essence of the partners coming to the union seems to be the last consideration. An overloaded Heart chakra might seek sex through blind need and cling too hard, negating themselves and elevating their partner to a status of power through obsession—there's little possibility of balance in such an exchange or partnership.

Seeking sex for pure personal pleasure is a hard problem to address because there is typically little motivation to change this behavior when the sex seeker sees few negative consequences and ample opportunity. However, that is only because the person with the blocked Heart chakra has not experienced the much more intense, pleasurable, and complete experience of sexual pleasure that is based in total spiritual union with a beloved intimate partner rather than the shallow physical pleasure of the hookup.

Sex and the Passionate Sacral Chakra

But let's not forget the second chakra, or Sacral chakra, where all that passion and pleasure begins. Masculine and feminine energy may meet at the Heart chakra, but the physical, earthy, sensual-pleasure part of sex comes from the second chakra.

If the second chakra is blocked, it becomes difficult to experience physical pleasure during sex, and this physical pleasure—and all its associated chemical signals in the body—is an intrinsic part of the sexual experience. The second chakra also reflects the body's fertility and creativity, which sexual energy can illuminate. A closed second chakra blocks off all those other wonderful, rich aspects of sexual union.

This can lead to periods of sexless relationship(s), where the partners often cannot articulate the problem in an otherwise loving union. Reconnecting to passion can immerse the partners in emotional vulnerability and physical sensitivity. Care must be taken. Vocalizations from the Sacral chakra (see Chapter 15) can help partners who are lost to find each other in the second chakra, *Svadhisthana,* which is "the dwelling place of the self" where they will meet in "the sweetness" of their sexual union.

Remember that in Tantra, physical pleasure is a manifestation of Divine ecstasy. It is not something to feel guilty about or to be suppressed. The intimate union of your bodies and spirits is something to celebrate, honor, and revel in, as you join totally with another human being. Without it, sex is just an exercise, like doing sit-ups. You must allow yourself to be present in the moment to acknowledge and welcome the Divine energy your partner brings to this moment. You are given permission to explore, to seek union in the other, to feel pleasure, and to bestow pleasure.

An overloaded Sacral chakra can get in the way of sexual pleasure, too. The second chakra is the source of feelings, emotions, and passions. If you get too needy, too clingy, or too desperate because of an overloaded Sacral chakra, the whole experience goes out of balance. This could lead to unbalanced personal power in the Solar Plexus chakra and to the ultimate out-of-balance nature of your relationships through the Heart chakra. An overload might also lead to engaging in sex purely out of selfish reasons. If you feel empty inside, you might believe merging sexually with another will fill your cup. It might fulfill you in the moment, but when the event is over, the emptiness returns. Ideally, sexual union is about the merging of equally potent energies, and if you can fill yourself up without needing someone else to do this task, sex can reach the next level of true connection and ecstasy.

Ideally, when the passionate Sacral chakra is open, balanced, and strong, the physical arousal and pleasure you will get from sexual union will be enough to make you weak in the knees. When your Heart chakra is open, balanced, and strong as well (surging with the power push of the Solar Plexus chakra), you'll have plenty of inner space for masculine and feminine energies to merge into one complete and realized whole as your body merges with another body that is experiencing the same thing. Two become one, and that one becomes sacred.

The Sacral chakra is located just above the genitals. An exercise to help open and energize the second chakra is to get very close to your partner and press your second chakras together—abdomen to abdomen. (You can be clothed or not.) Stay in this position for a full five minutes, looking at each other directly in the eyes (which also opens the Heart chakra). Don't speak or move. (Laughing a bit or giggling might be unavoidable.) This is an intense exercise and more difficult than it sounds, but it can really get the passion of the second chakra flowing.

One of Tantra's more talked-about techniques involves the notion that if orgasm can be suppressed intentionally, sexual energy will move back up toward the Crown chakra, rather than out of the body. The theory goes that sexual energy is so potent and powerful that releasing it through orgasm wastes it on mere physical pleasure. Instead, by becoming aroused and then directing the energy up through the *sushumna nadi* toward the Crown chakra, all that potent energy stays within the body and moves the consciousness closer to enlightenment, which is the ultimate blissful ecstasy.

Can't All the Chakras Have Some Fun?

Kundalini energy can't move up the spine seeking her masculine counterpart if any of the chakra doors are slammed shut, and each and every chakra plays its own role in the sexual experience. The more open and balanced all your chakras, the more complete your union will be.

Regular chakra work, regular yoga, regular massage, and yes, regular sex with a loving partner will all contribute to healthy, open chakras, but as further motivation, here are each chakra's contributions to your great sex experience:

- The healthy first chakra, or Root chakra, makes you feel secure enough that you can reach out to another human being without feeling like your own identity is at risk. The first chakra also takes care of your basic needs, so you don't have to worry about the unpaid electric bill or getting enough to eat when you are trying to focus on more elevated pleasures.

- The healthy second chakra, or Sacral chakra, provides actual pleasurable sensations within the body, the ability to feel your own body and the body of someone else, and a steady emotional connection with your partner. Swellings of passionate feeling and the desire to reach out and merge with another body also come from here.

- The healthy third chakra, or Solar Plexus chakra, gives sexual union power and volatility. It is the part of you that recognizes yourself as an individual and the other person as a different individual. It is also the part that gives you the courage and fortitude to step forward and extend a metaphorical hand to another human being, which isn't always easy to do.

- The healthy fourth chakra, or Heart chakra, serves as the energetic "bed" on which feminine and masculine energies consummate their union. This exact center of the chakras is the meeting ground for Earth and Heaven, and it also enhances sexual union with sensitivity, compassion, sacrifice, the desire to please someone other than yourself, and ultimately, love that far exceeds pure physical sensation.

- The healthy fifth chakra, or Throat chakra, provides a mental context for physical union. This is where we understand what sex is, as well as what it means. We speak to our partners from here, but we also listen, not just to the other's words but to actions, movements, and expressions. Without this capacity, sex withdraws into the purely physical without understanding of its implications, without a true understanding of the other person, and without any heightened sense of the meaning of union.

- The healthy sixth chakra, or Third Eye chakra, adds subtlety and nuance to the sexual experience. Without intuition, sex can become basic and desensitized, but with the health of the sixth chakra, each partner becomes keenly aware of what the other needs. This kind of mutual awareness catapults sex out of the realm of the ordinary or of duty to make it an art form. The sixth chakra adds the embroidered details to the Tantric weaving.

- The healthy seventh chakra, or Crown chakra, brings sex out of the physical world and adds the final Universal dimension that makes sex not just pleasurable but Divine. With seventh chakra involvement, sex is still a union of two bodies, but it also represents the union of body and Spirit, of Heaven and Earth, and of the human with the Divine.

Chakra Bonding for Better Sex

So, how can *you* have yourself some sacred sex? Try these Tantric-inspired techniques, some to try with your partner and some just for you, and remember, practice makes perfect!

Down-Under Workouts for Greater Orgasmic Control

You can't run a marathon without getting in shape, and you can't expect to have an intense prolonged sexual experience without getting in shape, either. Yet, to build up sexual energy for a more complete and total merging experience, you can't just rush through sex and fall asleep. You need to take some time.

But that takes stamina and the ability to control the rush to pleasure. Regular cardiovascular exercise actually goes a long way toward improving sexual strength. It also improves stamina, so you will be less inhibited, have more fun, and maybe even experience more intense sexual pleasure longer.

However, you can also spot-train for better sex and better orgasmic control. Both men and women have muscles around their sexual organs and pelvic floor that help to control and sustain orgasms. If you tend to be highly orgasmic and reach orgasm too quickly, toning these muscles can help you control that rush to pleasure. If you have trouble having an orgasm at all, toning these muscles can finally make the Big O a reality in your life.

To begin conditioning this area, squeeze the pelvic floor muscles and release them in a pulsing movement. This is the same muscular contraction you would use to stop the flow of urine. (This applies to both men and women.) These are sometimes called Kegel exercises.

Once you get the feel of it, do 10 repetitions. A few hours later, do it again. If you can do this a few times a day and gradually work up to about 50 reps, your muscles will be in great shape for whatever challenges they might encounter.

Shakti and Shiva

Sometimes husbands, wives, boyfriends, girlfriends, can be so … *annoying*. They don't load the dishwasher the right way, they take your phone charger without asking, or they forget to pick up the laundry. They have that little habit that just drives you *crazy*. But guess what? As much as your partner is a faulty and sometimes irritating human, she or he (or they) is also Shakti (Goddess energy) or Shiva (God energy).

We're not talking about idol worship here. We're not even talking about religion. We are talking about union because you are also a Goddess or God, the embodiment of Divine energy. When it comes to sex, you have to let all those annoying things go. What's more, you have to … or shall we say, you *get to* … worship your partner for the Divine embodiment she or he (or they) truly is.

This brings a whole new energy to sexual union, one that can completely transform your relationship. If your first reaction is something to the effect of, "You want me to worship him? I don't think so!" or "Worship her? Don't I do enough for her already?" then we have news for you. You need to work on your Heart chakra.

Part of the potent power of sacred sexual union is in the merging of equal opposites, but the only way for that to happen is for both partners to open their hearts and fall down on their knees in worship of the other. It doesn't work if only one person does this, but if neither one does it and if nobody wants to go first, then real union will never happen. One of the secrets of Shakti (the power to Become) and Shiva (Pure Being) is that mutual worship breaks down all barriers of separateness, ego, and the false idea that we are alone. If you worship your partner, your partner is likely to fall down in gratitude and worship you. This is human nature, and the beginning of an understanding of Divine union. Although mutual worship probably won't be easy or fast-acting, when equal forces meet with open hearts and a sense of commitment, it can, and quite often does turn into something beautiful.

Of Lingams and Yonis

Two of the sacred symbols of Tantra are the *lingam* and the *yoni*. The *lingam* is, essentially, a sacred phallic symbol that represents male energy and is depicted as a penis-like shape. The *yoni* is the sacred symbol of the female sex organs, representing female energy, and is depicted as a vagina-like shape. In ancient statues from India, these two symbols are often joined together and represent the energy that fuels the entire Universe.

Another potent and energy-generating activity is to massage each other's *lingam* and *yoni* (take turns) without coming to orgasm. Focus on total relaxation. When excitement builds, stop. Wait. Then start again when the energy dies down. This gradual building up increases sexual energy to levels far beyond what can be achieved in regular sexual contact. Touch and worship your partner's *lingam* or *yoni*, but keep pulling back until the energy has built to a peak.

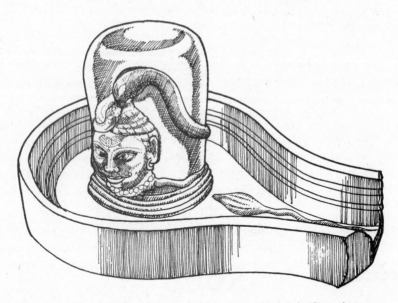

Ancient Hindu sculptures embrace the union of feminine (yoni) *and masculine* (lingam) *energy.*

We can't be responsible for what might happen next, but we hope you will keep exploring, keep coming together in union with your opposite, and keep worshipping the Goddess and God you seek for, and find, in each other.

Meditating: Root to Crown

As just about anybody who meditates regularly can tell you, meditation can be tough. It doesn't seem so hard, really. You just sit there, counting your breaths and trying not to think, or something like that, right?

Actually, meditation means many different things, depending on which tradition you explore. Meditation can be sitting with an empty mind, sitting with a completely mindful mind, counting breaths, chanting a mantra, focusing on a visual point, contemplating a question, or communing with Spirit or a Higher Power. It can happen while sitting or lying down, walking or dancing, laughing or spinning, or making love.

It can also center around the chakras.

Chakra Meditation

Despite all the many techniques and traditions, meditation almost always has the same goal: to expand the boundaries of awareness until the mind moves beyond its individuality and experiences unity with all things or with Divine Spirit. But most meditators can't just sit down and slip right into *samadhi*—the last of the Eight Limbs of Yoga, as described by Patanjali in the *Yoga Sutras*—and the direct experience of the unity of all things. Meditators need some techniques to help get them there.

One of the most common and proven techniques is to focus the mind on one thing. This trains the mind to concentrate and helps combat scattered thinking and excessive mental chatter. In chakra meditation, instead of a mantra to chant or an object to gaze upon, the objects of contemplation are the chakras.

Chakra meditation is incredibly relaxing and also an excellent way for beginners to test the waters of guided meditation. In a guided meditation, the meditation leader reads or speaks the meditation, leading the meditators through the steps. You don't have to try to clear your mind because you have someone else's voice and a story or visualization you will focus on. Guided meditation is an easy way to start learning how to meditate because it takes a little less discipline than just clearing the mind or focusing without anyone's help.

In particular, chakra meditation gives the mind something interesting, varied, beautiful, and self-involved to focus on—*way* more fun than just sitting there not thinking. As you get better at meditating on your own chakras, you can progress beyond hearing a guiding voice and meditate on your chakras without assistance.

Chakra Meditation How-To

Chakra meditation isn't difficult. However, it will be easier and more effective if you follow a few simple guidelines.

Who's Talking?

Obviously, you can't read these meditations out loud and also do the meditation at the same time. Instead, you could record your voice reading the meditations with your smartphone or audio recorder and then play them back.

If you are in a committed relationship, ask your intimate partner (or someone whose voice you love) to read or record the meditation for you. Once you are familiar with the meditation, you won't need to hear it anymore because you can just go through it in your head.

You can do the chakra meditations in this chapter separately, such as one per day, or you can do them all in one longer session. How long each will take depends on how fast you (or your partner doing the reading) read the words and how much time you give to the pauses; allow yourself about three to five minutes for each.

Why are these meditations better than just using a downloaded app? These guided meditations were created specifically for your chakra healing. By recording them, you've used your Throat chakra to communicate to your very own *prana* lifeforce. By following the meditation, you follow your own voice, or the voice of your loved one, allowing that energy to be the catalyst that activates and heals your chakras.

Set the Mood

Before you jump right in, set aside time during which you won't be disturbed by noise or interruptions, including texts, social media, children, or pets. Take out your ear buds and turn off your phone if necessary. Turn off the television. You want it to be as quiet as can be. (You only need 20 to 30 minutes to do all the meditations.)

If you simply must, you can play relaxing mood music, too, but it should not contain any vocalizations. Turn the volume low enough that the music doesn't interfere with the sound of the voice guiding you through the meditation. Any music should enhance, not compete with, the meditation.

Find a place to meditate. Ideally, it should be a clean, uncluttered spot that relaxes you, but do the best you can. Choose the room that makes you feel the most relaxed. If it helps, drape sheets, scarves, or saris over clutter and turn down the lights. Many people find candlelight relaxing.

We don't all have the luxury of a spare room or extra, unused space in our homes, but if you do, you might consider turning that spot into a meditation space. Keep your meditation space very clean and uncluttered with simple décor that makes you feel calm and peaceful. Many people with meditation areas set up an altar with items on it for meditative focus, such as candles, crystals, shells or leaves for the Elements, or pictures or statues of spiritual leaders or religious figures. Add a yoga mat and a folded blanket or meditation cushion. This room or space does *not* need a computer or a television, but it can benefit from beautiful art, especially in the colors of the chakras that you most want to heal.

Getting Into Position

Sit or lie down in a position that keeps your spine straight and expanded. You don't want to be hunched over, twisted, or moving. The best positions are either:

- Sitting cross-legged on a folded blanket with your spine lifted and straight. Roll your shoulders back and down, relax your arms naturally, and place your hands on your knees.

- Lying on your back on a yoga mat or a blanket on the floor in Corpse pose (see Chapter 7) with your arms slightly away from your body with your palms facing up, and with your legs stretched straight out and relaxed. If you tend to easily doze off, we recommend you do these meditations in a seated versus a supine position.

Now you are ready to meditate on your chakras. Record your voice reading each of these meditations, or ask your loved one to read them aloud for you. Relax, breathe naturally, and listen, following the words and focusing your consciousness according to the directions.

Whether you or someone else reads this meditation for playback on a recording or is reading aloud for you as you meditate, make sure to read it in a slow and calming manner. It can even help to make your voice almost a monotone. Also, do we have to tell you that when the following meditation text reads "[*pause*]," you are supposed to wait briefly but not actually say the word "pause"?

Root Chakra Meditation

Relax all the muscles in your body and soften your breath. Close your eyes. [*pause*]

Take a long, slow, and deep inhalation. As you exhale, imagine pure *prana* energy funneling down into the base of your spine. Your first chakra begins to glow a deep, hot red, like the molten core of the Earth. Your hips feel heavy, as if made from dense stone that sinks into the ground, cradled by the Earth. You feel warm, still, settled, calm, serene, and absolutely safe. [*pause*]

Now, imagine you are standing at the base of a vast cliff of rock that rises high above you into the sky. The cliff face is full of deep crags and crevices, and you can barely see the top, rising into the clouds. Before you, you see a cave, the entrance lit with the rosy glow of candles, the scent of cedar, and the ground carpeted with soft moss; the walls are smooth and clean. Look at the entrance to this cave and contemplate what might be inside. [*pause*]

Step forward and enter the cave. As soon as you step inside, you see that the cavern is vast and spacious with a high vaulted ceiling. The air moves as if by a gentle breeze through the stillness, warm and comfortable. Candles flicker everywhere, casting a deep red glow over the cave's interior. The moss carpet gives way to smooth stone. Walk further into this room and look around. [*pause*]

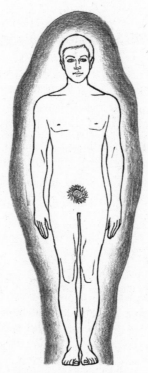

Energizing your Root chakra.

You notice another opening at the back of this room. It is also lit by candles that flicker warmly, so you walk into this second, smaller chamber. The room is completely empty except for the candles along the walls and a natural square-shaped stone in the middle of the room. You walk over to the stone and sit on it, making yourself comfortable. You feel as if you can sit cross-legged without any effort. [*pause*]

As you sit, you begin to feel as if you are a part of this vast mountain. Inside this cave, sitting on this stone in this private room, you realize the room was designed just for you because this is your place to be safe. You feel deeply anchored to the Earth as you breathe the mountain's inner air, feeling the height of the mountain rising above you as your own height. You *are* the mountain. You feel the cliff's crags and shelves as the vast topography of your own mind, and the mountain's weighty authority as your own inner resource, nourished and supported by the planet. [*pause*]

Feel your first chakra slowly spinning and strengthening, opening to the Earth's reassuring body and drawing the strength of stone and mountains from its core. The ruby-red color washes over you, the candles flare with the power of the Earth, and your first chakra flashes into full awareness. Inhale deeply then exhale, feeling pure *prana* energy move down your spine into your first chakra, illuminating the red wheel with sparkling light. [*pause*]

When you are ready, slowly rise from the stone bench, walk slowly out of the small room, through the larger room, and back out of the cave. Look back up the cliff face and know that you are the mountain. [*pause*]

When you are ready, slowly move your fingers and toes and rock yourself gently back and forth. Open your eyes, and return to stand for a few moments in the strength of yoga's Mountain pose. Breathe. Return to your day with your Root chakra energized and healed.

Sacral Chakra Meditation

Relax all the muscles in your body and soften your breath. Close your eyes. [*pause*]

Take a long, slow, and deep inhalation. As you exhale, imagine pure *prana* energy funneling down into your abdomen, just behind your navel. Your second chakra begins to glow a deep fire orange, like the light from a torch. Deep inside your abdomen, you begin to feel the movement of waves, as if it contained a vast ocean inside your abdomen with a confident tide, rocking your body with its ebb and flow. [*pause*]

Imagine you are standing on a wide, white beach with grassy dunes behind you and an immense sea before you. It is dawn, and the Sun ☉ hasn't yet risen above the ocean; the whole sky is colored a brilliant orange with washes of pink and textured with deep blue and purple clouds like the wisps of smoke. Watch the sky for a while and feel the intensity of its vastness. [*pause*]

Now, turn your gaze down to the water, which extends as far as you can see. The surf is calm and steady, with waves starting from far back and rolling gently in to break and wash calmly over the sand. Step into the water and let it surround your ankles and shins. The water is warm and swirls around you as the sky begins to brighten, the orange grows lighter and warmer, and the clouds part. The surf grows stronger and the waves pulse and flow against your knees and thighs. Feel the sea and the depths of emotion swirling with the Water element. [*pause*]

You move forward and dive into the water, letting the swirling warm sea caress your back and shoulders, your neck, and your face and hair. You come up out of the water and begin to swim, and the swimming is completely effortless. You look around, and the sea has become like a mirror. You ease onto your back and float on the quiet surface of the sea, gazing at the warm orange sky and letting the water rock you. [*pause*]

Feel your second chakra slowly spinning and strengthening, opening to the Water element's gentle pulse and flow, and drawing the energy of movement and grace from the depth and breadth of the sea. The flaming orange sky washes over you, and your second chakra flashes into full awareness. Inhale deeply and then exhale, sending pure *prana* energy down your spine into your second chakra, illuminating the orange with sparkling watery light. [*pause*]

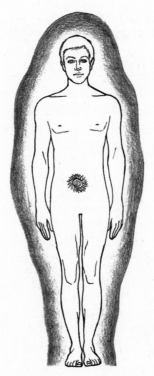

Energizing your Sacral chakra.

When you are ready, you begin swimming again, but you don't have far to go because you are almost back to shore and back to those who love you. The sea has carried you safely to the place where you belong. Your feet find the sand, and you walk out of the water as the Sun ☉ rises behind you into the sky, bathing the beach, the dunes, and your body in warm light. Turn to look back at the sea, feeling the windswept spray of seawater on your face like teardrops, and know that you are the sea. [*pause*]

When you are ready, slowly move your fingers and toes and rock yourself gently back and forth. Open your eyes, breathe, and return to your day with your Sacral chakra energized and healed.

Solar Plexus Chakra Meditation

Relax all the muscles in your body and soften your breath. Close your eyes. [*pause*]

Take a long, slow, deep inhalation. As you exhale, imagine pure *prana* energy funneling down into your chest and pooling at the base of your rib cage, which is the dwelling place of the brilliant jewel. Your third chakra begins to glow a dazzling gold, like a jewel beaming sunlight. Deep inside you, begin to feel a center of warmth in your stomach that spreads through your middle torso like a radiating Sun ☉. [pause]

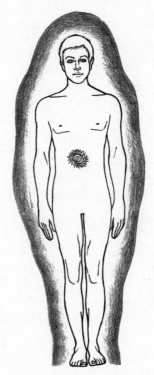

Energizing your Solar Plexus chakra.

Visualize yourself standing on a tall platform in the middle of a field covered in sunflowers for as far as you can see in every direction. The huge flowers wave gently in the breeze. The sky is brilliant blue with no clouds, and the Sun beams down on the field with warm rays. You can feel the warmth on your skin, and everything looks dazzlingly beautiful—the waving acres of yellow sunflowers on thick green stalks, the bright blue sky, and the golden light. [*pause*]

Now, look up at the blue sky that is full of depth. You lift your arms up above your head to embrace the Heavens, and you feel yourself rising, as if lifted by the rays of sunlight, rising up off the platform and high over the field. You look down and see flowers for miles. Look up and feel the wind rushing past your face, then clouds, and then nothing. You are rushing through space but always with your eye on the Sun's fire, flying like an arrow, and arms outstretched. You begin to play, stretching your arms out to the side like a superhero, swimming as if you were moving through a sea, turning somersaults and throwing both arms back to plunge headfirst toward the solar fire. Feel how fun it is to fly. [*pause*]

As you get closer and closer to the Sun, you feel the warmth, but the heat of its rays doesn't burn you. Instead, they feel like gentle pulsations of warmth. As you get closer, you see how huge the Sun is—a massive spinning sphere of fire and lava that is molten and invigorating. You hold your breath, put your arms over your head, press your palms together, and dive straight into the Sun's vital energy, leaving ripples on the surface. Inside, you realize you are floating and suspended in the middle of the Sun, supported by light and the Fire element. You see Earth, far away, green and blue, and spinning around you. You smile as you realize that suddenly, just for a few glorious moments, the Earth really does revolve around you! [*pause*]

Feel your third chakra slowly spinning and strengthening, opening to the Sun's power and rays of light as it flashes into full awareness, with light pouring out of your body's center core in rays that reach far beyond you and merging and becoming the light of the Sun. Inhale deeply and then exhale, sending pure *prana* energy down your spine into your third chakra, setting the golden jewel aglow with sparkling rays of light. [*pause*]

When you are ready, relax into the Sun's warmth and begin to slowly float down, and then pick up speed, not falling but flying back toward the Earth where our entire world exists because of the Sun. Now, you are returned to the field of sunflowers where you land gently to stand tall and strong back on the platform. The Sun beams inside your core, infusing your liver, your kidneys, and stomach with strength of clarity. You feel great personal power, tempered by warmth and charisma. You turn your face back up to the Sun and know that you are the Sun. [*pause*]

When you are ready, slowly move your fingers and toes and rock yourself gently back and forth. Open your eyes, breathe, and return to your day with your Solar Plexus chakra energized and healed.

Heart Chakra Meditation

Relax all the muscles in your body and soften your breath. Close your eyes. [*pause*]

Take a long, slow, deep inhalation. As you exhale, imagine pure *prana* energy filling your heart. Your Heart chakra begins to glow bright, deep forest green, surrounding a beautiful blood red rosebud. Deep inside your lungs, you begin to feel a flowering with each breath, as if your chest is filled with vines and leaves slowly unfolding and the rosebud at the center gently blossoming. [*pause*]

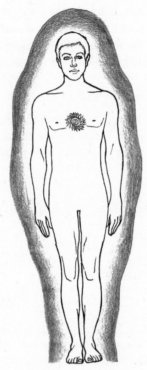

Heart chakra.

Imagine you are standing at the base of a huge leafy tree with a thick, knotty trunk and hundreds of magnificent sturdy branches lushly covered in brilliant green leaves. You look up through the branches and see layers of leaves and twigs. Feel the roots under your feet and look up at the branches extending into the sky. Reach out and grab hold of the thick sturdy bark and begin to climb. [pause]

It feels good to feel your core strength as you pull yourself up the tree. Whenever you need a branch to hold or a knot to stand on, there it is. You climb easily and freely, higher and higher until you can't see the ground anymore. Still, you climb higher until the branches begin to thin and you realize you are almost at the treetop. You can see light above you now, so you climb faster. At the very top of the tree, you find a seat in a wide V-shaped branch. You can see for miles and miles—fields, mountains, forests, a meadow, and blue sky. [*pause*]

A gentle wind rises, and the tree begins to sway back and forth, rocking you like a swing. You can smell the scent of lavender rising from the meadow. At the tip of each tree branch, tiny buds burst into more leaves, filling up all the spaces beneath you, so you feel completely secure and nurtured by this wise and sentient tree. The leaves brush lush against you, rustling in the Air element, making gentle whispering that sounds like "far, far, far...." [*pause*]

Feel your fourth chakra slowly spinning and strengthening, opening to the green leaves and powerful branches. The tree glows with a green light, and your heart feels as if it were a bud bursting open upon its leaves, flashing into the full bloom of awareness. Green light pours from your lungs, filling up your chest and flowing out into your shoulders and arms and down into your fingertips. Inhale deeply and then exhale, sending pure *prana* energy into your fourth chakra, illuminating it with sparkling, leafy-green light. [*pause*]

When you are ready, begin your descent, climbing easily back down the tree, through the branches and leaves that move to support and care for you. You feel deeply loved and nurtured. Finally, you reach the ground. You are at peace with yourself and your loved ones. Rooted back on Earth, you look up, your gaze following the sturdy trunk up into the branches and leaves of the magnificent tree, and know that you are the tree. [*pause*]

When you are ready, slowly move your fingers and toes and rock yourself gently back and forth. Breathe. Open your eyes, and return to your day with your Heart chakra energized and healed.

Throat Chakra Meditation

Relax all the muscles in your body and soften your breath. Close your eyes. [*pause*]

Take a long, slow, and deep inhalation. As you exhale, imagine pure *prana* energy rising up into your throat. Your fifth chakra begins to glow bright sapphire blue, like the blue of the brightest expanse of sky or the clearest river run. Inside your throat, you feel a gentle, subtle vibration that slowly grows and grows until you realize music resonates in your body. [*pause*]

Imagine you are walking through the woods along a river's bank on a path covered in pine needles. Trees surround you on either side, and sunlight pours through between the branches as the river burbles and flows. Among the trees, the wildlife watches you. Birds flutter back and forth between the branches. A fox darts inside a hollow log to your right, and you catch just a glimpse of his big, fluffy tail. In the river that runs alongside the path, you see a beautiful iridescent-scaled fish jump above the rocks and splash seamlessly under the water again. Everywhere you look, you see animals, and you know this is their home. Space and time fill the air around you as the sounds of the woods and river come to your ears. You know you are welcome to be at home here as well. [*pause*]

You come upon a large log between the path and the river. It looks comfortable, so you sit and settle in where a thick branch makes a perfect rest for your back. Lean into the log, relax, and listen. [*pause*]

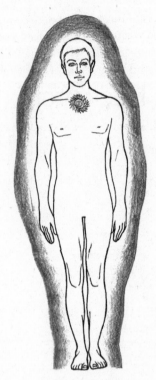

Throat chakra.

The first sound you recognize is birdsong, and their unique melodies weave into one another like a chorus of voices. Then you hear the honest, gentle background sound of the river pouring over rocks as it moves through the woods. The wind in the pine trees adds another layer of sound … the pattering rustle of poplar trees and the soft swishing sound of oak trees. Then you hear finer sounds: the air, the sunlight hitting the forest floor, the movement of clouds in the sky above, the planet Earth spinning in the Heavens, and the solar system turning like a giant chakra. Everything in the Universe makes a sound, and all the sounds harmonize into beautiful celestial music. [*pause*]

Feel your fifth chakra spinning and strengthening, opening to the song of the Earth and sky and the sound of being. The forest glows with blue light as it sings, and your fifth chakra flashes into full awareness. Inhale deeply and then exhale, sending pure *prana* energy into your fifth chakra, illuminating it with sparkling blue, sound-drenched light. [*pause*]

When you are ready, take a deep breath, rise from the log, and walk back down the path following the river. With your being in tune with celestial music, you feel ready to raise your body's voice in unison, clear and strong. As you leave the woods, you turn, look, and know that you are the singing woods. [*pause*]

When you are ready, slowly move your fingers and toes and rock yourself gently back and forth. Breathe. Open your eyes, and return to your day with your Throat chakra energized and healed.

Third Eye Chakra Meditation

Relax all the muscles in your body, and soften your breath. Close your eyes. [*pause*]

Take a long, slow, and deep inhalation. As you exhale, imagine pure *prana* energy rising up into your forehead and pooling just above the space between your eyebrows. Your sixth chakra begins to glow a deep indigo-purple, like a dark amethyst with an inner glow that illuminates your mind with a wash of gentle violet light, like the sky at dusk or at dawn. [*pause*]

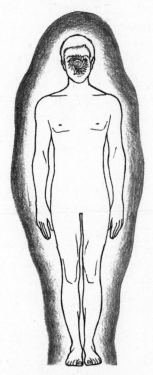

Energizing your Third Eye chakra.

Imagine that you have a chamber inside your head, and its door is in your Third Eye, just above the space between your eyebrows. When you want to go inside yourself to think, figure out what to do about something, contemplate your beliefs, or just get away from it all, you can go into this chamber, close the door, and have time completely to yourself. Visualize stepping inside and closing the door behind you. Look around. The chamber can be any shape, any size, any color, or any style you want. What will you make of it? Does it have windows? Does it have carpet, wood, or a thicket of thyme groundcover for a floor? What color are the walls? (Does it have walls?) Anything you envision for the chamber happens before your mind's eye. Create your chamber now. [*pause*]

You can furnish the chamber with anything you like. Do you want a luxurious bed in the corner or a fireplace, fountain, pool, or steamy hot tub? Do you want a desk, table, magnificent kitchen, cushioned window seat? Chandeliers? Candles? Shelves of books? An easel? Will there be a poet's garden to muse in? Your chamber may be full or almost empty. If you add something and you don't like it, you can make it disappear again. Move things around until you get the chamber exactly the way you want it. Don't worry about making permanent decisions, either. The next time you come to your chamber, you can manifest it completely anew. How does your chamber look today? Furnish your mind's eye chamber now. [*pause*]

Find a comfortable spot in your chamber to sit and get comfortable. Let your mind open to what you need right now. Why do you need time alone right now? What are you looking for? What answers do you seek? [*pause*]

As you sit in quiet contemplation, feel your sixth chakra slowly spinning and strengthening, opening to the inner turning that is yours in this chamber. See the room growing lighter until your sixth chakra flashes into full awareness. Inhale deeply and then exhale, sending pure *prana* energy into your sixth chakra, illuminating it with sparkling crepuscular violet light of the Celestial element. [*pause*]

When you are ready, take a deep breath, stand, walk to the door, open it, and then turn back to see your beautiful thought chamber; know that the room, *in* your mind, is a manifestation *of* your mind. Only you can create the space to tap into its deep inner wisdom. [*pause*]

When you are ready, slowly move your fingers and toes and rock yourself gently back and forth. Breathe. Open your eyes, and return to your day with your Third Eye chakra energized and healed.

Crown Chakra Meditation

Relax all the muscles in your body, and soften your breath. Close your eyes. [*pause*]

Take a long, slow, and deep inhalation. As you exhale, imagine pure *prana* energy rising into the crown of your head and pooling at your seventh chakra, which begins to glow like a sparkling diamond rotating slowly about an inch above your head. As you focus on this brilliant jewel, it begins to change; its brilliant multi-colored rays unfold into a beautiful white lotus flower with one-thousand petals, which is the sacred Thousand-Petaled Lotus shining with the Goddess and God joined in the Thought element. [*pause*]

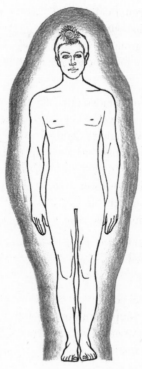
Energizing your Crown chakra.

You are piloting a small spaceship through the Universe. Although you've never been trained to do it, you already know exactly how to operate the controls and you fly easily past thousands of stars and spinning planets. Your ship has windows on every side, and as you fly, easily avoiding collisions, you can see the velvety blackness of space and the brilliant luminous celestial bodies all around you; these clouds of dust seem to be lit from within—lazy meteors and soaring comets with long glowing tails. Far off in the distance, you see a glow brighter and more incandescent than all the other dazzling stars and planets. It looks like a giant star. You turn your ship to fly toward it, and as you get closer, you see it is a solid sphere, not a star. It has a stable surface that radiates an inner light. You land, step out of your ship, and you know you will be able to breathe. As your feet touch down, you begin to glow, illuminated by the infused light of the surface. Begin to explore, filled with a quiet calm; as you walk, the surface of this celestial body undulates and glows, changing shapes, rising up into undulating waves of natural forms and then sinking back into itself so that the landscape you walk over appears in constant flux. Yet your footing is never unsure. Every manifesting shape looks and feels familiar. Stop and watch the surface of this glowing landscape shifting. [*pause*]

You hear a low humming wind whispering a message of the ancestors directly into your soul: your knowledge is their knowledge, spanning the generations for all time. As you listen and try to understand, you feel your seventh chakra slowly spinning and strengthening; the Thousand-Petaled Lotus that is your seventh chakra begins to open, petal by petal, unfolding to the Universe as a flower in full blossom and circling to sit above your head's crown.

Suddenly, you understand that just when you have reached the threshold of finally comprehending what life is, there will always be more and a never-ending unfolding. Your seventh chakra flashes into full awareness, and suddenly, you understand that it is all one—you, the planet Earth, stars, meteors and comets, clouds and sky, sea, forests and trees, and mountains and cliffs. It is *all* you, and you are a part of the All—the Source—rising like a wave and then falling back into Universal consciousness. Inhale deeply and then exhale, sending pure *prana* energy into your seventh chakra, illuminating it with sparkling diamond light. [*pause*]

When you are ready, take a deep breath, and then walk back to your ship, climb inside, close the door, and rise back up off this strange yet familiar celestial body. As you lift off, turn back to see its surface glowing in the Heavens with the Thought element, and know, too, that you are its glowing surface. When you return to Earth, you will be Earth as well, and everything on Earth will be you. [*pause*]

When you are ready, slowly move your fingers and toes and rock yourself gently back and forth. Breathe. Open your eyes, and return to your day with your Crown chakra energized and healed.

Tarot Chakra Meditations

Feeling like you want to check in on how well *all* your chakras are cooperating? A seven-card Tarot Chakra reading will give you insights into your chakras, whether they are in or out of balance. For this reading, you can do two versions. One uses Tarot's Major Arcana cards, which will tell you how your chakras are balanced with the karmic forces of Fate and Destiny in your life; the other version uses Tarot's Minor Arcana cards, which tells you how your chakras are responding to the daily activities of your life—your Free Will decisions. For these readings, all cards should be oriented in the upright position before shuffling the Tarot deck.

Tarot's four suits—Wands, Cups, Swords, and Pentacles—each correspond to one or more of the body's chakras (see Chapter 4). If you are new to the Tarot, there are many books and websites that will tell you more about the individual Tarot cards and how to interpret their meanings in readings. It might be a good idea to have a Tarot primer on hand while doing these healing chakra Tarot readings.

Tarot Suit	Tarot Meaning	Chakra Correspondence
Wands	Creativity, Inspiration	Third, or Solar Plexus Fifth, or Throat
Cups	Compassion, Love	Second, or Sacral
Swords	Action, Thought	Fourth, or Heart, Sixth, or Third Eye
Pentacles	Abundance, Wealth	First, or Root
Major Arcana	Destiny, Source	Seventh, or Crown

Chakras and Your Fate

For this reading, separate Tarot's 22 Major Arcana cards from your deck. Shuffle the Major Arcana cards while thinking about the questions you might have about your life's path, your life's goals, and your needs and desires. When you are ready, choose seven cards and place them faceup in a vertical column, starting at the bottom with the first card revealing your Root chakra and the seventh card at the top of the column revealing your Crown chakra. Ask yourself the question: *how can I understand my life force Destiny?*

1. Look deeply into the Major Arcana card for each chakra to understand its relationship to your security (first chakra, or Root chakra), your passion (second chakra, or Sacral chakra), your power (third chakra, or Solar Plexus chakra), your compassion (fourth chakra, or Heart chakra), your voice (fifth chakra, or Throat chakra), your thought (sixth chakra, or Third Eye chakra), and your soul (seventh chakra, or Crown chakra).

2. Take a look particularly at the first, fourth, and seventh cards to examine the balance presented in your life journey's path to enlightenment. The first card, revealing your Root chakra, shows where your karmic journey begins and what your life force needs for you to feel safe to set off on your path. The seventh card, revealing your Crown chakra, shows where your karmic journey arrives and where your life force finds its place in the Universe. The fourth card, revealing your Heart chakra, gives insights into the balance needed to bring the karmic journey's start and its destination into harmonic resonance. This card is the key to understanding how you will unite what might seem like dissonant or even opposing forces.

3. Take a look at the flow of energy that moves through the Major Arcana cards for keys to unlock the *Kundalini* serpent power that will kick your life force *prana* into high gear. This is your karmic Destiny on steroids. But remember, be safe—*Kundalini* energy and karmic Destiny are an intense combination. It will take much deep thought to understand the Tarot cards' message here.

Chakra and Your Daily Choices

To understand how chakra energy informs the daily choices of your Free Will, repeat the steps above, this time using only the Minor Arcana suits of the Tarot deck: Wands, Cups, Swords, and Pentacles.

- As you analyze the Tarot cards, double the energy of any Minor Arcana card in the reading whose suit matches the one corresponding with that chakra. For example, the Three of Cups landing as the card revealing the second chakra, or Sacral chakra.

- If the number of the card also matches the chakra it reveals, triple the energy of that card in the reading. So, for example, the energy of the Two of Cups landing as the card revealing the second chakra, or Sacral chakra would be tripled.

- The seventh, or Crown chakra is revealed by the energy of a Major Arcana card. You'll want to shuffle the Major Arcana cards and choose one to add to the Minor Arcana card you've previously placed there to reveal the Crown chakra. The two cards together will give added insight into the Free Will choices that inform your soul's karmic Destiny.

Using the Tarot to do healing chakra readings is only one more way to use correspondences to deepen chakra meditations. Go back to Chapter 4 to study the associations listed there, as well as Chapters 7 through 13 on the individual chakras, Root to Crown. Look for things that resonate with you, as tools to further your meditative chakra healing.

You may want to initiate a practice of meditation by exploring color theory or supplementing your diet with chakra-related foods. In Appendix A, you'll see how to use an astrological birth chart to explore your unique chakra energy. The more you discover about your own chakras by exploring their correspondences, the deeper your chakra meditations will become, and the more fruitful their results will be.

Especially if you are not the kind of person who can do traditional meditation (maybe all you do is sit or lie on the floor and watch the minutes tick by) without losing interest, incorporating yoga, herb gardening, love of gemstones, or other interests into your meditations can give you ways to enhance your understanding, allowing you to think deeply and nurture your path to chakra healing.

Part 5

RELAX, RELEASE, RESTORE, RENEW

Now it is time to learn even more advanced ways of doing healing work through your chakras. We start with a chapter on how to go deeper into finding and releasing blockages in your chakras, using yoga poses and other basic physical movements. We move on to show you how visualization can be a powerful tool for chakra healing and maintenance, and then we get super spiritual with a lesson on your very own astral and causal bodies. An appendix explores how to use your astrological birth chart to understand your unique chakra energy and how you can best heal your chakras to become your best self.

Chapter
18

Partner Chakras:
The Power of Two

"People … people who need people … are the luckiest peeee-pllllle, in the wooooorld …." Okay, we'll stop. We realize you really don't want to hear us do karaoke versions of 1960s Streisand hits. However, we dabble in song just to make a point: chakras seek each other.

Chakra magnetism is one of the coolest things about chakras, and we have a theory about it. We think that maybe the reason humans are such social animals, always seeking companionship—friends as well as sexual partners and soul mates—is because our chakras are drawn energetically to the chakras of other people. Maybe that's one of our primary connections.

In the same way that making a particular sound can tone and tune up the chakras (see Chapter 15), so can close contact with the chakra of another. The best thing about synchronizing your chakras with someone else's chakras is that chakras don't synchronize their blocks or overloads. The healthiest, most-balanced chakra opens or balances the less-balanced chakra, and if you and a partner have different chakra strengths, each one's strength will benefit the other without any negative effects from unbalanced chakras. In other words, only good can come of chakra partner work. Synchronized chakras are not codependent—they are co-inspiring!

That's what this chapter is about. We show you how to tune up your chakras with some simple exercises with another person. This can be your partner, your soul mate, or your friend. You can even do these exercises with your children, although they work best if you are approximately the same size, so your chakras line up.

First, let's talk about why chakra synchronizing works.

Chakra Synchronicity

If you hold a pendulum over a chakra, the *prana* energy in that chakra will rise toward the pendulum like a bubble seeking the surface of the water or a piece of iron drawn to a magnet, like a portal.

That's because *prana* tends to seek other *prana*. You can actually feel this magnetic-like attraction. Rub your two palms together briskly until they begin to feel warm. Then close your eyes (so you aren't distracted by visual stimulus) and put your palms close together—but not quite touching—in front of your heart. Move them slowly wider apart and then closer together. Pay close attention to the feeling in your palms. Can you feel the energy buzzing and flowing from one palm to the other? Can you feel it pulling as you pull your palms apart, as if your *prana* wants you to hold the energy in your palms together? Take a look again at the illustration in Chapter 1 that shows how you can feel the magnetic energy of the Heart chakra between your palms. You even have small chakras in both your palms as well, and they seek each other's energy. Maybe that's why it feels so good to hold someone's hand. Your hand chakras are communing.

We believe our chakras are attracted to the chakras of other people, and we also believe our chakras are attracted to the chakras of animals. Yes, animals have chakras, too, which can open and close or get blocked or overloaded, much the same as ours do. In an animal, the Root chakra lies at the base of the tail; the Passion chakra lies in the lower abdomen; the Solar Plexus chakra lies at the base of the rib cage; the Heart chakra lies at the heart; the Throat chakra lies in the throat; the Third Eye chakra lies at the forehead; and the Crown chakra lies at the highest point of the skull. Perhaps that's why people are so fascinated with animals and why we have developed such close and meaningful relationships with our dogs and cats.

Chakras are not only about our shared humanity, but they are also about our shared vitality as sentient beings. You might even experience the vital *prana* of plants, especially trees. Have you ever stood back-to-back against the trunk of an old-growth tree and felt the life force energy coursing through it? All that lives possesses this Divine *prana* life force. So, when we damage another living being, we damage ourselves. This is why it is so important to honor the *prana* life force in all that lives—not just in our garden or community but also everywhere on the Earth.

The Yin-Yang Connection

Chakras also attract each other because of yin and yang. In case you don't remember the yin-yang discussion in Chapter 3, the concept of yin and yang comes from China and says that yin and yang are opposite but balancing forces inherent in everything. Yin is the lunar, feminine, cooling, receptive, wild, undisciplined energy of Earth. It is also the energy of *Kundalini*. Yang is the solar, masculine, heating, forceful, disciplined, structured, spiritual energy of the Sun ☉, and it is the masculine counterpart to *Kundalini*, which is Shiva in Indian philosophy. Yin urges yang into a more sensual and joyful appreciation of life, while yang urges yin into a more evolved spiritual understanding of existence.

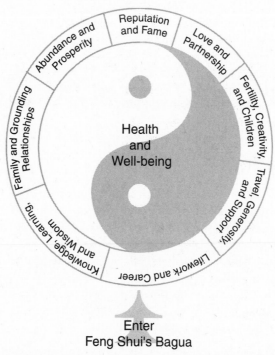

Enter
Feng Shui's Bagua

Yin and yang also influence the Eastern practice of Feng shui which studies the flow of energy through personal spaces. Think of the areas in Feng Shui's Bagua (like an energy map) as the chakras of your house!

The yin-yang symbol is a circle that is half black and half white, with a swirl of each fitting inside the other, and a dot of the opposite color inside each swirl. It represents ultimate balance. You have both yin and yang energy in you, and every one of your chakras has yin and yang energy spinning inside it.

According to the Chinese, all things seek to balance their yin and yang. You can apply this to the chakras in different ways, but let's take the Heart chakra as an example. When your Heart chakra is blocked and you have a hard time giving and receiving love, you might have too much yang, which is more intellectual and spiritual and less immersed in communion with the physical world. If, on the other hand, you give love too easily with wild abandon and don't logically consider the consequences of being too open or letting others manipulate you because you love them so much, you might have too much yin.

But put an overloaded Heart chakra or a blocked Heart chakra right up against a healthy, balanced Heart chakra that processes energy according to its nature, and the blocks can melt and the overloads even out. The two Heart chakras synchronize, always balancing out according to the healthiest chakra.

Another way to look at it is that the *prana* energy within your chakras is like water that always seeks to rejoin the sea. All chakras—indeed, all bodies—have within them an innate sense of what it feels like to be open and healthy, because an open healthy chakra has direct access to Universal *prana* that flows in and out of it. The sea doesn't seek to flow up into the rivers, dams, and lakes, and Universal *prana* doesn't align itself with blocks or overloads. Instead, when a troubled chakra detects a healthy chakra, it tends to align itself with that chakra because it recognizes its true nature.

Chakra Partner Exercises

This tendency of the chakras to seek and balance each other makes partner work a natural way to clear blocks and balance overloads in your own chakras. This kind of work can be as simple as a hug offered in greeting. When you hug someone (of course, with their agreement to the act), many of your primary chakras are put into direct contact with each other—especially at the chest, heart, and throat. That feels good for both partners (both giver and receiver), and that's probably part of why hugs have been proven to be physically and psychologically beneficial. The strongest of each of the chakras helps open the weaker of the chakras, getting them all spinning and active again. Hugs are particularly beneficial for opening the Heart chakra. (See the "Heart-to-Heart" exercise later in this chapter.)

Also, a willing but awkward hug can serve as an acknowledgment of the hope for connection or even the first step toward an enduring energetic bond. We can often begin to feel an attraction of *prana* energy even at a socially distanced six feet of intervening space. At this social distance, direct eye contact connects the Third Eye chakras, and a vocal greeting by name connects the Throat chakras, enhancing that shared fellow-feeling of *prana* energy. In the time of the COVID-19 pandemic that began in 2020, virtual communication through social media proved surprisingly therapeutic in supportively connecting life force energy. By creating online communal choral or musical events—again highlighting the shared strength of the upper Universal Throat and Third Eye chakras—people held together when the physical bond remained socially distant; an isolated world joined in an unprecedented show of human connection.

You and your partner, friend, or family member can help each other even more, with targeted chakra partner work practiced together. As long as you choose someone you trust, these partner chakra exercises can really affect your own chakras. Plus, partner work is mutually beneficial, so your strongest chakras can greatly affect your partner, too. Never do chakra partner work with a reluctant or unwilling partner, just as you would never condone unwanted physical touch. Partner chakra work should be shared—it should never be forced. Both partners must be willing to participate. It is okay to have a shy or skeptical partner, just never an *unwilling* one.

Two consenting intimate partners making love is the ultimate chakra partner exercise. When you make love with your partner, you are not only aligning your Heart (compassion) chakras, but you are also aligning your Root (safety), Sacral (passion), and Solar Plexus (power) chakras—all the worldly chakras that ground you and give you access to an appreciation of the physical world. Remember, the Root chakra is the Earth element, the Sacral chakra is the Water element, the Solar Plexus chakra is the Fire element, and the Heart chakra is the Air element. When you kiss, you are aligning your Throat (communication) chakra and Third Eye (mind) chakra, too. The Throat chakra is the Sound element, and the Third Eye chakra is the Light element. Yes, a really good kiss can stimulate the *prana* energy of these upper Universal chakras, enhancing your natural intuitive communication and communal sense of knowing.

Meditation: Back-to-Back Chakra Alignment

We usually think of the chakras from the front of the body, but they are actually inside the body, in the middle, and their energy emanates from the back of the body, too. However, the fronts of our bodies represent our vulnerable, personal selves (the yin side of the body), while the backs of our bodies represent our more detached, Universal, Spiritual selves (the yang side of the body).

For this reason, back-to-back partner work is a great place to begin. Both partners won't feel quite as vulnerable or nervous if they line up their Universal sides, as opposed to their personal sides. Sitting back-to-back is also an excellent way to meditate in sync. You just focus on meditating, and each partner's spiritual nature will become ignited by the close contact of your Spiritual sides and the alignment of your chakras, making meditation easier and more effective.

You can meditate back-to-back with a partner anytime, but in this exercise, meditation is a preparation for other, more personal chakra work because it increases each partner's immediate awareness of his, her, or their chakras. You don't have to think about the other person's chakras at all, and even though you aren't doing anything purposefully, your chakras will be aligning and strengthening each other, just because of their close contact.

As for what *you* have to do with conscious intention, just think of this exercise as tuning in to your chakra channels so you can get the station to come in without any static. Then you can listen to the music.

1. Position a folded blanket on the floor or in the middle of a yoga mat. Sit back-to-back with your partner, so that each of you is sitting on the opposite edge of the blanket. Your lower backs should be in alignment, and you can rest against each other a touch, just so that you can feel where your lower backs come together as much as possible without one person pushing into the other. If you and your partner are of great height disparity, the shorter partner can sit on a pillow or blanket so that your lower backs will align. You should both be sitting up straight.

2. Imagine you are both rising up from the crown of the head to straighten your spines. Breathe naturally and listen to your breath. Don't worry about how your partner is breathing, although you might find that your breath naturally begins to synchronize with your partner's breath without any effort. Just keep focusing on your own breath. This is the time to center your mind on you and your own chakras, so you are in the right mode to do more with them in subsequent exercises. If you need to readjust or have any concerns, just say so. It is perfectly okay for you to talk, or laugh for that matter.

3. Now it's time to tune in to your chakras. You each have a job to do. You are going to take turns naming the chakras, and as you do, both partners focus all their attention on their self-named chakra. Choose who will go first.

4. The first partner says, "Root. Safety." Bring all your attention to your own Root chakra. Don't worry about feeling your partner's chakra right now. You are back-to-back, so that part will take care of itself. Just think about your own. Feel your Root chakra spinning at the base of your spine. Imagine its red color and its power to ground you. Breathe normally and feel your chakra for about one minute. It's okay to use a timer on your smartphone or watch while you do this.

5. The second partner says, "Sacral. Passion." Bring all your attention to your own Sacral chakra, and feel it spinning just below your navel. Imagine its orange color and feel its power to move you and inspire your emotions and creativity. Focus on your chakra for about one minute, breathing normally.

6. The first partner says, "Solar Plexus. Power." Bring all your attention to your Solar Plexus chakra, and feel it spinning at the base of your rib cage and through your liver, kidneys, and stomach. Imagine its yellow color and feel how it projects your own personal power and confidence, giving you the will to act, change, and make things happen. Focus on your chakra for about one minute while breathing normally.

7. The second partner says, "Heart. Compassion." Bring all your attention to your Heart chakra, and feel it spinning around your heart and through your lungs, in the center of your chest. Imagine its green color and feel how it infuses your entire torso with compassion, love, and healing energy. Focus on your chakra for about one minute, breathing normally.

8. The first partner says, "Throat. Communication." Bring all your attention to your Throat chakra, and feel it spinning in your throat, right behind the hollow between your collarbones. Imagine its blue color and feel how it ignites your inner sense of perception, discerning the truth of situations and being able to speak and listen with intelligence and clarity. Focus on your chakra for about one minute, breathing normally.

9. The second partner says, "Third Eye. Mind." Bring all your attention to your Third Eye chakra, and feel it spinning in your forehead, just above the space between your eyebrows. Imagine its deep indigo color and feel how it activates your intuitive intelligence so that you know much more than you can perceive with your five senses. Your inner knowing glows. Focus on your chakra for about one minute, as you breathe normally.

10. The first partner says, "Crown. Soul." Bring all your attention to your Crown chakra, and feel it spinning just above the crown of your head. Imagine its pure purple or pure white color, and feel how it opens to a sense of knowledge and power, of Spirit that is beyond you in the Universe and yet within you, connecting you to everything and to the Source of All. Focus on your chakra for about one minute, as you breathe normally.

11. The second partner says, "Return." Breathe deeply and bring your awareness back to the external world. Feel your partner's back against yours. Both partners rock back and forth gently to reenergize their legs. Slowly lean forward and come back up to standing. Face your partner, bring your palms together in front of your heart, and say, "Thank you."

Having a clear, conscious intention is one of the most important things you can do to increase the effectiveness of any chakra work. Before you begin any chakra exercise, whether with a partner or alone, always set your intention. What do you want to happen? Just think about the answer for a moment, or fill in the blank to this sentence:

"Right now, I do this because _____."

Your answers will vary, but they might be something like:

- "Because I want to open my heart."
- "Because I want to feel more confident in who I am."
- "Because I want to say what I really mean."

Setting your intention isn't just good for chakra work. It is good to do before you attempt anything, whether you are working on a project for your job ("because I am committed to fulfilling my role in the team"), taking a yoga class ("because I want to feel stronger and more flexible today"), or just getting ready to cook dinner ("because I want to nourish myself with good food").

Now you are ready to do more.

Line-Up: Chakras Palm-to-Palm

This exercise is excellent for romantic partners because it really brings two people closer together and can generate strong feelings of compassion and even desire. However, this is not a sexual exercise; it is an intimacy exercise.

This exercise is designed to help increase your feelings of integration as a couple, but it also works very well for two friends who are not romantically involved, helping them to forge a deeper and more meaningful connection. It is also incredibly healing because throughout the exercise, you join palms with your partner, so the healing energy that flows from your Heart chakra out through your palms is twice as strong as it mingles with your partner's healing energy.

This exercise is also ideal for aligning and balancing all the chakras—yours and your partner's—because you work through each chakra, as you did in the first exercise. In this one, however, because you are face-to-face, focusing on the more vulnerable and personal sides of your bodies, and consciously connecting your chakras, the intimacy effect of the partnership is more intense and powerful.

Before you begin, decide who will start when cueing each chakra. If you just finished the previous exercise, switch who goes first. Spend about 30 seconds on each chakra. If you know one or both of you is having issues with a particular chakra, allow a little more time with that chakra—up to one minute.

1. Stand in yoga's Mountain pose (see Chapter 7), about two feet from your partner, face-to-face. Both partners stand with their feet shoulder-width apart. Arms hang at your sides. Stand up straight, lengthen the sides of your body as you pull your shoulders up, and then roll your shoulders back and lower them, opening and raising your chest. Move your upper inner thighs apart and back, and keep your

tailbone tucked under. Keep a very slight bend in your knees. Stand comfortably and breathe normally.

2. Both partners hold out their arms and grasp each other's wrists with straight arms. Bend your knees and stick your buttocks way back as you pull against each other, like you are waterskiing. You may need to take a step back to find the correct balance. Keeping your arms straight, stretch your arms and shoulders while keeping your armpits lifted. Get in sync with each other's energy.

3. Stand, release wrists, step closer to your partner, and then hold out your hands at the level of your Heart chakra, palms facing your partner. Touch your palms to your partner's palms.

4. Close your eyes, keeping your palms together. The first partner says, "One." Both partners focus all their attention on the energy of their first chakra, or Root chakras. Imagine your first chakra's deep red color and vigorous spin at the base of your spine, and then imagine it moving outward like a funnel to join the energy of your partner's first chakra. You are rooted together like a great double-trunked tree. Visualize each chakra growing and strengthening, opening fully and coming in line with its fellow chakra. Both chakras fill up with energy and powerful red light. Keep the connection between your palms.

5. After about 30 seconds, the second partner says, "Two." Both partners focus all their attention on the energy of their second, or Sacral chakras. Imagine your second chakra's fiery orange color and flowing, undulating spin in your lower abdomen, and then imagine it moving outward like a funnel to join the energy of your partner's second chakra. You are joined by your emotions. Visualize each chakra growing and strengthening, opening fully and coming in line with its fellow chakra. Both chakras fill up with energy and fiery-orange light. Keep the connection between your palms and all your lower chakras.

6. After about 30 seconds, the first partner says, "Three." Repeat the process for the remaining chakras. For each chakra, both partners focus all their attention on the energy of that chakra, imagining the color (yellow for the third chakra, or Solar Plexus chakra; green for the fourth chakra, or Heart chakra; blue for the fifth chakra, or Throat chakra; indigo for the sixth chakra, or Third Eye chakra; purple or white for the seventh chakra, or Crown chakra) and the chakra's energetic spin. Then imagine the chakra's energetic spin moving outward like a funnel to join the energy of your partner's corresponding chakra and connecting you. For each chakra, visualize your joined chakras growing and strengthening, opening fully and coming in line with its fellow. Throughout the exercise, keep the connection between your palms and all your lower chakras.

7. After you have finished the seventh chakra, or Crown chakra, wait about another 30 seconds, and the second partner says, "Open your eyes." Look directly into your partner's gaze. Put your palms together in front of your Heart chakra and say to your partner, "Thank you."

Chakra partner work should be fun and lighthearted because if one person begins to feel intimidated or manipulated, their chakras might close reactively for protection. Laugh, smile, be supportive of each other, and have a good time. The more open you are, the more open your chakras will be.

A Hug a Day: Chakras Heart-to-Heart

Is a hug a day good medicine? You know it is. When you hug someone, your Heart chakras touch and they get a chance to fortify and strengthen each other. Because the fourth chakra, or Heart chakra, is the source of healing energy in the body's energy system, hugs are particularly alchemical.

When two Heart chakras physically make contact, the combined energy becomes greater than the sum of their parts and infuses both partners with a real feeling of well-being and increased inner healing.

1. Find a willing partner, of any size. Kids are great. Open your arms.

2. Instead of putting your right arm up over your partner's shoulder and your left arm under their right arm (the typical hug move), go the other way: your left arm over your partner's shoulder and your right arm under your partner's left arm. This puts your actual hearts closer together.

3. Squeeze and hold for at least 10 seconds. Don't worry about what your Heart chakra is doing because it knows exactly how to heal. Work up to 30-second hugs.

4. Repeat several times daily.

Hugging seems simple, even a formality, but regular Heart chakra bonding with other human beings not only makes you feel better, but it increases your sense of connectedness with all life. When you feel connected, you feel happier, calmer, and more satisfied with your life. Studies also suggest that regular hugs actually boost your immune function. We suggest you work up to 10 of them a day, if possible.

According to a study conducted at the University of North Carolina, hugs increase the body's production of oxytocin, the chemical that makes you feel emotionally connected to and nurturing toward other people. According to the study, when two people hugged for 20 seconds, oxytocin levels increased, especially between people who already love each other. Oxytocin doesn't just make you feel nurturing toward someone. It has also been shown to reduce the risk of heart disease. At the same time, levels of cortisol—the notorious "stress hormone"—decreased during the 20-second hug. Cortisol has also been linked to heart disease. Is it a coincidence that touching Heart chakras decreases the risk of heart disease? We don't think so.

For more advanced Heart chakra work, explore healing through alternating forward and backward bends. In a forward bend, you bear and protect the open Heart chakra of your partner. In a backward bend, your own open Heart chakra soars and exalts your partner's steady, calming Heart chakra.

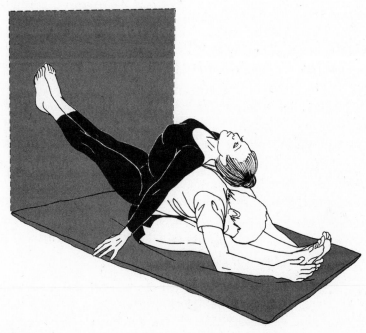

Take turns exploring your Heart chakras by sharing forward and backward bends. How open is your Heart chakra to your partner? This pose can be seen as a metaphor for the yin and yang balance of partnership through your Heart chakras.

Clear Sight: Chakras Third Eye-to-Third Eye

The sensitive fifth chakra, or Third Eye chakra, is particularly susceptible to the energy of others, so even though this is a quick exercise, it packs a punch. Don't be alarmed if you "see" things during this exercise. Opening the intuitive intelligence of your chakra so close to someone else's can cause visions to happen. If you want this intuitive sight to happen, stay very calm, breathe deeply, and really concentrate on opening your Third Eye chakra like a window.

You might see symbolic images or events related to yourself or to your partner during this exercise. If you do, talk about it with your partner to figure out if what you see means something to either one or both of you. If you don't see anything, that's okay, too. Intuitive communication comes in many forms, and it isn't always trying to tell you something. Even when your intuition is silent, this exercise is healthful and strengthening to your sixth chakra.

1. Stand face-to-face with your partner, about six inches apart, in yoga's Mountain pose (see Chapter 7), with your feet a little less than shoulder-width apart, your arms at your sides, and your back straight.

2. Look your partner in the eye and begin breathing together to a count of about five seconds inhaling and five seconds exhaling. With each inhalation, imagine the crown of your head rising to expand and make space inside your body. With each exhalation, imagine your body expanding, so that your energy reaches out in every direction.

3. Keep breathing together. Slowly, so you don't bump heads, both partners lean in toward each other and touch foreheads. Synchronize your breathing by tuning in to the sound of your breath and your partner's breath. You can both close your eyes.

4. Stand with your foreheads touching for 10 breaths. An inhalation and an exhalation is one breath. After the tenth breath, open your eyes. Slowly separate and return to Mountain pose. Share with each other what you felt. You can do this exercise a few times if you or your partner felt you were on the verge of seeing or feeling something extraordinary and you want to give the exercise more time to do its work. Share your visions and explore their meaning(s).

Touching your Third Eye to someone else's Third Eye is a powerful exercise, so don't overdo it. You should not hold this connection for more than 20 breaths unless you both have a lot of practice meditating and are both comfortable with the experience. Otherwise, the physical posture can strain your back, and the intense electrical energy through your Third Eye chakras could cause a chakra imbalance, opening your Third Eye chakras too much and at the expense of your other chakras.

Tree pose: Chakras Side-to-Side

More and more research is being done to show the sentient nature and collective intelligence of forests. Now more than ever, the Earth's forests are an important presence. Our forests are the Earth's lungs. To understand the communal breadth and width and reach of a tree, begin by standing at your partner's side, touching only shoulder-to-shoulder, each of you in yoga's Tree pose with the opposite knees drawn up. Hold the pose and look out upon your shared view. You see together, but you *know* each other through your close proximity and shared pose. Open your heart by taking deep, full breaths into your lungs in unison. Inhale, hold your breath, and exhale. Do this for at least 30 seconds and for up to 1 minute.

Once you have both grounded and opened yourselves by standing side-by-side in yoga's Tree pose, it is time to reach for each other. Once alone together, you will now reach out to grow and entwine yourselves just as old-growth trees do in a forest stand. If one or both of you loses your balance as you reach for each other, don't worry—it is part of the process. You are aiming for the ultimate goal of shared strength, grounded vision, and the free movement of *prana* life force energy up and down through your bodies as you breathe together. Feel the intense knowledge that concentration and cooperation grow between you as you hold Partner Tree pose.

Open your chakras side-by-side with yoga's Partner Tree pose. Hold each other's feet and rest your opposite hands on the small of your backs. As you stand your ground together, feel your chakras opening and spreading like branches of two trees growing and intertwining their energies.

Marvel at the great sentient power of Earth's living lungs—its forests—and as you experience the vision of an open shared vista, stand entwined together as one with the Universe. Hold Partner Tree for as long as you are able or until you tire. Gently release the pose. Press your palms to your Heart and say to your partner, "Thank you."

Savasana: Chakras Crown-to-Crown

In this easy but enlightening exercise, you and a partner lie in the classic yoga pose called *Savasana* or Corpse pose (see Chapter 7), but you lie with the crowns of your heads touching (or very close together). This joining of Crown chakras magnifies the energy in each person's Crown chakra, attracting more external *prana* to flow into all your chakras and encouraging all your internal *prana* to flow upward. You might feel a strong sense of connectedness to all life and a deep sense of well-being during and/or after this exercise. You might also feel more oriented toward your spiritual side and in touch with the Universe.

If the Crown-to-Crown seventh chakra exercise becomes too intense, do something grounding afterward, like eating something or exercising your body.

Before you begin, set a timer for 10 or 15 minutes.

1. Position two yoga mats or blankets on the floor, end to end. Each partner sits in the middle of the mat, back to back with the other partner. Lie down slowly, being careful not to knock heads, and adjust so that the crowns of your heads are touching.

2. Shift your shoulder blades back under you so your chest lifts and your shoulder blades feel like they are cradling your heart. Relax your low back and slightly tuck your tailbone. Feel your neck and shoulders release. Let your arms rest loosely at your sides and let your feet fall open.

3. Close your eyes. Relax your jaw, your mouth and your teeth, and your tongue. Let your eyes sink and relax the inner corners of your eyes. Relax your ears, neck, shoulders, and chest. Relax your arms, elbows, wrists, and hands. Relax your stomach, abdomen, hips, legs, knees, ankles, and feet. Let your entire body sink into the ground. If you lose direct contact with your partner's head, that's okay. Your seventh chakras are already joined.

4. Remain in a totally relaxed position and focus on the sound of your breath, letting your mind relax. When thoughts come to you, let them go. Thoughts will continue to arise, so acknowledge them without judgment, and then let them float away. Stay in this position for about 10 minutes. You don't have to think about, visualize, or do anything about your seventh chakra during this exercise. It is an open portal to the Universe, the *prana* life force energy that flows in through you, through your partner, back out, and in through your partner, through you, and back out in a great circle (like a giant chakra or spiral galaxy) that grows stronger and brighter with every breath.

5. When the time is up, very slowly move your fingers and toes to reorient yourself to the physical world. Slowly bend your knees and roll over to your right side. When you are ready, slowly sit up, put your palms together in front of your heart, rest a moment, then say to your partner, "Thank you."

If you don't have anyone at home who you can do this chakra partner work with, enlist an interested friend or even someone from your yoga class. Show them this book and tell them what you'd like to try. When the right partner comes along for this kind of chakra healing work, you'll know it. Your experience of relationship(s) and feelings of belonging on the Earth and in the Universe will deepen and open, even as you find yourself grounded and centered within.

Chapter
19

Chakra Visualizations

Some people come into this world automatically able to see chakras—not just their own, but everybody else's, too. Even as kids, they go through life wondering what those colored lights on everybody's bodies are, or they just accept that everyone has them and don't think to question it.

For most of us, however, seeing one's own chakras seems a little bit like seeing one's own soul. We might not really believe we can see our chakras because they don't have a physical form. Seeing mysterious energy centers in our bodies seems a little incredible—more like something we could imagine happening than something we believe could *really* happen.

But it *can* happen. Regular seeing—the sight from our eyes—is one of our physical senses, which is the realm of the three lower chakras. Seeing chakras is a more advanced skill than regular seeing because it is based on finely tuned intuition. This intuition requires more mature development in our three upper chakras, and that takes a little more work.

Seeing Is Believing

You could read this book from the beginning all the way to this point and still not totally believe chakras are a real thing. Maybe the closest you come to believing is considering that the chakras are nifty metaphors for the human spine and nervous system or that the concept of chakras and their symbolism are such useful tools for explaining and understanding the human psyche.

Even if we only see the chakra system as one giant physiological or psychological metaphor, chakras make sense and are rewarding to explore. You might be thinking, "Yes, I have trouble opening up to love, so my Heart chakra is 'blocked.'" Perhaps you think, "The *idea* of a blocked Heart chakra *symbolizes* my problems opening up to love. That makes sense to me, so now maybe I can do something about it."

That's all fine and good. It's a little like doing yoga for exercise rather than for spiritual enlightenment. It works, it's certainly not harmful, and it's fun. It makes you feel good, so you do it, even if it doesn't mean the same thing to you as it does to someone who follows the yoga path— all of it, not just the poses—to become enlightened.

However, once you start to *see* your chakras, you might be ready to take this whole chakra thing (and this whole yoga thing, for that matter) to the next level. Seeing your chakras—although certainly not infallible proof of their existence (our senses can play tricks on us)—can certainly make them more real to you, especially when what you see makes perfect sense with how you feel and how your life works.

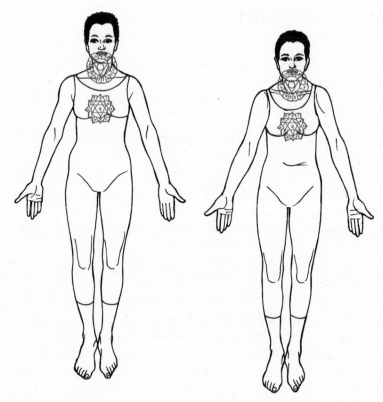

A quick way to visualize your chakras opened and aligned is by practicing yoga's Prana Arch pose. You can practice this pose anywhere, anytime. In the illustration, you can see how the Heart and Throat chakras are energized as your posture improves and your palms open, fingertips stretching toward the floor.

Imagination vs. Perception

When working on chakra visualization, a lot of people ask (and many more probably wonder silently) something along the lines of, "How do I know I'm not just imagining this?" Imagination can be vivid, so it's perfectly natural to wonder whether your chakra perceptions are valid or not.

Because the chakras are not physical structures, the line can get blurry, especially because the imagination is a tool for developing visualization skill. However, imagination can get in the way of intuition, like the person who is always sure she shouldn't get on that plane because she *just has a bad feeling,* when in reality, her imagination is just being fueled by anxiety about the flight, the trip itself, or anything else.

But intuition is the key to telling the difference between imagination and perception. Intuition's messages come through when you can calm the mind's chatter through the practice of meditation (via learning how to withdraw the senses and concentrate on a single point, eventually training the mind to quiet).

The only way to do *that* is to practice, practice, practice. Meditate on a regular basis and train your mind to see beyond the part of it that thinks to the vast being beyond thought. Esoteric? You bet, but it works, and it's a practice worth doing if you want to really tell the difference between what your mind thinks and what your mind *knows*. Now, letting go of the rational mind to accept intuitive sight can become a lifetime pursuit.

However, we aren't going to require you to meditate an hour each day for the next decade before you'll be able to know how to intuit your own chakras. Just know that the more you meditate and the more you learn to still your mind, the more you will be able to do the exercises in this chapter with the confidence that you are authentically sensing and *seeing* your chakras.

There is an old Zen saying about seeing the Moon's ☽ reflection in a pond. If the surface of the pond is agitated and full of ripples, the Moon's reflection won't look anything like the Moon. That agitation—those ripples—are your constant thoughts and feelings, which disturb your ability to perceive truth. When the pond is perfectly still, however—when your thoughts and feelings withdraw and stay quiet—then you can see the Moon's reflection. You can perceive the truth. And you can see your chakras. However, you can still see a scattered, fragmented reflection in an agitated pond. You can continue to look even as you work on calming the waters. This kind of work might even inspire you to meditate more.

If you are fascinated by creative visualization and how to see intuitively, you are probably open to learning about the concept of psychic intuition. For more insights on honing intuitive sight, you'll want to read *The Complete Idiot's Guide to Psychic Intuition, Third Edition* by Lynn A. Robinson and LaVonne Carlson-Finnerty (Alpha Books, 2012).

Chakra Survey

You could go to a mirror and look long and hard at your body, and if you are like a few gifted people, you might be able to begin to perceive your chakras. But again, most of us need more help than that. Although chakra seeing is different from imagining, it can start with imagining via visualization.

Visualization uses the imagination as a structure to help the mind perceive what is really going on. It can be a highly effective tool to plumb the depths of the subconscious where much of our knowing and the source of our intuition lives. This is also the source of our knowing whether our chakra visualization is accurate.

When you get more experienced, you can look at all your chakras in one session, but to get started, it's a good idea to work on them one at a time. This will allow you time to perceive more instead of being tempted to rush through. Do one a day, or do them one after the other for as long as you can pay attention. Let's start with your first chakra, or Root chakra. Are you ready to take a look?

As with other visualizations in this book, you can record yourself or someone else reading these exercises. Or you can read them over a few times before you do them, and if you think you remember well enough, just follow the steps as you recall them. For each exercise, prepare by arranging a yoga mat or blanket on the floor or on a firm surface. Put a pen and notebook (or your tablet or laptop computer) nearby. After you finish each exercise, record your thoughts. These recollections might be useful later as you progress and improve in your visualization skills.

Root Chakra: The Red Door

1. Lie down on your back in a comfortable place in yoga's Corpse pose (see Chapter 7), with your arms slightly away from your body, palms facing up, legs relaxed, tailbone tucked under, shoulder blades tucked down and under, and your head and neck completely at rest. Let your feet fall open. Close your eyes.

2. Inhale deeply, filling your lungs fully from the bottom, into the middle, and into the chest, to a slow count of 10. Hold your breath for three seconds at the top of the inhale. Then, exhale slowly and deeply over the count of 10. At the bottom of the exhale, hold your breath for one second.

3. Repeat this long, slow breath seven times, continuing with short retentions after the inhalation and exhalation.

4. After the seventh breath, begin breathing normally, but imagine that all your breath flows in and out of your first chakra, or Root chakra. Focus all your attention on how that chakra feels.

5. Imagine you are standing in front of a white house with a red door. This might be a house you dream about sometimes, a house you used to live in, or a house that you make up entirely; however, it should feel comforting.

6. Walk up to the front door. Notice what it looks like, how it is designed, and what shape it is. Notice what kind of doorknob it has. Put your hand on the doorknob. Feel its weight, temperature, and texture. Open the door and notice that it is a heavy, sturdy, and secure door. Step into the house.

7. Inside, you see the room you have entered. Look around the room and notice what it looks like. Don't try to impose any qualities on the room; just look at what you see in your mind's eye. As you look around, you notice another red door on the far side of the room. Walk over to it and open it. You see a staircase with dim lights along the banister. Step onto the landing and close the door behind you. There are seven stairs going down. Descend the stairs until you reach the bottom.

8. At the bottom of the stairs, you find yourself in a dark room lit by a red glow. In the middle of the floor, you see a large circular pane of glass, about six feet in diameter and like a window in the floor. You walk over to it and look down. Behind the glass, you see a deep, glittering, ruby-red wheel spinning, and you know this is your Root chakra. Sit down on the floor and watch it for a while.

9. As you observe your chakra spinning, don't try to impose any thoughts or feelings on what you see. Just look and note the impressions that come to your mind. In particular, pay attention to the shade and brightness, size and shape, quality of the edges, speed and direction of the spin, and anything unusual in the details you notice.

10. When you feel like you have looked long enough, imagine standing up, bowing to your Root chakra, turning away, climbing the stairs, opening the door, walking through the main room, opening the front door, stepping out of the house, closing the door, turning to look at the red door, and then walking away.

11. Slowly move your fingers and toes, bend your knees and hug them to your chest, roll over to your right side, and when you are ready, sit up and open your eyes. Breathe.

Sacral Chakra: Fire and Water

1. Sit comfortably on a folded blanket with your legs crossed. Breathe deeply in and out seven times, just as you did for the first exercise. When you have completed those seven breaths, begin breathing normally, but focus all your breath on your second chakra, or Sacral chakra, as if you were breathing in and out from your abdomen.

2. Imagine walking through the woods at sunrise. The Sun ☉ is just barely visible through the tree branches, which are losing their leaves. It is autumn and orange and yellow leaves flutter down from the trees and carpet the path, so each step is cushioned and soft.

3. You come to a clearing next to a small stream. In the center of the clearing is a fire pit with a campfire burning brightly inside a circle of stones, as if it is waiting for you. You sit on a small log next to the fire with the stream behind you.

4. Warm your hands at the fire, and throw sticks and leaves on it to keep it fueled. The fire makes you feel happy and content, and you stare into it, fascinated by the movement of the flames. You can hear the sound of the water running over its rocky streambed behind you. Watch the fire and listen to the stream.

5. As you continue to observe, the sound of the stream begins to combine with the sound of the fire. The flames begin to change, melting down into each other and swirling into a bright orange eddy and into what looks like a whirlpool of fire, right there on the forest floor. The spinning watery fire stays within the circle of rocks of the fire pit. You lean forward to watch it, and you know it is your second chakra.

6. As with your Root chakra, watch and notice the Sacral chakra's specific qualities. Make a note to remember any unusual details.

7. When you think you have seen deeply enough, stand, turn away, and walk back through the woods. When you are ready, gradually open your eyes. Breathe.

Solar Plexus Chakra: Here Comes the Sun

Let your third chakra, or Solar Plexus chakra help you visualize more intensely.

1. Sit comfortably on a folded blanket with your legs crossed. Breathe deeply in and out seven times, just as you did for the previous exercises. Imagine your sitting bones grounding down onto the Earth and safely anchoring you.

2. When you have completed those seven breaths, begin breathing normally, but focus all your breath on your Solar Plexus chakra, as if you were breathing in and out from the base of your rib cage.

3. Imagine you are standing in a wide-open, rolling field of green grass on a sunny day. The sky is perfectly blue with no clouds, and the Sun ⊙ has risen to about a 45-degree angle from the ground. Look all around you and take in everything you see.

4. Now look at the Sun. It doesn't hurt your eyes, and you can see its bright, glowing golden shape. As you stare, you notice the Sun is spinning like a spiral galaxy, and you can see all the movements of fire and light on its surface as it spins. You know this is your Solar Plexus chakra, right out here in the open, beaming down on the world, unafraid.

5. As with your other chakras, observe this chakra's shade and brightness; size and shape; speed and direction of spin; watch and notice anything new or unusual. Spend as much time as you need to observe, allowing thoughts and impressions to be received without judgment.

6. When you think you have seen enough, imagine lying down in the soft grass of the field and closing your eyes. Feel that Sun on your skin, and see its filtered light through your eyelids. What else do you see? What impressions, shapes, and forms swirl inside your inner vision?

7. When you are ready, gradually open your eyes. Breathe.

Heart Chakra: Heart-Felt

Your beating heart and *prana*-filled lungs can tell you a lot about your internal balance and how it reveals your compassionate growth, so look closely!

1. Lie down on a yoga mat or a folded blanket in Corpse pose (see Chapter 7). Breathe deeply in and out seven times, just as you did for the previous exercises. When you have completed those seven breaths, begin breathing normally, but focus all your breath on your fourth chakra, or Heart chakra, as if you were breathing in and out in harmony from the heart of your compassion.

2. Now imagine you are walking through a city. The streets are busy with people walking and riding bicycles. Some people run and some stroll, but everybody is smiling or looking contented. You walk down a wide sidewalk, passing people who smile at you. The sidewalk isn't crowded but has a lively energy. Look around at the people, buildings, lampposts, squares of the sidewalk, and the occasional trees and flowerbeds. Notice all the granular details you can about this friendly city as you walk.

3. Now you see a glass building on your right, but the glass is fogged, so you can't see what is inside. The building has an arched door painted bright green with a brass handle. Open the door and step inside.

4. You are inside a vast greenhouse. The vaulted ceiling is glass, and all the walls are glass. The air is humid and fragrant with the smell of greenery and flowers. All around you are trees, vines, ferns, flowering bushes, and trays of seedlings. The city outside and the greenhouse within exist in perfect harmonic balance. Look around the greenhouse.

5. You walk through the greenhouse to the other side, where you see there is another, smaller room, also made of glass. You step inside and see that the room is filled with orchids. In the middle of the room is a small fountain issuing steam. You walk between the tables with the trembling orchid flowers and step up to the fountain.

6. The fountain is set inside a wide silver bowl about four feet in diameter. The jets quiet, and as the spray falls back down into the water, the water in the base of the

fountain begins to swirl like a whirlpool. You gaze into the fountain and see the base is green with soft moss. The water swirls softly over the moss, and then it begins to take on the color of the moss until the swirling water becomes a swirling green light, and you realize that this swirling fountain is your Heart chakra.

7. As with your other chakras, watch and notice this chakra's shade and brightness, size and shape, speed and direction of spin, and anything new or unusual. Spend as much time as you need to observe, allowing thoughts and impressions to be received without judgment.

8. When you have seen deeply enough, step back from the fountain, turn, walk back out of the room full of orchids, back through the greenhouse, and back out the green door, and onto the friendly street. When you are ready, gradually open your eyes. Breathe.

Yoga's Downward-Facing Dog pose moves energy in the form of heat from the Heart chakra to your hands and feet. Visualizing this energy transfer while you hold the pose can help you to feel the release and flow of prana energy throughout your whole self.

Throat Chakra: To Tell the Truth

What happens when you examine your ability to use intuitive perception as a means to nurture insightful communication and creativity? What truth will you find yourself able to tell? What do you see now—unseen only a moment before—that you *know* to be true? Healing potential lives in that discovered truth, resounding within you. Once creatively expressed, it could be a truth that will change you forever, and maybe even change the world.

1. Sit comfortably on a folded blanket with your legs crossed. Breathe deeply in and out seven times, just as you did for the previous exercises. Imagine your sitting bones grounding down onto the Earth, anchoring you safely. When you have completed those seven breaths, begin breathing normally.

2. Imagine you are sitting in a tent. The wind blows the tent flaps open and shut, and you can see the Sun ☉ outside; inside the tent it is cool, dark, and calm. You sit on the ground and in front of you is a big blue crystal ball, about two feet in diameter, sitting on a solid granite pedestal. You gaze into the crystal ball and marvel at the swirling blue designs inside it.

3. You ask the crystal ball a question—anything you want to know. You stare into the crystal ball and watch shapes and images begin to form. They speak to you and show you the answer to your question. The answer might not be direct or make sense right now, but just take it in.

4. After you've received an answer, look deep inside the crystal ball. The blue swirls begin to take form and organize, and they begin to rotate inside the crystal ball such that the entire inside of the crystal becomes a swirling wheel of blue energy. The blue becomes an expanse of blue upon which to express your creativity. You realize that this is your fifth chakra, or Throat chakra.

5. As with your other chakras, watch and notice this chakra's qualities. Remember anything that appears new or unusual. When you think you have seen enough, stand up, turn away, and walk to the opening in the tent. Step out into the Sun ☉. When you are ready, gradually open your eyes. Breathe.

Third Eye Chakra: A Mirror to Nature

Tap into your intuition by examining the view from your mind's eye.

1. Sit comfortably on a folded blanket with your legs crossed. Breathe deeply in and out seven times, just as you did for the previous exercises. Imagine your sitting bones grounding you onto the Earth, anchoring you safely.

2. When you have completed those seven breaths, begin breathing normally, but focus all your breath on your sixth chakra, or Third Eye chakra, as if you are breathing in and out from your forehead.

3. Imagine you are standing in a dark room lit only by candles, in front of a huge mirror. The mirror has no frame. It is just a big piece of glass about the size of a large door and is secured firmly against a wall. Step up to the mirror and look at yourself. Notice what you look like in this mirror.

4. Now you notice in the mirror that there is a blue spot on your forehead. Step closer and look at your forehead in your mirror reflection. Look very closely. As you move closer, you see a dark, violet-blue spinning circle right in the middle of your forehead. It begins to grow until it comes to its full size, and you know this is your Third Eye chakra. Examine it. See how it moves as you move and expands when you stay still and breathe into it.

5. As with your other chakras, watch and notice your Third Eye chakra's shade and brightness, size and shape, speed and direction of spin, and anything new or unusual. You know you are observing the nature of your own mind—your mind's eye. Spend as much time as you need to observe, allowing thoughts and impressions to be received without judgment.

6. When you think you have seen deeply enough, imagine placing your hand gently over your forehead. When you take your hand away, the chakra mark on your forehead is gone. You know it has moved within you. Turn away from the mirror and leave the room.

7. When you are ready, gradually open your eyes. Breathe.

Crown Chakra: Higher Power

1. Sit comfortably on a folded blanket with your legs crossed. Breathe deeply in and out seven times, just as you did for the previous exercises. Imagine your sitting bones grounding you onto the Earth, anchoring you safely.

2. When you have completed those seven breaths, begin breathing normally, but focus all your breath on your seventh chakra, or Crown chakra, as if you were breathing in and out from the crown of your head.

3. Close your eyes and continue to breathe, but as you do, imagine that you are not breathing out of your own power. Imagine the Universe as breath moving in and out of you, inhaling through the crown of your head as you exhale, and exhaling into the crown of your head as you inhale.

4. Now breathe normally. Imagine yourself walking in a procession of finely dressed people down a deep-purple carpet through a magnificent hall. As you walk, you realize the procession is centered around you. The people in front and behind are your Spirit Guardians, and people on either side cheer for you. You look down and see you are wearing a long robe covered in gold and silver embroidery and studded with beads and jewels that shine with every color. You continue to walk until you are led into a great room and up seven steps, and you are guided to sit on a beautiful throne.

5. You sit on the throne cushions, which are luxuriously comfortable and soft. You put your arms on the golden armrests, which are inlaid with pearls and diamonds. You run your hands over the jewels in the throne, and then you look up and see that everyone is watching you and smiling with reverence and joy. What does the room look like? What do the people look like? Who are they?

6. Now, a young girl and boy walk toward you. They have pure-white hair, pale skin, and eyes of a bright, royal purple that are unlike any eyes you've ever seen. They are twins. Together, they carry a purple cushion, and on it is a beautiful crown fashioned as a Thousand-Petaled Lotus and completely encrusted with diamonds. The diamonds sparkle with inner fire. The twins ascend the seven stairs and kneel before you, holding out the Thousand-Petaled Lotus crown.

7. You lean over to look, and you see that inside the lotus blossom crown is a swirling white light. It grows and overtakes the crown, the cushion, and the twins, so all you see is this beautiful light. It rises up in front of you and turns so you can see it, spinning at your eye level about one foot in front of you. Look at it. Watch how it moves and what it looks like. You realize this is your Crown chakra.

8. As with your other chakras, watch and notice this chakra's shade and brightness, size and shape, speed and direction of spin, and anything new or unusual. Marvel at its pure beauty. Spend as much time as you need to observe, allowing thoughts and impressions to be received without judgment. Let the chakra live in front of you for as long as it likes.

9. When you think you have seen deeply enough, reach your hands out and take the chakra. It solidifies again, becoming the diamond-encrusted Thousand-Petaled Lotus blossom crown. The twins are back, kneeling before you, holding the cushion, and with heads bowed in respect. You place the Thousand-Petaled Lotus crown on top of your head. Everyone in the great room begins to applaud, but the applause grows fainter and fainter, and then the whole magnificent hall disappears. All that is left is you, the crown, the breath, and light. Feel this and let it hold you for as long as you like.

10. When you are ready, gradually open your eyes and stretch. Feel the *prana* life force move within and around you. Breathe.

Understanding What You See

If you've done all seven exercises, you've made it to an important place. You've seen all your chakras. This is just the beginning if you choose to continue working on this skill. Eventually, you will be able to see your chakras clearly and directly, without the aid of visualization exercises. You will be able to go further, see more deeply, and evaluate your chakras' health more easily. Now, however, it's time to interpret what you have seen.

Remember that chakras can change from moment to moment and from day to day. What you saw during your exercises are snapshots. Your chakras might appear and behave completely differently the next time you look. As with measuring chakras, seeing chakras is most effective if you practice on a regular basis. If one of your chakras is always smaller, always spins counterclockwise, always has a dark spot in the lower left corner, or always has a dent on the top, you will understand that you have a chronic issue to deal with.

Look over your notes and notice which chakras seemed to be the brightest, the biggest, and the fastest moving. These are likely to be your strongest, most-open chakras. Notice which chakras seemed to be darker, smaller, slower moving, or even not moving at all. These chakras are more likely to be your blocked chakras.

When chakras have holes or rips in them, you are having a problem in that chakra. You are missing something or have been hurt, or you might have a health issue related to that part of your body. The same holds true for dark spots, although these are more likely to be things in that part of your body or life that you don't want to see, so you hide them—whether consciously, or unconsciously.

Chakras with wavering or blurry edges—especially if they are very large—might be overloaded. Overloaded chakras also tend to move more slowly because they are having trouble processing all that energy.

When a chakra rotates counterclockwise, it might be regrouping, reenergizing, or purging negative energy, which signifies healing. A counterclockwise-rotating chakra might be blocked.

For quick reference, use this guide to interpret what you see, but also remember that a counterclockwise, dark, or particularly slow or large chakra in *you* might not mean the same thing as it means in someone else. As you consider, even meditate, on what you see in your own chakras, keep asking yourself, "Does this feel true?" When it does feel true or when your interpretation resonates with your experience and you get that *aha* feeling, that's a thumbs-up sign from the Universe that you're onto something.

CHAKRA CHARACTERISTICS

Quality	Possible Meaning
Bright	Healthy
Dim	Blocked
Larger than other chakras	Overloaded
Smaller than other chakras	Blocked
Same size as other chakras	Healthy
Round	Healthy
Elliptical	In healing process or semi-blocked
Depressions or dents	Blocked
Bulges	Overloaded
Tears or rips	Sign of trauma or disease
Holes	Weak spots, insecurity in semi-blocked
Dark spots	Hiding some aspect from yourself
Wavy or blurry edges	Overloaded
Unevenness or anomalies on the top of the chakra	Problem with a spiritual or intellectual aspect of the area
Unevenness or anomalies on the bottom of the chakra	Problem with a physical/sensory or practical aspect of the area
Unevenness or anomalies on the right side of the chakra	Problem with yang/masculine energy related to the area
Unevenness or anomalies on the left side of the chakra	Problem with yin/feminine energy related to the area
Faster spin than other chakras	Overloaded
Slower spin than other chakras	Blocked
Spin similar in speed to other chakras	Healthy
No spin/static	Blocked
Clockwise spin	Healthy
Counterclockwise spin	In healing process, purging negative energy, or blocked

Developing Your Chakra Vision

The more you work on seeing your chakras, the easier it gets. As you develop your skills, you can adapt the exercises in this chapter to see *all* your chakras. For example, when you visualize a red door in the first exercise, you could make the door white this time. Visualize the house with seven floors. As you go from one floor to another, you see different lights illuminating the floor, which represent each respective chakra. Climb from floor to floor until you reach the house's seventh floor, where all the colors merge into bright white light.

With regular practice, you can move beyond visualizations. During meditation, just focus on each chakra and see it in your mind's eye. Eventually, you might even be able to look at yourself in a real full-length mirror and see your chakras. Keep practicing. With time, you might even be able to see other people's chakras, too. Everybody has different ways of seeing, so when you find yours, there is no limit to what you will be able to see.

Chapter
20

Physical, Astral, Causal: Three Bodies, One You

Let's just say you are so inspired by this book that you're dreaming of learning Sanskrit and flying off to India to study with a Tantric master. Fantastic. We're happy to have helped fuel your inspiration. However, we are guessing that while you find chakra and yoga philosophy somewhat interesting, you likely are more interested in your chakras as a way to help you feel better and evolve in your personal life—right there in the comfort of your home. We think you'll find this last short philosophical chapter interesting because it takes the theoretical concept of the chakras as well as the right-here, right-now reality of chakras beyond your body.

Actually, that's not entirely accurate. It takes the concept and reality of the chakras to the next *level* of your body—and the next level after that.

Your Three Bodies

You know all about your *physical body*—the body you can see and feel, comprised of your bones, muscles, organs, and physical features, as well as your physical feelings like pain and pleasure. But did you know you also have an *astral body* that permeates and extends slightly beyond your physical body? This is your energy body, and it is the realm of your *nadis* and your chakras. But your body-ness doesn't end there. You also have a *causal body,* and it permeates and extends to about a foot beyond both your physical and astral bodies. This is the realm of the soul and the essence of you that lives on when your physical body ceases to exist. This is one of the basic ways that yoga philosophy understands the body.

At least, that is a simplified explanation of yoga's subtle bodies. We aren't going to bore you with the details of the entire cosmic infrastructure as yoga philosophy describes it. However, we do want to walk you through the basics of the three bodies because understanding what they are, how they are different, how they interact with each other, and what they have to do with your chakras can help you understand yourself better.

That's because there are many different theories on the different subtle bodies, including how many there are and what they are called. Some theories, for example, name five bodies: the physical, etheric, astral, mental, and causal bodies. However, just as there are many chakras—and we only discuss seven of them in this book—for our purposes, we have chosen to limit our discussion to the physical, astral, and causal bodies. We did this with the full recognition that not everybody interprets things the same way we do, and not everyone who writes about such matters has learned about them from the same sources or traditions.

The Physical Body: Blood, Guts, and Glory

We don't have to introduce you to your physical body. You already know it well. This body is made up of your bones, muscles, organs, and blood. The physical body has legs and arms, a torso, a face, hair, fingernails, toenails, and teeth. It has hands that grasp and feet that walk the ground. This is the body that gets headaches and pulled muscles and that loves to eat, sleep, and have sex. This body breathes air, drinks water, and needs to sleep. It is the body people recognize as *you.*

The chakras don't live in the physical body, which is why you can't see them (without intuitive training, of course!). Everyone can see the parts of the physical body, inside and out, whether with the naked eye, with a microscope, or with medical equipment, such as X-ray machines and MRIs. Yet, chakras exist within (and outside of) the physical body, and structures within the physical body, such as clusters of nerves, particular glands, and certain organs, relate to and respond to the energy of the chakras.

The Astral Body: *Prana* Central

Your physical body breathes in air, but with every breath, the astral body also breathes in the *prana* life force. The astral body permeates the physical body and exists inside of it, but it is also bigger than the physical body and extends anywhere from a few inches up to about a foot beyond the physical body. You move your arm, and your astral body's "arm" moves, too, as the energy imprint and aura of the physical body's arm.

The astral body is your energy body. It is the realm of thought and also the place where *prana* moves through you, in and out of you. This is the body that contains the meridians doctors use for acupuncture and Shiatsu massage. They put needles in and press points on your physical body, but they are doing it to manipulate the energy flow within your astral body.

The astral body contains not just the primary meridians but thousands and thousands of energy channels like a network of rivers and streams on a planet. At every intersection between two or more energy channels, there exists a chakra. Although this book focuses on the seven primary chakras along the midline of the body, there are thousands of other chakras of various sizes and strengths, all over the body.

Because your chakras exist in the astral rather than the physical body, you can't see them through normal visual means (see Chapter 19). However, they are hard at work bringing *prana* into your body and processing it. This is *prana* transforming your physical qualities into energy, which your chakras process and then respond to by getting bigger or smaller, brighter or dimmer, or changing shape or speed. Once the chakras process what is going on in your physical body, those events become a part of your energy body and a part of your thoughts, feelings, and the energetic expression of yourself.

The astral body is also the source of your aura, the energy field in and around every person or object, and the outer boundary of the astral or energetic body, which is larger than the physical body. In the same way that you can learn to see the chakras, you can also learn to see your aura, and the auras of others. Some people believe auras can be photographed using a technique called Kirlian photography, although not everybody agrees that a Kirlian image really does show the aura.

Seeing auras is interesting, and is a great way to get a sense of the astral body. It is also (arguably) easier than seeing chakras. The auras encircle all people and objects like a whole-body halo. We could write a whole separate book about auras and using them to diagnose problems and improve your life, but for now, we'll just say that people have auras of different sizes, shapes, and colors, and like chakras, auras can change depending on what you are doing, feeling, thinking, and experiencing. If you stand in front of a mirror and relax your eyes, you might be able to see your aura. If you practice, you might eventually begin noticing other people's auras.

Some people practice astral projection, a conscious and purposeful out-of-body experience in which the astral body leaves the physical body for a while. This is a difficult practice that not everyone is able to master, although some people crave it and strive for it. Others believe astral projection doesn't exist and is really just dreaming. There is a tradition of astral projection in certain cultures, such as among certain Native American tribes. However, like all other aspects of the astral body, the phenomenon can't be measured or proven using society's current tools and techniques, which are limited to the phenomena of the physical body.

The Causal Body: Universal You

The causal body permeates and interpenetrates the physical and astral bodies; also, it extends beyond these bodies to form a sort of egg shape around you that extends approximately two or three feet beyond your physical body. The causal body carries the seed energy of *you*, which some people think of as the soul.

Even when your physical body is gone to dust and your astral body dissipates into the ether, your causal body remains.

According to the Law of Karma, the causal body carries on into the next reincarnation. The Law of Karma is an ancient Eastern concept that says, in essence, that there is no good or bad, only action and reaction, or cause and effect. Everything you do, and everything that happens, is imprinted on the Universe and will eventually be balanced by other actions or happenings. Reincarnation is the belief that the soul is reborn many times into different physical bodies.

Reincarnation will take the form of a new physical and astral body, but the causal body will be the same. Karma is commonly discussed in terms of past lives because the actions of an individual can become imprinted on the causal body, and the individual can carry that imprint from one life to the next, so that what happens in one life can be the reaction to what happened in a previous life.

Although the chakras exist within the astral body, they are also a link between the physical and causal bodies because the result of *prana* processed through the chakras is part of the imprint upon the causal body. In other words, all three bodies are linked, and what links them most potently are the energy vortexes that are the chakras.

Chakras: Three Bodies, One You

When we envision the three bodies—physical, overlain by astral, overlain by causal—we like to think of the chakras as a row of buttons down the middle, holding them all together. The physical body is like the bottom layer of clothes, and the causal body is like the top layer. The astral body floats between them, with the chakras buttoning them all together into one whole being: you.

Understanding that you are more than your physical body—that your energy has a body, and your soul has a body, too—can help you to understand how much bigger and more important you are than you might have thought—and what potential you have for evolution. Your chakras anchor you to that something bigger. They are the means for accomplishing a better, more complex, more amazing, and eventually enlightened you.

Sure, it's all a bit esoteric, but think of it like this: You are more than your physical body. You are more than your thoughts. You are more than your soul. But you are *all* those things, and the common thread between them all is the thread running from the base of your spine to the crown of your head.

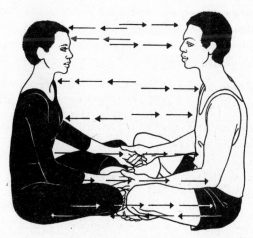

Connecting to your partner's chakra energy means joining your astral and causal bodies as well as your physical ones.

Your chakras help to take a piece of the Universe's consciousness and mold it into an individual body-mind-spirit. You are here now for a reason, and your chakras are here to help you figure out what that reason is.

Life is funny. So full of challenges, pain, and separation, it is also so full of connection, beauty, and joy. Life isn't meant to be easy, but it is a gift that we get to be here, manifested in life and inhabiting these bodies on this beautiful Earth for a little while. It's so fortuitous that we have our very own chakras as tools to make the most of our lives. And when do we finally make the most of living? Do we do so in this lifetime or over the course of a thousand lifetimes? The point is that we have the *opportunity* to make the most of being alive. And having our seven chakras (and all the others) is part of that opportunity. So, what are you waiting for?

Stepping into Love

The end goal of our journey on this Earth and through this life, according to yoga, is to finally fully understand that we are part of the Universe's consciousness—an integral part. When we see that and when we have finally learned all the lessons we have come here to learn, we take the final step. We move beyond ourselves and into the bliss of enlightenment, which is purely love. Finally, in the end, we get to turn in those bodies—all three of them—and drop back down like a wave rolling up a beach and falling back into the ocean.

You don't have to believe in reincarnation to understand the chakras, but if you do believe in reincarnation, you can see that you could live a thousand lives in a thousand physical bodies with a thousand different sets of chakras, all plugging away to make it work—to help you *see*. When you've learned everything you need to learn, at long last, you get to go home to the primal consciousness where you started. Maybe this is how the Universe itself evolves, tiny bit by tiny bit, part by part, or heart by heart.

Or maybe you don't believe in reincarnation. It doesn't matter because where the chakras are concerned, it comes to the same thing. You are here, inside layers of bodies and layers of meaning, feeling, and understanding. You are right here, right now, here to learn how to be something bigger than yourself—to remember who you really are. The chakras spin and churn and process your energy to help you see the truth. When you finally do, you get to step back out of those bodies—those temporary tools—back into the great healing current of love. You were born there, and in the end, it's where you belong.

The chakras are such powerful tools for this ultimate process of transformation that we sincerely hope you will continue to work on them, feel them, measure them, look at them, contemplate them, and heal them. We believe that only through the evolution of one person here, one person there, each person at a time, will the human race ever really move to the next level of consciousness and awareness. By healing our chakras, we give expression to the empathic promise of humanity as it evolves toward love. And this happens without a need for artificial intelligence or genetic manipulation. It happens with *you*. We see a future for humanity that sparkles with promise and glows with hope, despite all our Earthly challenges, and it is a future *you* can help grow. As *you* heal through your chakras, the Earth heals as well, restoring the elements and all that lives.

We can *all* help grow the future of the human race together because when we change ourselves, we change the world. Happiness, peace, and love are powerful and infectious. When you find them within yourself, they radiate from your life, from your chakras, from your very pores, and everyone around you feels the difference. Let your chakras help you become that difference, and we promise to keep working on ourselves, too.

You hold within you the Sun ☉ and the Moon ☽ and all of the Universe. As you join your palms in yoga's Prayer pose, inhale and feel prana *flow to your Heart chakra. As you exhale, feel that energy flow toward Heaven and Earth. Namaste We honor the Divine Light within you.*

The light within us recognizes and honors the light within you. May we all go forth with grace, secure in our Root chakras, passionate in our Sacral chakras, powerful in our Solar Plexus chakras, loving in our Heart chakras, truthful in our Throat chakras, intuitive in our Third Eye chakras, and filled with the bliss that flows into our Crown chakras from the love that catalyzed us.

And may we shine.

Chakras and Your Astro Birth Chart

The ancient intuitive art of astrology has gained a renewed relevance in our own time as powerful computer algorithms are making it easy to create and interpret personal birth charts. While a professional astrologer still has a human advantage in helping you understand what is revealed in your chart (the intimacy of face-to-face human communication allows for a direct connection that facilitates truly personalized astrological insights), a computer chart can be a fun way to begin exploring what astrology means beyond just following your daily Sun sign horoscope.

Your Astro Birth Chart

Calculating a birth chart used to be a laborious process, but a computer can now do the calculations instantly and with astonishing precision. All you need to do is enter your birth date and as precise a birth time as possible for the time you were born. (Hopefully, you'll be able to get hold of your birth certificate, and you won't have to rely on your parents' memories of that fateful day!) Also, you will need the precise location of your birth. (Your birth certificate can be helpful for this, too!) If you don't know the time you were born, astrologers will use noon as your time of birth. Once the calculations are completed, your birth chart wheel will show a representation of your personal planets, signs, and houses. In essence, your birth chart is a map of the Heavens at the precise minute and place of your birth (a lovely metaphor for your place in the Universe!).

If you are into astrology and want to learn more about all the intricacies of reading charts and how to interpret astrological cycles, read Madeline Gerwick's book in the *Awakened Life* series, *Astrology: An Enlightening Primer for Starry-Eyed Beginners* (Alpha Books, 2020). This wonderfully comprehensive book gives beginners a solid introduction to astrology's signs, planets, and houses, as well as a few more advanced concepts such as aspects, transits, and progressions. It's a great book to have on hand while you're learning how to harness the wisdom of the Heavens to help you understand your place in the Universe—why you are here on Earth and what this life means for you—as well as helping you problem solve and plan for your future.

We'll be taking a look now at the noon chart for Michelle Obama, which is shown here with the birth chart wheel, as well as the aspect grid (an advanced tool that calculates the angle of relationship between planets and reveals extra meaning).

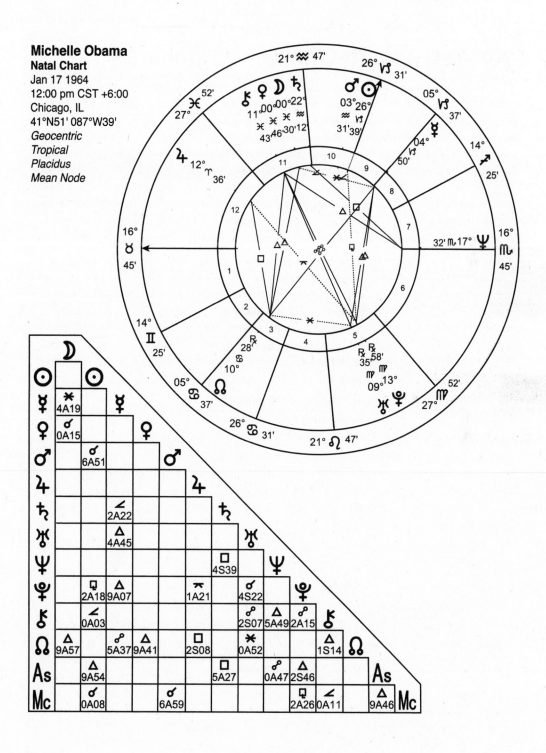

Michelle Obama
Natal Chart
Jan 17 1964
12:00 pm CST +6:00
Chicago, IL
41°N51' 087°W39'
Geocentric
Tropical
Placidus
Mean Node

Astrology for the Awakened Chakras

To see how the seven chakras are revealed in Michelle's birth chart, find the planet placements in her signs and houses.

MICHELLE OBAMA'S PLANETS IN THEIR SIGNS AND HOUSES

Planet	Sign	House
Sun ☉	Capricorn ♑	Tenth
Moon ☽	Pisces ♓	Eleventh
Mercury ☿	Capricorn ♑	Eighth
Venus ♀	Pisces ♓	Eleventh
Mars ♂	Aquarius ♒	Tenth
Jupiter ♃	Aries ♈	Twelfth
Saturn ♄	Aquarius ♒	Eleventh
Uranus ♅	Virgo ♍	Fifth
Neptune ♆	Scorpio ♏	Seventh
Pluto ♇	Scorpio ♏	Fifth

Listed in the chart above are Michelle Obama's *personal* planets, signs, and houses as they appear in her birth chart. As you learned in Part 3, each chakra has its own *natural* planets, signs, and houses that correspond with it. You can review a chart of natural astrological correspondences for the chakras at the end of Chapter 13. These natural correspondences reveal the essential astrological nature of each chakra. A person's individual chart placements reveal the astrological spin on the chakras revealed *just for them.*

To understand how Michelle's chakras are revealed in her chart, examine her personal planet placements.

Root Chakra: Saturn ♄ and Uranus ♅

Michelle's personal Saturn ♄ is in Aquarius ♒ in the eleventh house. This Saturn shows an innovator in achieving visionary goals who is surrounded by like-minded people who can make long-term dreams come true. Michelle's personal Uranus ♅ is in Virgo ♍ in the fifth house. This Uranus shows unexpected change to a shrewdly ordered plan that means taking a creative risk on romance, fun, and family. Michelle's Root chakra is secure in setting big goals and dreams, and it seems she listened to her Uranus to take a risk on an unlikely guy who proved a perfect life partner for her life's work—personal and professional.

Sacral Chakra: Jupiter ♃ and Neptune ♆

Michelle's Jupiter ♃ is in Aries ♈ in the twelfth house. This Jupiter is super-expansive, super-charged, and ready to go big with a creative passion that is transformational on both personal and societal terms. Michelle's Neptune ♆ is in Scorpio ♏ in the seventh house. This Neptune holds dreams with passionate intensity for primary relationships. Michelle's Sacral chakra contains almost explosive creative energy matched only by the big dreams she holds for her family and loved ones.

Solar Plexus Chakra: Mars ♂ and Pluto ♀

Michelle's Mars ♂ is in Aquarius ♒ in the tenth house. This Mars is an electric thinker who is ready to fight for the social good. Michelle's Pluto ♀ is in Scorpio ♏ in the fifth house. This Pluto views the soul's journey with passionate intensity (amplified as Pluto is Scorpio's natural ruler, with Mars as co-ruler) and has the ability to take risks in love and family. Michelle's Solar Plexus chakra finds great power in fighting for family and the social good, which are bound together in the core of her being.

Heart Chakra: Venus ♀

Michelle's Venus ♀ is in Pisces ♓ in the eleventh house. This Venus is a dreamy visionary and then some and loves to bring the right people to the right goals and watch wonderful things happen. Michelle's Heart chakra wants the best for people and wants the best people to help make visionary dreams happen in real life.

Throat Chakra: Mercury ☿

Michelle's Mercury ☿ is in Capricorn ♑ in the eighth house. This Mercury is about constructing a message that is transformational, almost a rebirth. This could be a personal rebirth found within the new path Michelle created through her choice of marriage partner. This path continues to evolve and grow as it twists and turns to the future. Michelle's Throat chakra is sounding the call for a better future, and this is a truth and a message she shares with her partner.

Third Eye Chakra: Sun ☉ and Moon ☽

Michelle's Sun ☉ is in Capricorn ♑ in the tenth house. This Sun is a builder for the public good. Michelle's Moon ☽ is in Pisces ♓ in the eleventh house. This Moon trusts the intuition of her dreams and visions and has the ability to be surrounded by the right people to realize the dreams she knows can be possible. Michelle's Third Eye chakra trusts in herself—in her inner knowing and in her real-world experience; she knows what she sees and what she can do.

Crown Chakra: Bliss

Michelle's Crown chakra is Divine, as is every human being's Crown chakra. The Crown chakra is beyond astrology, but we can see a clear pattern of the direction Michelle's *Kundalini* energy can take from Root to Crown. Michelle's chakras spin with a clear energy and focus. Looking at the astrological birth chart energy of your chakras can help you determine hints and patterns to direct the course of your own Divine energy. It can help lead you toward awakened chakra healing for your highest good.

Aspects for Extra Meaning

For an advanced astrology tool, you can look at the aspect relationship between planets in your birth chart. Aspects are the angles that planets make to each other, which can be beneficial or challenging. To reveal nuances of how chakra energies can influence one another, list the major aspects in the triangular aspect grid accompanying your birth chart, and then add the chakra for each planet. The resulting chart will tell you how your chakras spin together in beneficial or challenging ways. Let's look at Michelle Obama's chakra aspects.

MICHELLE OBAMA'S CHAKRA ASPECTS

Planet/Chakra	Astro Aspect	Planet/Chakra
Mercury ☿ *Throat*	Sextile ✶ (harmonious)	Moon ☽ *Third Eye*
Venus ♀ *Heart*	Conjunct ☌ (strong benefit)	Moon ☽ *Third Eye*
Mars ♂ *Solar Plexus*	Conjunct ☌ (strong benefit)	Sun ☉ *Third Eye*
Uranus ♅ *Root*	Trine △ (favorable)	Mercury ☿ *Throat*
Neptune ♆ *Sacral*	Square □ (challenging)	Saturn ♄ *Root*
Pluto ♇ *Solar Plexus*	Trine □ (favorable)	Mercury ☿ *Throat*
Pluto ♇ *Solar Plexus*	Conjunct ☌ (strong benefit)	Uranus ♅ *Root*

By examining the relationships between and among the chakras in aspect to each other, you can begin to see further patterns in the way Michelle Obama's chakras interact with each other. Note that all but one of her aspect relationships is beneficial—her Sacral chakra is in challenging aspect to her Root chakra. This means that Michelle's passions and her safety are often in tension with one another, and bravery (or caution) may be required to chart the right energetic course. This is an area that may need extra healing for Michelle.

Looking at your astrological aspect chakra relationships can help you identify areas of special sensitivity for healing or areas where you are strong or have room to grow.

Index

B

C

D

F

G

soul, 194

Spirit, 192

grace (second chakra), 99

grounding

first chakra, 77–78

poses (sixth chakra), 186

guided meditation, 242

H

Hatha yoga, 42, 48, 86

Headstand yoga pose (seventh chakra), 203–204

healing

first chakra blockages, 83–84

first chakra overloads, 86

second chakra blockages, 103–104

second chakra overloads, 107

third chakra blockages, 122–123

third chakra overloads, 124–125

fourth chakra blockages, 145–146

fourth chakra overloads, 148–149

fifth chakra blockages, 164–165

fifth chakra overloads, 167

sixth chakra blockages, 182–183

sixth chakra overloads, 184–185

seventh chakra blockages, 199–200

seventh chakra overloads, 202

Healing Sounds, 227

health issues

first chakra blockages, 82–83

first chakra overloads, 85

second chakra blockages, 103

second chakra overloads, 105

third chakra blockages, 121–122

third chakra overloads, 123–124

fourth chakra blockages, 144

fourth chakra overloads, 147

fifth chakra blockages, 163

fifth chakra overloads, 166

sixth chakra blockages, 182

sixth chakra overloads, 184

seventh chakra blockages, 198

seventh chakra overloads, 201

healthy chakras, 49–51

Heart chakra. *See* fourth chakra

Hinduism, 23

hugging, 270

I

ida nadi, 31–34

imagination (sixth chakra), 176

inner fire (increasing), 219

insomnia, 212

Introduction to Chi Kung, 35

Intuition chakra. *See* sixth chakra

ishvarapranidhana, 24

Iyengar, B.K.S., 32

J

Jhalandara Bandha, 61, 169

Jnana yoga, 49

Johari, Harish, 95, 113

journal, 27

Judith, Anodea, 22, 96, 156, 174, 190

Jung, Carl, 47

Jupiter (second chakra), 110–111

P

U

V